Leadership Without Borders:
Successful Strategies from
World-Class Leaders

Leadership Without Borders:
Successful Strategies from World-Class Leaders

Ed Cohen

John Wiley & Sons (Asia) Pte Ltd

Other Wiley Editorial Offices

John Wiley & Sons, Inc., 111 River Street, Hoboken, NJ 07030, USA
John Wiley & Sons Ltd., The Atrium, Southern Gate, Chichester PO19 BSQ, England
John Wiley & Sons (Canada) Ltd., 5353 Dundas Street West, Suite 400, Toronto, Ontario M9B 6H8, Canada
John Wiley & Sons Australia Ltd., 42 McDougall Street, Milton, Queensland 4064, Australia
Wiley-VCH, Boschstrasse 12, D-69469 Weinheim, Germany

Library of Congress Cataloging-in-Publication Data:

ISBN: 978-0-470-82227-2

Wiley Bicentennial Logo: Richard J. Pacifico
Typeset in 11/14 point, Meridien by Superskill Graphics Pte. Ltd.
Printed in Singapore by Saik Wah Press Pte. Ltd.
10 9 8 7 6 5 4 3

For Pris, my beloved and my best friend, who opened the world to me and without whom I might never have had my first international stamp in my passport. And for my daughter, MacKenzie, who at age 15 was brave, curious, adventurous, and open to moving to the other side of the world when we relocated from the United States to India.

Contents

Acknowledgments

I am deeply grateful to B. Ramalinga Raju and the leaders of Satyam Computer Services, who supported my efforts to collect information, conduct interviews, and bring to life *Leadership Without Borders*. I am grateful to Vira Komarraju, Madhavan Sanjeevi, and A. V. Vedpuriswar for their support and encouragement.

Thank you to each of these global leaders for their outstanding contributions: Dr. Mukesh Aghi of Universitas 21 Global, Antonio Alemán of Vodafone, Marjan Bolmeijer of Change Leaders, Dr. Frank-Jürgen Richter of Horasis, V. Shankar of Standard Chartered Bank, Dr. Ralph Shrader of Booz Allen Hamilton, and Geoff Taylor of Nike. Thank you also to the world-class leaders who participated in the interviews.

I have learned that it truly takes a solid global team to author a book and I am thankful to the Satyam Thought Leadership team – Maya Mohan, Bindu John, Srabani Deb, Sunil Kumar, Himanshu Davada, and the eSupport team – and to the entire Satyam School of Leadership team for their contributions. Thank you to Hemant Kumar and Bijan Sinha for your creative graphics arts. A special thanks to Nishi Levitt and to Joshua Craver for trusting me when I said, "Come to India with me to build the Satyam School of Leadership." You are both colleagues I have watched grow into true global leaders over the many years we have known each other. Thanks to everyone who assisted in my search for successful global leaders, including John Ballantine, Robert Bjork, Sunita Lanka, Ego Onwuka, Dharam Paluru, Lakeesha Ransom, and Michael Su. Special thanks to Daniel Blair, Andrew Paradise, Wei Wang, and Clover Soares of ASTD for partnering with Satyam on the Global Leadership Survey and for analyzing the results.

I am grateful to all my global colleagues, teachers, and mentors, who throughout my journey have shared their stories and taught me so much, especially, A. S. Murthy Garu, B. Rama Raju, Ram Mynampati, Vijay Prasad, Hari T., Shailesh Shah, Tamar Elkeles, Mukesh Aghi, Rebecca Ray, Abdul Rasheed Miya, Ralph Shrader, Sam Strickland, Horacio Rozanski, Leslie Gilbert, Joe Garner, Dan

Lewis, Heather Burns, Davide Arpili, Sheila Haji, Elaine Boomer, Jay Davis, Nicola Dingemans, Neil Gillespie, Pat Harbour, Chuck Jones, Karen Barley, DeAnne Aguirre, Joyce Doria, Marty Seldman, Marie Lerch, Susan Cipollini, Frank DeVita, and Elliott Masie.

I wish also to express my great appreciation to Marcel Ferraz, who dedicated a great deal of time to reviewing, collating, searching for quotes, and debating his position throughout the drafting of the manuscript. Marcelo, you are a true future global leader.

I am grateful to Ibanga Umanah, who dedicated six months to the research, collation, and analysis of data. He also reviewed and edited the text, scheduled and conducted interviews, developed ideas, and discussed and debated topics with me. Ibanga, without you, this book would never have happened. You are a future global leader who compelled me to be a better leader as you captured my total respect and admiration.

I would like to thank the outstanding professionals at John Wiley & Sons (Asia) Pte. Ltd., including Nick Wallwork, publisher, Cynthia Mak, assistant marketing manager, Louise Koh, publicity executive, Jessie Yeo, production executive, Robyn Flemming, freelance copyeditor, and J. C. Ruxpin, the design company, for the cover. I am especially appreciative of Janis Soo, managing editor, who was always responsive and whose opinions and experience I greatly value.

And, to my best friend, Jay Golub, who has been a major influencer in my life for the past 40 years, thank you for coming up with the idea for the title, *Leadership Without Borders*. If not for you, the book might have been called *Borderless Leadership*.

I am grateful to Priscilla Nelson, an outstanding executive coach and global learning leader who has worked with hundreds of senior executives over the past 25-plus years. Pris is my coach, my teacher, my mentor, my best friend, and the one I have been blessed to be married to for close to two decades. Thank you for always being there for us.

Finally, I would like to acknowledge my late mother, Bernice Ruth Cohen, who, as a single parent, worked two jobs while raising me with the right values, instilling in me the importance of learning, and teaching me the value of relationships, while being my greatest fan.

Leadership Without Borders is truly a global effort.

Foreword

Truly global leaders are hard to find. While an overwhelming majority of people surveyed by my colleagues at The Gallup Organization claim to be good leaders, very few have any experience in leading across borders. Herein lies the challenge for our future.

The organizations we work for are "going global" at a pace that is unprecedented in our world's history. I have yet to meet an organizational leader without aspirations of serving people around the world. Every day, thousands of businesses set up virtual storefronts on the web, offering their products or services to consumers from Berlin to Budapest, from Boston to Bangkok.

While technology is making the dream of a truly global marketplace a reality today, we as human beings are now slowing things down. We are armed with the means for reaching out and interacting across borders, yet we do not. Instead, many of us remain in our comfort zones, and spend most of our time working with those who are nearby. The borders that exist today are not created by a lack of transportation or technology ... they are created by a lack of human connections.

In *How Full Is Your Bucket?* (Gallup Press, 2004), which I co-wrote with Don Clifton, we explored the impact of interactions between people. We discovered that seemingly small moments accumulate and have a profound effect on our health, longevity, achievement, and overall well-being.

In my second book, *Vital Friends* (Gallup Press, 2006), I explored the advantages of very close friendships in organizations. After surveying more than 10 million people (in 114 countries), we discovered that people who have a "best friend at work" are seven times as likely to be engaged in their jobs as those who don't. We also found them to be significantly more productive, to have higher customer engagement scores, and to maintain better safety records on the job. Unfortunately, most of us fail to nurture the connections that make us great.

As you will learn in *Leadership Without Borders*, building sustainable and diverse networks is one of the main challenges leaders face today. If you step back and look at your own network today, what could you do to increase its bandwidth?

In addition to building stronger networks, we all have a great deal to learn if we want to be better leaders for our world's future. And no one understands this better than Ed Cohen. While Ed has embodied global leadership in his own life and career, perhaps most importantly, he is a world-class student and teacher on this subject. Ed has interviewed hundreds of leaders over the years, listening carefully to their stories, and then sharing this collective knowledge for the benefit of many others.

For those of us who are still working to be more global leaders, Ed's insights have illuminated a path for understanding and development. As I read *Leadership Without Borders*, each chapter challenged my assumptions about what it takes to lead in this new world. Drawing on decades of study and stories that bring it all to life, *Leadership Without Borders* reveals what it will take to build a global constituency of your own.

As you read this book, I encourage you to keep a very open mind as you learn from these successful global leaders. Whether you are in a major leadership role today, or aspire to be a global leader in the future, it all starts with curiosity, a little learning … and a lot of listening.

Tom Rath
Author of *Vital Friends*
Co-author of *How Full Is Your Bucket?*

Introduction

IN THE BEGINNING, A GLOBAL LEADERSHIP JOURNEY...

My own *Leadership Without Borders* journey began in 1988. I was 29 years old and didn't even have a passport. I met my wife Priscilla through our work together. We each owned training businesses. We decided to merge our businesses and, over time, our lives. When Pris and I selected our wedding date, we were faced with a key decision: where to go for our honeymoon. We agreed the ideal place would be Europe. At the time, our company, Innovative Resources, based in Orlando, Florida, was new, profits were slim, and a trip to Europe was more of a dream than a real possibility. Nevertheless, Pris has always believed in the law of attraction and simply said, "We should put it out there. Something good is sure to happen."

The next day I was teaching a computer course when a participant approached me and asked whether Innovative Resources would be willing to consider a barter agreement. She explained that she worked for an international airline. "We would like to attend more courses, but our budgets are rather tight just now. How about we trade? We could take a few computer courses with your company in exchange for credit toward travel on our international airline." I know this sounds bizarre, but it really happened!

The day after our wedding, November 19, 1989, passports in hand, Pris and I boarded our international flight. We landed in Luxembourg, stepped off the plane, and walked to the immigration desk, where I proudly handed over my shiny new passport to the immigration officer. Thirty seconds later, I had my very first international travel stamp! Two tattered passports, more than 150 stamps, and eight visas later, I have had the opportunity to visit and/or work in 32 countries,[1] many of which we continue to return to. Each new country, each new encounter, offers a unique opportunity. Knowing how to maximize those opportunities is what separates the best global leaders from the rest of the pack.

The *Leadership Without Borders* research came about as a result of our relocation from Northern Virginia, in the United States, to Hyderabad, India. In Northern Virginia, I had been the strategic leader for Booz Allen Hamilton's corporate university, which took the number one spot in the 2006 *Training Magazine's* Top 100 ranking.[2] Then, Satyam Computer Services came along and made me an offer I found impossible to refuse; move to India and develop a world-class leadership and research development program complete with a 240,000-square-foot, brand-new facility waiting for the new leader to complete the interior design. Satyam is a global consulting and IT services firm offering a wide array of solutions, from strategy consulting right through to implementing IT solutions. When I was first approached I was extremely impressed by Satyam's commitment to learning. The company's vision was to launch the Satyam School of Leadership to develop its top leaders and fuel the leadership engine, in order to maintain the company's phenomenal, sustained growth. When Satyam first listed on the Bombay Stock Exchange in 1991, it had 100 associates and had just tipped the US$1 million revenue mark. In 2001, when it listed on the New York Stock Exchange, it had 10,000 associates. Today, there are more than 35,000 associates located throughout the world and Satyam has tipped the US$1 billion mark. This type of growth requires the right people, processes, and technologies to sustain it. More importantly, from my perspective as a learning leader, it requires a solid commitment from the top that acknowledges the importance of strong leaders and learning.

Early in the process, I had the opportunity to meet with the chairman of Satyam, Ramalinga Raju – or "Raju," as he is called. Raju and his brother, Ramu, who is the firm's managing director, founded Satyam and inspired its growth from a small company to a global player in the enterprise solutions marketplace. Raju's passion for leadership and learning was clear and contagious. He described for me the concept of full life-cycle leadership, and explained how leaders at Satyam were empowered to run full life-cycle businesses as chief executive officers of their own businesses. This sense of independence and interdependence resonated with me. It represented a true shift in how leaders manage in global, knowledge-based firms.

Pris (who is now Satyam's global head of executive coaching

and mentoring) and I were so sold on the value proposition of the Satyam School of Leadership, we sold our home and our cars, packed up our belongings, and with our 15-year-old daughter, MacKenzie, and Jasper the schnoodle (half-poodle, half-schnauzer), boarded a flight to India to begin our global adventure.

As I wondered what competencies, behaviors, and values would be expected of me in my new role, I realized I had many questions about leadership for which I sought answers:

- How do successful global leaders maximize people differences?
- How do successful global leaders maximize technology?
- What insights could other global leaders provide to ease the transition of new global leaders and enhance the experience of current global leaders?
- What advice do successful global leaders have for future global leaders?

Once we were settled in Hyderabad, the fifth-largest city in the country and known both for its rich history and culture, and for being the technology center of India, my new team, along with the research team at the American Society for Training and Development (ASTD), launched a Global Leadership Survey. We sent it to senior executives around the world, and received responses from executives who, in total, have lived and worked in approximately 60 countries. We followed this up with extensive interviews of more than 50 global leaders representing a multitude of countries, industries, and backgrounds. The insights collected from the Global Leadership Survey and interviews form the basis of this book. *The detailed analysis and report from the Global Leadership Survey is available from ASTD at www.astd.org.*

HOW THIS BOOK IS ORGANISED

Leadership Without Borders comprises 14 chapters divided into two main parts.

Part 1: Global Leadership Competencies provides valuable information on global leaders from survey respondents, interviews, best practices, and profiles of world-class leaders who have lived and worked in more than 60 different countries.

- *Chapter 1: The New Global Frontier* provides a context for prioritizing global leadership competencies and an overview of the five key areas: leadership characteristics, global business acumen, worldview, people leadership, and business leadership.
- *Chapter 2: Global Leadership Characteristics* presents information on traits – "Who you are," and core values – "How you are."
- *Chapter 3: Global Business Acumen* presents the eight most critical areas for leaders to understand: business terminology, regional and global economics, global finance awareness, strategic marketing, organizational behavior, enterprise knowledge management, operations management, and business innovation.
- *Chapter 4: Worldview* identifies the importance of gathering information from multiple sources, and demonstrates how to enhance and maintain the broadest perspective of the world.
- *Chapter 5: Global People Leadership* presents, from the perspective of the complexities of global leadership, views on how world-class leaders adjust their style, expectations, and timelines to achieve the same outcomes as they would in their country of origin. They recognize the power that comes from harnessing the strengths of the team's background, experiences, cultures, and traditions within the context of what will work in each situation and each market.
- *Chapter 6: Global Business Leadership* presents, from the perspective of the complexities of global leadership, views on business complexities, strategy and vision, usage of technology, alignment, structure and change, extreme networking, and prioritization of time and outcomes.

Part 2: Successful Strategies from World-Class Leaders provides the serendipitous opportunity to learn from the experiences of eight exceptional global leaders. Their stories reinforce the global leadership competencies discussed in Part 1.

- *Chapter 7: The Artistry and Science of Global Leadership.* Dr. Mukesh Aghi, chief executive officer, Universitas 21 Global (U21Global), Singapore, provides insights into the artistry and science of global leadership by taking us back to the roots of global leadership. Mukesh shares stories, both his own and from others, that address the manner in which globalization has changed the world, coupled with an assessment of the impact the explosion of technological advances has had on the global nature of leadership today.
- *Chapter 8: Satyam: The Creation of a Global Company.* B. Ramalinga Raju, founder and chairman of Satyam Computer Services, India, takes us on the journey through six orbits that have solidified the success of this global company.
- *Chapter 9: Transitioning to a Global Mindset.* V. Shankar, global head of corporate finance with Standard Chartered Bank, Singapore, provides a history, context, and perspective on how companies around the world are transitioning to a global mindset. V. Shankar discusses how organizations – a collection of individuals united by a common purpose – combined with the forces of globalization, technology, and information explosion have changed the economic landscape.
- *Chapter 10: Booz Allen Hamilton's Global People Strategy.* Dr. Ralph Shrader, chairman and chief executive officer, Booz Allen Hamilton, in the United States, provides a first-hand account of the transition from several distinctly different cultures to one global culture. Ralph provides historical perspective and stories to illustrate the steps taken in the next evolution of the firm's global people leadership strategy.
- *Chapter 11: Global Risk Strategies.* Geoff Taylor, director of risk management with Nike Europe, Middle East, and Africa Region, Nike European Operations Netherlands BV, discusses the case for why global businesses must have a new focus on risk awareness and management. Geoff provides concrete steps for developing a solid enterprise risk management strategy with the right support from the top to ensure its success.
- *Chapter 12: Vodafone Change Leadership.* Antonio Alemán, business unit managing director, Vodafone Spain, shares his views on the key elements required for successful integration of a local subsidiary into a multinational group, and the lessons

learned. Antonio demonstrates how applying the benefits of globalization, without losing local identity, and at the same time transitioning employees to a global mindset in an international environment, achieves greater long-term results.

- *Chapter 13: Managing Your Global Leadership Development.* Marjan Bolmeijer, chief executive officer, Change Leaders, Worldwide and Frank-Jürgen Richter, president, Horasis, Geneva, Switzerland, provide insightful learning activities for current and future global leaders wishing to expand the bandwidth of their cultural sensitivity, get the right global feedback, and chart the cultural mosaic of their world.

The stories and views presented in this book provide a solid foundation for commencing, continuing, or validating your global leadership journey. Each chapter ends with a number of global leadership viewpoints to assist you in building your own checklist of global leadership knowledge, skills, and behaviors that you can start to use right away.

- Finally, *Chapter 14: Conclusion* provides guidance for future global leaders, and final viewpoints from the more than 50 world-class leaders who contributed to this book.

Endnotes

1   Aruba, Australia, Austria, Barbados, British Virgin Islands, Canada, Curaçao, Denmark, Dominican Republic, France, Germany, Hungary, Iceland, India, Italy, Jamaica, Japan, Kiribati, Luxembourg, Malaysia, Mexico, Monaco, Netherlands, Panama, Singapore, South Africa, Switzerland, Thailand, United Arab Emirates, United Kingdom, United States, and Vietnam.
2   Joseph Kornik, "Booz Allen Hamilton Puts People First," *Training Magazine*, March 1, 2006.

Part 1

Global Leadership
Competencies

Chapter 1

The New Global Frontier

WELCOME TO THE NEW GLOBAL FRONTIER

Significant changes have occurred since the emergence of the knowledge economy, demanding a recast of many of the roles of leaders. Today's leaders live and work in countries other than their home country, manage multinational teams, and have customers from all over the globe. According to Nigel Andrews, venture capitalist and governor of London Business School, and Laura D'Andrea Tyson, dean of London Business School, "Markets are multinational. Communication is global, instant, and constant. In this environment of – pardon the clichés, but they are all quite real – 24/7 contact, triband cell phones, the BlackBerry, frequent-flyer families, airport-lounge showers, long-distance teams, and extensively extended enterprises, the successful executive has to be flexible, multifaceted, and global."[1] Anyone who is working either outside their country of origin or with others from outside their country of origin needs to demonstrate an effective blend of global competencies. This is even more critical for leaders and requires blending cultural definitions of leadership with multiple geographic influences.

More and more, the internet and other means of rapid communication are allowing diverse groups of employees to come together to work and learn from each other. Ian Davis and Elizabeth Stephenson of McKinsey & Company believe, "More transformational than technology itself is the shift in behavior that it enables. We work not just globally but also instantaneously. We are forming communities and relationships in new ways. More than two billion people now use cell phones. We send nine trillion e-mails a year. We do a billion Google searches a day, more than half in languages other than English. For perhaps the first time in history, geography is not the primary constraint on the limits of social and economic organization."[2] Yes, we live in a web-enabled world; yet, we travel more than ever, encountering new people, new places, and new cultures. According to the International Air Transport Association, international travel is expected to grow an average of 5.6% per year between 2005 and 2009. The top five markets expected to grow are Poland at 11.2%, China at 9.6%, Czech Republic at 9.5%, Qatar at 9.2%, and Turkey at 8.9%.[3] According to a *Business Week* article by Beverley Fearis, "Business travel remains strong in most regions of the world, according to the latest finding from the airline industry. Significant growth in airline capacity particularly in Asia Pacific, the Middle East, Africa, and Europe indicates a continued upturn in business travel in these regions."[4]

Today, a leader might be from India working for an Indian-owned company and assigned to work in the United States. Another may be from France, working for an Australian-owned company and living in China. In my case, I am an American working in India for an Indian-owned company. Yet another person might work for a company headquartered in one part of the world and be assigned to a region in another part of the world. Wherever they are, all these people can connect simultaneously (with some creative and respectful time zone planning) to make key decisions that instantly influence organizations on a global scale. Welcome to the new global frontier.

Let's define some key terms used in this book:

- **Global:** of, relating to, or involving the entire world; worldwide.[5]
- **Leadership:** the office or position of a leader, capacity to lead, the act or an instance of leading.[6]
- **Global leadership:** leaders capable of succeeding across the globe.

THE ORIGINS OF *LEADERSHIP WITHOUT BORDERS*

Leadership Without Borders started as a way for me to learn how to be successful in my new role as head of Satyam School of Leadership in Hyderabad, India. I had never lived overseas or worked for a non-American company, and things weren't going quite as I had thought they would. The leadership techniques I had used successfully in my home country weren't working for me in this new part of the world. As I struggled with my own learning curve, I realized that, in today's world, many other people were embarking on the same type of leadership journey as myself, or would likely do so at some point.

At Satyam, my journey, and that of my colleagues, towards *Leadership Without Borders* comprised three stages:

1. We conducted a Global Leadership Survey.
2. We interviewed more than 50 leaders who have lived and worked in more than 60 different countries.
3. We sought advice and counsel from those successful global leaders, which we distilled into the suggestions and insights contained in this book.

The ASTD/Satyam Global Leadership Survey

In August 2006, with assistance from the American Society for Training and Development (ASTD), we surveyed 1,500 business leaders, receiving more than 200 responses from 16 countries. Nearly half of them (41%) were vice presidents or above (see Figure 1.1), and 45.2% of them had been in a position of leadership for more than 12 years (Figure 1.2). The majority of the leaders surveyed (63.0%) had advanced degrees. They worked for organizations in a variety of industries, with professional, scientific, and technical services cited most frequently (46.5%). Most of the organizations they led had locations in several countries, with 68.8% of them having locations in more than five countries.

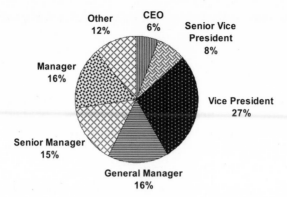

Figure 1.1   Designations of respondents from the ASTD/Satyam Global Leadership Survey

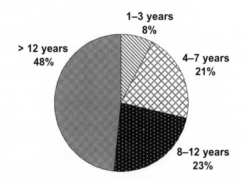

Figure 1.2   Leadership tenure of respondents from the ASTD/ Satyam Global Leadership Survey

Global Leader Interviews

We then asked participants in the survey if they would agree to be interviewed. Of the 200-plus respondents, we interviewed 10 and then sought another 45 who had lived and worked in different parts of the world, in order to have a broad global representation.

The average leadership tenure of these 55 global leaders was 14.8 years. They had each lived and worked in an average of three different countries. In total, they had lived and worked in more than 60 different countries (see Figure 1.3). In the previous two years, they had each travelled to an average of 10 different countries. Sixty-two percent were fluent in at least two languages, with 36% being fluent in three or more (see Box 1.1).

GLOBAL LEADER INTERVIEWEES FEATURED IN THIS BOOK

Erna Adelson,
Sony Electronics

Davide Arpili,
AlixPartners, LLP

Luc Bollen,
Hilton Hefei (China)

Mary Capozzi,
Best Buy Company, Inc.

Fernán R. Cepero,
The YMCA of Greater Rochester

Thomas Czaplicki,
Johnson Controls, Inc.

Dominique de Boisseson,
Alcatel China Investment Co. Ltd.

Umesh Kumar Dhoot,
Indian Oil Corporation, Ltd.

Avery Duff,
Rolls-Royce International, Ltd.

Lisa Earnhardt,
Royal & SunAlliance

David Gee,
Eli Lilly Japan K.K.

Alicia Goodman,
Taylor Nelson Sofres PLC (TNS)

Jeanette Harrison,
American Express Company

Stephen Heathcote,
Association of Chartered Certified Accountants (ACCA)

Steve Hoke,
Church Resources Ministries

Oliver Huegli,
UBS Service Centre (India) Pvt Ltd.

Angela Hyde,
AstraZeneca

Kent Jonasen,
A.P. Moller – Maersk A/S

Danny Kalman,
Panasonic Europe Ltd.

Karl-Heinz Lensing,
Kathrein Mobilcom Brasil LTDA

Stefan Mahrdt,
International Bank based in Sri Lanka

Elliott Masie,
The MASIE Center & Learning Consortium

Ideval Munhoz,
Satyam Computer Services, Ltd.

Kal Patel,
Best Buy Company, Inc.

Clive Pegg,
Bayer CropSciences AG

Hugh Peterken,
International Federation of Red Cross and Red Crescent Societies

Srinivas Prasad,
GlaxoSmithKline, Consumer Health Care

Mahesh Pratapneni,
IndyMac Bancorp, Inc.

Navi Radjou,
Forrester Research

Vladimir Raschupkin,
Rolls-Royce International

Tom Rath,
The Gallup Organization

Jair Ribeiro,
Braxis IT Services

Sam Sahana,
International Air Transportation Association

Marty Seldman,
Seldman Learning, Inc.

Giorgio Sfara,
Ministry of Foreign Affairs, Italy

Siow Choon-Neo,
Federal Express Pacific, Inc.

Bonnie Stoufer,
The Boeing Corporation

Oern Stuge,
Medtronic, Inc.

Phillip Styrlund,
The Summit Group

Raymond Tamayo,
Citigroup Inc.

Bill Thoet,
Booz Allen Hamilton

Elizabeth Haraldsdottir Thomas,
World Health Organization

Nils Thorsen,
Ernst & Young

William Vincek,
MGI PHARMA, INC.

In Chapters 2–6, you will have the opportunity to read their profiles and gain insights from each of them.

BOX 1.1   LANGUAGES SPOKEN FLUENTLY BY INTERVIEWEES

Arabic	Hebrew	Oriya
Bahasa Malaysia	Hindi	Portuguese
Chinese	Italian	Russian
Danish	Japanese	Spanish
Dutch	Kannada	Swedish
English	Malayalam	Tamil
French	Marathi	Telugu
German	Norwegian	Yuman
Gujarati		

Distillation of the Advice and Counsel from Successful Global Leaders

The third stage in developing *Leadership Without Borders* was distilling the advice and counsel given by our interviewees into strategies for success that anyone can use. Those strategies are summarised below and form the backbone of this book.

SUCCESSFUL STRATEGIES FROM WORLD-CLASS LEADERS

Successful global leaders are entrepreneurial. When most people hear the word "entrepreneur," they think "business owner." But the Merriam-Webster dictionary defines an "entrepreneur" as an innovator; one who recognizes opportunities and organizes resources to take advantage of the opportunity. In this context, everyone has the ability to be a successful global entrepreneur.

There are two types of leaders – those that *use* the best talent and those who *develop* the best talent. Ralph Nader said, "The function of leadership is to produce more leaders, not more followers."

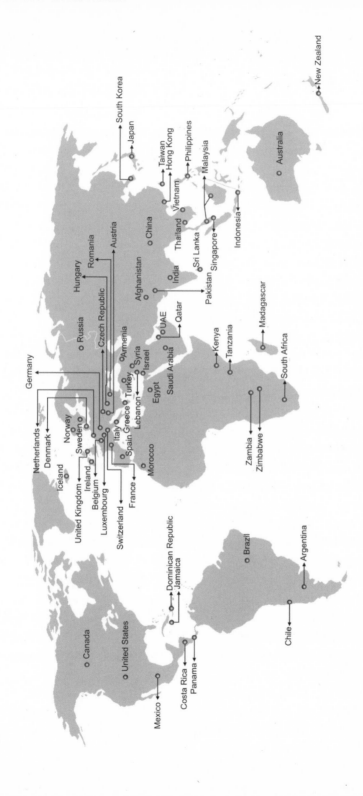

Figure 1.3   Countries where interviewees have lived and worked

Successful global leaders understand that developing talent is a top priority and therefore grow more leaders by constantly developing and assisting in the growth of their careers.

Successful global leaders understand the "business of global business." Deep domain and/or functional knowledge may take people up the career ladder, but the leaders we spoke with understand that this isn't enough. They understand the need to know the business of global business, including being technology perceptive, demonstrating financial acumen, and being skilled in the areas of strategic marketing, enterprise knowledge, organizational behavior, and operations management. They also successfully balance tactical work and strategic work, so that they both produce and lead simultaneously. Successful global leaders understand the need to balance time spent in thinking, doing, and communicating. As Mahatma Gandhi said, "Happiness is when what you think, what you say, and what you do are in harmony."

Successful global leaders lead others by influencing them. Mentoring, coaching, and teaching are three primary roles that leaders must master. People no longer want to work in settings where the leaders are authoritarian micro-managers. They want to work for leaders who empower them; someone who can, according to Peter Drucker, "lift a person's vision to higher sights, they raise a person's performance to a higher standard, building a personality beyond its normal limitations." Successful global leaders delight stakeholders. Within every organization, there are multiple stakeholders, including employees, investors, customers, and society at large. Leaders balance their efforts in order to enhance stakeholder delight and ensure the success of their organizations. In addition, they understand that a multifaceted, diverse workforce is better prepared to take full advantage of opportunities that result in mega-innovation and limitless creativity.

Finally, successful global leaders share a set of core vales, such as integrity, excellence, respect, and perseverance, and a set of traits such as desiring to learn, enjoying differences, and seeking to understand others.

GLOBAL LEADERSHIP COMPETENCIES

Before globalization of the workplace, leadership competencies were usually prioritized as shown in Figure 1.4.

1. *Geographic competencies* (within the context of where one works) include cultural differences, business protocols, and business legalities.
2. *Corporate and proprietary competencies* include internal culture, institutional business protocols, and proprietary skills; these competencies distinguish companies from each other.
3. *Functional and market competencies* include the skills necessary to provide the services or products offered.

The emphasis on geographic and corporate competencies in this model creates unnecessary barriers to success.

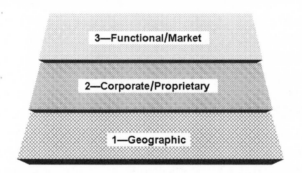

Figure 1.4 Pre-global leadership competency priorities

Today's companies must continually identify new, and extend existing, expectations about the competencies and characteristics required of their employees who are doing business in our increasingly global business environment. In order to be successful as global companies, our learning priorities need to shift from this focus on geographic competencies (where your company is located, or where you work), followed by organization-specific competencies, followed by functional and market skills. The global shift requires new competency priorities, as shown in Figure 1.5

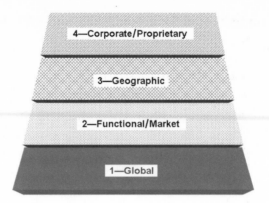

Figure 1.5   Global leadership competency priorities

1. *Global competencies* include a worldview, global business acumen, extensive networks, and change leadership skills, which provide the foundation for global success.
2. *Geographic competencies* (within the context of where one works) include cultural differences, business protocols, and business legalities.
3. *Functional and market competencies* include the skills necessary to provide the services or products offered.
4. *Corporate and proprietary competencies* include internal culture, institutional business protocols, and proprietary skills; these competencies distinguish companies from each other.

Priorities must shift to those illustrated in this model for global organizations to attain maximum success.

Our Global Leadership Survey respondents were asked what weighting their companies placed on each of these four competency areas. The results are shown in Figure 1.6.

The responses show that, overall, corporate/proprietary competencies have the highest weighting, followed by global, then geographic, and finally, functional/market competencies. Globalization demands that we shift our development priorities. At the foundation of the pyramid should be global competencies; above them, in decreasing order of importance, are functional/ market, geographic, and corporate/proprietary competencies. Global competencies break down barriers, enhancing performance and relationships and reducing an organization's reliance on

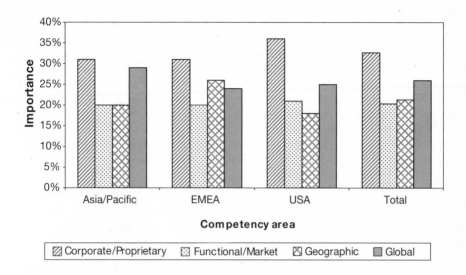

Figure 1.6 Competency priorities as perceived by respondents to the ASTD/Satyam Global Leadership Survey

corporate/proprietary competencies. While corporate/proprietary competencies are important in distinguishing organizations in a highly competitive world, they also create self-imposed barriers that diminish organizational performance and strain relationships.

What is the optimal formula for global leadership competencies? Based on our survey and interview results, we believe it should look more like the formula shown in Figure 1.7.

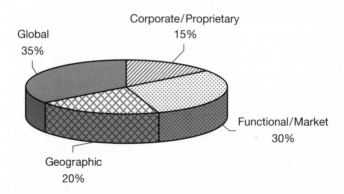

Figure 1.7 Competency priorities for optimal success as a global leader

CRITICAL COMPETENCY AREAS FOR GLOBAL LEADERS

Within the context of global competencies, survey respondents and our successful leader interviewees listed critical competencies needed to be a successful global leader in the following categories:

- Global business acumen: 29.5%
- Leadership characteristics: 16.6%
- Worldview: 12.5%
- People leadership: 27.2%
- Business leadership: 14.2%

The data suggests that while leaders recognize the importance of awareness of the global environment, it can be a challenging factor in running a team, and many organizations are therefore failing to make encouraging a worldview a key focus of their leadership programs. Here is what is included in each of the five critical categories identified above:

1. *Global business acumen* encompasses the ability to comprehend the business environment in its totality. This includes entrepreneurial and financial skills, profit and customer awareness, and domain, industry, and business knowledge.
2. *Leadership characteristics* encompass mental and emotional behaviors, including self-assurance, energy and enthusiasm, being learning-focused, and displaying empathy. It also includes a common set of core values, and the ability to remain authentic regardless of the situational and environmental challenges.
3. *Worldview* encompasses global environment awareness, cultural adaptation, and social, political, and economic trends. The common themes that emerged from our research – experience with foreign countries, years in leadership, and organization size – influenced our survey and interviewees' worldview responses. Variables related to foreign experience that influenced the worldview responses included number of countries traveled to for business, responsibility for staff in other countries, interaction with customers in other countries, and work experience in other countries. Leaders from larger

organizations were more likely to mention worldview than leaders from smaller organizations.

4. *People leadership* encompasses communication skills, ability to motivate and inspire people, human resource skills, networking, and development.

5. *Business leadership* encompasses strategic decision-making, efficient resource allocation, effective time management, problem-solving ability, ease in managing complexities, and flexibility. It also includes the ability to adapt leadership style to a variety of situations, creativity, innovation, and having a strategic/visionary mindset.

In the chapters that follow, we will focus on each of these five categories in the context of global competencies, providing stories, profiles, and practical information gathered from successful global leaders who have lived and worked in more than 60 different countries. As you read each chapter, take the time also to review the profiles of successful global leaders. Use their insights to assist you in developing your own action plan for success.

 ## Global Leadership Viewpoints

This chapter provided an overview of the information collected for *Leadership Without Borders* and provided a new way of prioritizing global competencies as the foundation of the competency pyramid. Along the way, we shared the following global leadership viewpoints:

- Significant changes have occurred since the emergence of the knowledge economy, demanding a recast of many of the roles of leaders. Today's leaders live and work in countries other than their home country, manage multinational teams, and have customers from all over the globe.
- More and more, the internet and other means of rapid communication are allowing diverse groups of employees to come together to work with and learn from each other.
- Successful global leaders are entrepreneurial; they understand the "business of global business"; they lead others by influencing

them, including through mentoring, coaching, and teaching; and they share a set of core values, such as integrity, excellence, respect, and perseverance, and a set of traits such as desiring to learn, enjoying differences, and seeking to understand others.

- Companies must continually identify new, and extend existing, expectations about the competencies and characteristics required of their employees who are doing business in our increasingly global business environment.
- At the foundation of the competency pyramid should be global competencies, then functional/market, geographic, and corporate/proprietary competencies.
- Global competencies break down barriers, enhancing performance and relationships, and reducing an organization's reliance on corporate/proprietary competencies.
- Corporate/proprietary competencies create self-imposed barriers that diminish organizational performance and strain relationships.
- Global business acumen encompasses the ability to comprehend the business environment in its totality.
- Leadership characteristics encompass mental and emotional behaviors, including self-assurance, energy and enthusiasm, being learning-focused, and displaying empathy. They also include a common set of core values, and the ability to remain authentic regardless of the situational and environmental challenges.
- Worldview encompasses global environment awareness, cultural adaptation, and awareness of social, political, and economic trends.
- People leadership encompasses communication skills, ability to motivate and inspire people, human resource skills, networking, and development.
- Business leadership encompasses strategic decision-making, efficient resource allocation, effective time management, problem-solving ability, ease of managing complexities, and ability to stay flexible. It also includes the ability to adapt leadership style to a variety of situations, creativity, innovation, and having a strategic/visionary mindset.

Endnotes

1   Nigel Andrews and Laura D'Andrea Tyson, "The Upwardly Global MBA," *Strategy & Business Magazine*, Fall 2004 (www.strategy-business.com/ press/16635507/04306).

2   Ian Davis and Elizabeth Stephenson, "Ten Trends to Watch in 2006," *The McKinsey Quarterly*, January 2006, p. 1.

3   International Air Transport Association, Five Year Forecast Shows Rapid Growth in Asia and Central Europe 2005–2009 Forecast Summary (www. iata.org/pressroom/pr/2005-10-31-01).

4   Beverley Fearis, *Business Week*, special advertising section, 2005, p. 1. © The McGraw-Hill Companies.

5   Merriam-Webster Dictionary online.

6   Ibid.

Chapter 2

Global Leadership Characteristics

INTRODUCTION

It was the summer of 1970, in Miami. As usual, I was working at my dad's petrol station, pumping gas. The day was hot and humid, as Miami is at that time of year. I heard the familiar *"ding-ding"* as a white Cadillac rolled over the cable, signaling the arrival of a customer. I walked to the car and asked, "How may I help you?" The driver, an elderly man, replied: *"Llena por favor mi tanque con el gas."* (Please fill my tank with gas.) Not understanding a word of Spanish, I said again: "How may I help you?", to which the man again replied: *"Llena por favor mi tanque con el gas,"* but this time pointing to the gas pump. I now understood that he wanted gas in his auto. (Back then, gasoline sold for 8 cents a gallon!) I filled the tank, he handed me some money, and I went to the office to get his change. By the time I returned he had driven off, leaving me with more than a $5 tip.

Señor Miguel became a regular customer. As his English improved, I learned he was a refugee from Cuba who had moved his family to Miami. I was fascinated to meet someone from another country and wanted to meet others. Over the next few years, more than 200,000 refugees from Cuba and Haiti settled in Miami, changing the culture of the city and my narrow perspective on the world forever. However, it wouldn't be until I was 29 that I would first venture outside the United States.

LEADERSHIP TRAITS AND CORE VALUES

Leadership characteristics divide into two categories: traits and core values. Leadership traits represent *WHO you are*. They develop over time. We don't know exactly how early our character traits develop, but once formed, they don't change quickly. Leadership core values represent *HOW you are* – the guiding principles for how everyone in an organization thinks and acts. We will examine both traits and core values from the perspective of world-class leaders who have shared with us their thoughts and successful strategies.

Leadership Traits Represent *WHO You Are*

According to Stewart Black and Hal Gregersen, "The general consensus seems to be that global leaders are born and then made... Since both global and domestic leaders lead, the fundamental difference is one of degree, not kind – but the difference in degree is not small. A domestic leader need only put his mind around one country, limited cultural paradigms, one political system, and one set of labor laws. A global leader must stretch his/her mind to encompass the entire world with hundreds of countries, cultures, and business contexts."[1] In other words, *all* leaders demonstrate certain leadership characteristics; what sets global leaders apart is that they exhibit a broader spectrum of these traits.

Global leaders who completed our Global Leadership Survey identified the following traits as being essential for world-class success:

- being open to new experiences;
- being curious about the world;
- being enthusiastic and energetic;
- being willing to listen and learn;
- being able to adapt rapidly to change;
- being willing to ask the right questions;
- being innovative and creative;
- being self-assured; and
- being results-oriented.

Just having these traits alone, however, won't ensure that a leader will be a successful *global* leader. As the leaders we interviewed indicated, the appropriate experiences, training, and opportunities to learn are still necessary.

Here is an excellent example of a young professional who exhibits all the traits shared by successful global leaders. I came to know Marcelo Santa Cruz de Freitas Ferraz when I first moved to India. At Satyam, we have a program called "Crossover," where young professionals from around the world move to India for a year or more to work for the company. This infusion of young professionals has helped to shift the culture at Satyam from an Indian-centric environment to a global one. Marcelo is a researcher. He now works with me and has spent countless hours reading and debating with me the merits of the topics set out in this book. Marcelo realizes that "cultural identity is what ultimately bonds groups of people. It is a must to understand the cultural backgrounds of others in order to successfully be a part of or lead diverse, multinational teams."

Marcelo was born and raised in São Paulo, Brazil. At 24 years of age, he has already lived in India, Hungary, and Lebanon. In addition, he has visited Austria, Belgium, Chile, the Czech Republic, France, Germany, Israel, Italy, Jordan, Mexico, the Netherlands, Poland, Romania, Serbia-Montenegro, Slovenia, Spain, Switzerland, Syria, Turkey, Ukraine, and the United States. Marcelo is fluent in Portuguese, English, German, French, and Spanish. He says, "Languages can reveal a lot of a society's values and perceptions. Learning a language is about enhancing the scope of people with whom you are able to communicate and it is about understanding how others use their language to process information."

This amazing young leader is on a quest to exemplify what global leadership is all about. Marcelo has all the traits of a global leader. He is open to new experiences, curious, enthusiastic, and energetic; he has a desire to listen and learn, is able to adapt rapidly to change, is willing to ask the right questions, is innovative and creative, self-assured, and is totally results-oriented. Most importantly, Marcelo recognizes the need to nurture his leadership traits so that he can hone his craft – global leadership.

We will now examine each of these leadership traits in turn.

Being Open to New Experiences

According to Peter Senge, "Effective leaders must cultivate open mindedness, in order to continually challenge their own favored views and to learn how to embrace multiple points of view in the service of building shared understanding and commitment."[2]

Davide Arpili
Director Performance Improvement Practice
AlixPartners, LLP
www.alixpartners.com

AlixPartners solves complex challenges. Since 1981, the firm has earned a reputation for hands-on problem-solving skills based on real-world operational, financial, and analytical expertise.

Davide Arpili works in the United States, and his country of citizenship is Italy. He has held leadership positions for more than four years. In the past two years, Davide has visited eight countries. His organization's official language is English. He speaks fluent English, German, Italian, Portuguese, and Spanish. Davide has lived and worked in Austria, Germany, Italy, Portugal, Spain, the United Kingdom, and the United States.

Global Leadership Insights
- Think global, act local.
- Choose flexible and open-minded team members capable of maximizing multiple nationalities and cultures.
- Listen, adapt, and evolve quickly.
- Know the language of business and the local culture.
- Use technology to create transparency and reduce barriers.

Always make sure that everyone is heard; this is especially important when the first language of the individual differs from that of the organization. You would say, "Let's go back for a second and listen to ...." The leader is responsible for balancing the relationships and improving the morale of the team. Allowing one culture to dominate others could impact the morale of the team.

Davide Arpili, of AlixPartners, LLP is originally from Italy. "When I studied for six months in Vienna, at 21, I became curious about what the world had to offer," says Davide. "Right from the start, I knew I had to be open to new experiences if I was going to be successful as a global leader." Bonnie Stoufer, at The Boeing Corporation (see profile in Chapter 3), says: "Be willing to jump out there and take a risk. Any time you make a job move, it broadens your perspective. Challenge yourself. Go where you don't know how to navigate, and be open to learning." Being open to new experiences allows leaders to gain new ideas, new points of view, and new experiences, but is being open enough? What drives global leaders to *seek out* new experiences?

Being Curious about the World

During the writing of this chapter, Ethan, a friend's four-year-old son, has been staying with us. He is curious about everything. When he sees something new, his eyes grow big and he says: "Look at that. What's that, Uncle Eddie?" or "Why is that like that?" The most successful global leaders retain curiosity as a trait as they grow older.

Marty Seldman, a colleague who is considered to be one of the world's most experienced executive coaches, having conducted in-depth, one-on-one coaching assignments with over 1,200 executives, agrees. "A key characteristic is *curiosity*; most people respond very well to someone who is curious." Nils Thorsen of Ernst & Young also agrees. "To be competitive as a global leader, be curious and ask questions of the people around you."

"Being global is about creating that spark of curiosity within yourself," says Kal Patel of Best Buy Corporation, Inc. "The real question is, are you curious about the world?"

Do you get energized and want to know more when you encounter something new, or do you simply look and then move on?

Marty Seldman, Ph.D.
Chief Executive Officer
Seldman Learning, Inc.
www.seldman.com

Seldman Learning offers a variety of programs, services, and materials with two main objectives: to help executives reach their full career potential; and to equip leaders with the necessary skills to create respectful, innovative, and ethical organizations.

Marty Seldman works in the United States, which is also his country of citizenship. He has held leadership positions for more than 20 years. In the past two years, Marty has visited two countries. His organization's official language is English. He speaks fluent English and Japanese. Marty has lived and worked in France, Japan, Morocco, Spain, and the United States.

Global Leadership Insights
- Demonstrate flexibility and self-awareness.
- Be a life-long learner.
- Influence and persuasion skills differ across cultures.
- Demonstrate organizational savvy.
- Be genuinely curious.

It is important to understand how each culture defines leadership. Most people will perceive others based on their cultural scorecard of norms and values. A leader needs to understand that the same behavior received positively in one culture may be received negatively in another. If you are genuinely curious, people will respond well to you.

Being Enthusiastic and Energetic

Elliott Masie (see profile in Chapter 3) is one of the most enthusiastic learners I have ever known. "You have to be excited about learning," he says. "You have to wake up in the morning, like Jack Welch said about GE [General Electric], excited every day, knowing you are going into work to learn something new. Getting on an airplane, having a teleconference, or a video-conference with people from other countries is when I learn the most."

According to Mary Capozzi, "The first six months working internationally aren't easy. Initially it takes a tremendous amount of enthusiasm and high energy."

When making choices, David J. Gee of Eli Lilly Japan K.K. advises: "As a leader you need to have high energy, and if you don't enjoy your life and your work, you can't maintain that high energy." In *The Leader of the Future 2*, Marshall Goldsmith writes, "Professionals need to look forward to going to work in the morning! The leaders of the future need to identify, support, and encourage passion in their professional employees. Leaders also need to 'lead by example' and demonstrate this same passion in their love for leadership."[3]

But, can energy and enthusiasm alone excite global leaders?

Being Willing to Listen and Learn

My mom used to say, "Son, you've been given two ears and one mouth for a reason." It took me a long time to recognize how important her advice was. Do you listen twice as much as you speak? The global leaders we interviewed nominated the ability to listen as an essential trait for success. "We make a lot of assumptions when leading domestically about knowing people and how they are going to respond, based on the fact that we speak the same language and grew up with similar cultures," says Mary Capozzi. "When leading globally, I don't have the same expectations. I know I don't know everything. I have to *listen* more carefully, and be *open* to differences." Dominique de Boisseson of Alcatel China Investment Co., Ltd. (see profile in Chapter 5) agrees. "Make sure you are ready to *listen and learn* every day." According to Jair Ribeiro of Braxis IT Services (see profile in Chapter 3), "It's a mistake to talk too much. Listen and don't be too impulsive about taking positions. Your intention and perception need to match your behavior." "A domestic company that's going global may be used to seeing a very simple picture around them; now they face thousands of new challenges," says Nils Thorsen of Ernst & Young. "To be competitive in this global paradigm, you need to ask questions of the people around you. Listen and have a thorough dialogue."

Nils Thorsen
Senior Manager
Ernst & Young
www.ey.com

Ernst & Young is a private accountancy consulting firm with nearly 114,000 employees stationed in 140 offices around the globe.

Nils Thorsen works in Denmark, which is also his country of citizenship. He has held leadership positions for more than five years. In the past two years, Nils has visited three countries. His organization's official language is English. He speaks fluent Danish, English, German, Norwegian, Spanish, and Swedish.

Global Leadership Insights
- Ensure that the organizational structure supports cross-regional collaboration.
- Understand the impact of your business on environmental and social sustainability in new areas entered.
- Use technology to share knowledge.
- Don't assume your culture is better than any others.

Utilize the productive and innovative forces of diversity. The difference in attitudes, spirit, and culture is a driver for innovation and doing things in a different way. See these differences as a productive force, as resources rather than as challenges or problems.

A domestic company or individual going global may be used to seeing a very simple picture around them, and may now face a raft of new challenges. To be competitive, ask questions of the people around you. Listen to and include the thoughts of others in your leadership of the company.

Do global leaders enjoy learning for the sake of learning, or do they learn in order to change and evolve?

Being Able to Adapt Rapidly to Change

Change is a constant. Change on a global level is far more complex because the scale and speed of change are dramatically greater. Being able to adapt to rapid changes, to different cultures and geographies, is an important leadership trait. "One of the big lessons I learned is that you have to be *curious*, and have an open mind," says Tom Rath of The Gallup Organization (see profile in Chapter 3). "You need to be willing to set aside your conventional wisdom, not only in terms of cultural sensitivities and localizing things, but also general belief systems, and political, economic, and religious issues." Erna Adelson of Sony Corporation says, "You need to have *appreciation* for other countries and cultures."

Having the ability to adapt rapidly to change is important, but does rapid change fuel or inhibit innovation and creativity?

Being Willing to Ask the Right Questions

I recently booked some travel for my family to Dubai. Much to my surprise, when the travel agent emailed me the reservation confirmation, I saw that we weren't sitting together. I called the agent and asked why. "You didn't request that you be seated together, so we assigned the best available seats to each of you," he replied. In talking further with the agent, I learned he had never been on a plane, and so had no context for anticipating something that I had taken for granted. I had to ask specifically. When you ask the right questions, you get the right answers. This becomes more apparent when working on a global scale. Successful global leaders are willing to ask the right questions and to be patient and tolerant until they get the answers they need.

Being Innovative and Creative

The world's most innovative companies, such as WL Gore, have created processes, systems, practices, and organizational structures that enable them to innovate continuously, as part of their organizational culture. Such companies are, alas, few and far

Kal Patel
Executive Vice President
International Strategy and Development
Best Buy Company
www.bestbuy.com

Best Buy Company, Inc. is an innovative Fortune 100 growth company that sells consumer electronics, home-office products, entertainment software, appliances, and related services.

Kal Patel works in the United States, and his country of citizenship is the United Kingdom. He has held leadership positions for more than eight years. In the past two years, Kal has visited nine countries. His organization's official language is English. He speaks fluent English and Gujarati. Kal has lived and worked in the United Kingdom and the United States.

Global Leadership Insights
• Have a strong, globally informed point of view about your context.
• Diversify your team to gain varied thoughts, strengths, and experiences.
• Develop a solid global technology platform.

Keep in mind that "global" doesn't mean just having many stamps in your passport. A global mindset is one with broad perspectives. If you make the mistake of equating travel with having a global mindset, you will miss the big challenge, which is to understand who you are as a person, through introspection. You need to have curiosity within yourself.

between. They are less concerned with what is happening in their own markets and industries because they are the leaders – their competitors are constantly kept off-guard by their innovations and struggle to know what these innovators know.[4] Even in the face of rapid and constant change, world-class leaders are inherently innovative and creative. It stems from their perpetual curiosity, combined with a keen ability to listen and learn. Innovative leaders marry the art of invention with the discipline of management. They are motivated by what is possible, not by what seems probable. They are willing to try out new ideas based on their possibility of success, rather than on measured success, and they consistently push the envelope – for themselves and all who follow. They fear stagnation more than taking risks; they are unflagging excellence junkies who resist the status quo and embrace failure as a step toward success. These leaders welcome change and challenge like fine, old friends. They are hungry for learning, stimulus, and discovery; they are motivated by their internal drive, rather than by external forces; they inspire others by "doing" and "demonstrating"; and they admit to a strong inner sense of direction, mission, or calling.[5]

Here is the true story of one such leader. In Hyderabad, there is a shop called Handicraft de India. The shop's owner, Showkat Khan, has just turned 30 and is one of the most innovative and creative leaders I have ever met. Khan, as everyone calls him, sets his prices in accordance with the Indian custom that truly embraces negotiating for goods. On any given day, Khan and his team bargain with customers who visit and select from the thousands of handmade crafts and carpets. Khan's business comes mostly from international visitors, with a smaller proportion from local residents.

Hyderabad isn't one of the most popular destinations in India, although the technology boom is changing that. Before I moved there, I had never heard of the city. Yet, it is steeped in history and in the traditions of southern India. Khan owns several shops in town, each with a different name. "Why don't you use the same name for all your shops?" I asked him. "Wouldn't the same name bring you greater brand recognition?" Khan replied, "When a customer comes into my store, if they don't find what they want or we cannot reach agreement on a price, then we tell them they should try the shop down the street." Each shop has a different name because his goal is that, wherever the customer ultimately purchases, they are buying from him, even though they may never realize it. Khan is a keen observer, especially of his foreign customers. By listening to his customers, he has figured out a successful strategy for capturing a greater share of the market – not by creating brand recognition, but rather, by avoiding it. I have spent many hours visiting Khan, getting to know him and his family, and with every encounter I learn something new from this young entrepreneur who has never

Mary Capozzi
Director of Operations
Best Buy Company, Inc.
www.bestbuy.com

Best Buy Company, Inc. is an innovative Fortune 100 growth company that sells consumer electronics, home-office products, entertainment software, appliances, and related services.

Mary Capozzi works in the United States, which is also her country of citizenship. She has held leadership positions for more than 20 years. Her organization's official language is English. She speaks fluent English and Italian. Mary has lived and worked in Belgium, Italy, and the United States.

Global Leadership Insights
- Connect with people; tell your story.
- Assess the strengths of the local team and use them wisely.
- Use technology to keep people connected, and to create buy-in from dispersed members.
- Understand that you don't have control over everything, and you'll sleep better.
- Be humble in the face of cultural differences with which you may not agree.

Learn about the cultures where your people are by taking the time to ask questions. Ask, "What was your worst experience with a foreign national coming over to work with you, and what was your best experience?" The responses will tell you everything you need to know about how that person perceives someone coming in and working with them from a foreign country.

traveled outside of India. If you ever find yourself in Hyderabad, pay a visit to Handicraft de India and ask for Khan. Tell him: "Ed sent me, and he said for you to give me a good price!"

Being Self-assured

Underlying all these traits is self-assurance, which comes from knowing who you are, feeling comfortable with ambiguity, and allowing things to work out. Several years back, I had the opportunity to hear Gerda Weissman Klein share her story about the time she spent in concentration camps during World War II. She was liberated in May 1945 in Czechoslovakia by an American soldier named Kurt Klein, who became her husband. Gerda completed her moving story by saying, "I learned that 90% of everything that you worry about probably will not happen and that the other 10% you cannot do anything about, so why worry?" Mary Capozzi of Best Buy agrees. "Very little keeps me awake at night now. Somewhere along the way I realized I didn't have as much control over things as I had previously thought. I used to worry about how people would react, and their buy-in. I realized that when I do my best, nothing is left to worry about."

"Don't lose hope," advises Giorgio Sfara of the Ministry of Foreign Affairs in Italy. "Always be convinced that there is a way out of a problem, and prove it with your actions." Effective global managers often display a good mix of self-confidence and humility. They are experienced enough to be both confident in their judgments and aware that there is seldom only one right answer to any issue of importance.[6] World-class leaders understand that they should adjust any display of confidence to the prevailing culture and the particular environment in which they are doing business. For example, in Japan, display of a high level of confidence might be perceived as being overly assertive or egotistical, while in the United States, the same behavior would be perceived as a positive leadership trait.

Being Results-oriented

World-class leaders say what they mean, and do what they say they will do. That pretty much sums it up!

David J. Gee
Director of IT (CIO Lilly) & Chief Privacy Officer
Eli Lilly Japan K.K.
www.lilly.com

Eli Lilly applies the latest research from its own worldwide laboratories, by collaborating with eminent scientific organizations, by making use of the most up-to-date technological tools, and by providing exceptional service to customers.

David Gee works in Japan, and his country of citizenship is Australia. He has held leadership positions for more than 16 years. In the past two years, David has visited 16 countries. He has lived and worked in Australia, China, Hong Kong, and Japan.

Global Leadership Insights
- It is most important to really enjoy what you do.
- Have a versatile leadership style.
- Attract and develop talent.
- Inspire trust – establish open and candid relationships.
- Use technology to help you stay connected.
- Adaptable – the world is changing quickly, so you must remain flexible and open to change.

Find role models to see what success looks like. Try to understand how that person operates and what makes them an *exceptional* leader. Look at your own strengths and adopt their best attributes. Don't be afraid to try this on. (Like a new pair of shoes, it may not feel comfortable at first.)

Core Values Represent *HOW You Are*

In Chapter 10, Dr. Ralph Shrader comments: "Booz Allen is a diverse community on many levels, but our core values unite us." Core values are the essential and enduring tenets of an organization; as guiding principles, they have a profound impact on how everyone in the organization thinks and acts. They are the soul of the organization.[7] When it comes to core values, Danny Kalman of Panasonic Europe advises: "Increasing amounts of people will be aware of the type of company for which they are working – does the organization have good ethics, values, and integrity? People want to be proud of their company, and will increasingly require corporate social responsibility in their companies." Therefore, it is important that a global leader share her or his values and align them to the company's mission.

Analysis of the Global Leadership Survey and following interviews identified 14 key core values of global leaders (see Table 2.1).

Giorgio Sfara believes that integrity and perseverance are essential if one is to be trusted.

Hugh Peterken of the International Federation of Red Cross and Red Crescent Societies agrees and adds: "Integrity and diversity are key to global leadership; you have to live both principles. You have to travel and work in different countries, build diverse teams, and always do what you say you will do!" Solid integrity leads to solid trust. What does trust look like? Trust is openness. Trust is valuing other people, such that you respect their opinions and perspectives. Trust means listening to others. It means moving outside your comfort zone and letting go of always doing things your way, or the way they have "always been done before."[8]

Several of our global leader interviewees discussed the need for work–life balance to be included on the core values list. Marty Seldman expressed his concerns as follows: "CEOs want to have a normal life, and balance is critical. But, with all the time zones, this has become a major challenge."

Luc Bollen, of Hilton Hefei in China, commented: "There is a new equilibrium in values, a shifting of priorities away from career towards family, community, and recreation. This is the case in Europe as well as China, especially in the urban areas such as Shanghai. People have started to pay attention to their health and leisure. They are no longer willing to 'die for their job' as they had in the past."

Many other leaders expressed the need for work–life balance to be given a higher priority, especially as the competition for talent continues to increase. "There needs to be a paradigm shift around career stability," says Hugh Peterken. "I don't think we adequately support workers in having families. Global leaders should engage in this debate. We need to view work and life balance as a competitive differentiator to recruit and retain the right talent."

Erna Adelson
Senior Vice President
Sony Electronics
www.sony.com

Sony Corporation of America is the US subsidiary of Sony Corporation, headquartered in Tokyo. Sony is a leading manufacturer of audio, video, communications, and information technology products for the consumer and professional markets.

Erna Adelson works in the United States, which is also her country of citizenship. She has held leadership positions for more than 12 years. In the past two years, Erna has visited two countries. She has lived and worked in Japan and the United States.

Global Leadership Insights
- Analyze business processes and systems from a global perspective. Determine which should be "centralized" and which should be "distributed" and locally unique.
- Set up internships/rotations between regions, as well as functions.
- Understand the sociology and history of countries, so that you know why things are the way they are.

There are different cultural approaches to authority, which will affect how you start, set, and execute initiatives. In some cultures, conflict is avoided. "Yes" doesn't always mean "yes." It is important to ascertain what people are really telling you, and to listen to more than their words.

A recent survey by the Association of Executive Search Consultants (AESC) indicated that a growing number of senior executives would turn down a promotion if they thought it would tip their work–life balance. "This should be a wake-up call to every employer," says Peter Felix, president of AESC. "The value gap between executives and employers is widening. Nearly half of the respondents are truly concerned that their work/life balance has changed for the worse in the last five years."[9] Clearly, this core value is on the minds of leaders across the globe.

Table 2.1 Key core values of global leaders

Core values	Behaviors
Conviction	Conveys sincerity and confidence in beliefs and decisions; willingness to make and stand by difficult decisions.
Diversity	Values different perspectives; builds multifaceted (see Chapter 5, "Global People Leadership"), diverse teams; seeks to understand what drives and motivates individuals.
Entrepreneurship	Recognizes opportunities and organizes resources to maximize them.
Excellence	Strives for excellence, which is not the same as perfection; recognizes that "excellence" may vary from country to country, depending upon the local context.
Fairness	Makes decisions that are fair and equitable.
Humility	Acts in the knowledge that he or she is no better or more important than others.
Integrity	Demonstrates honesty and makes ethical decisions.
Passion	Leads by example; demonstrates a high level of energy and enthusiasm.
Perseverance	Shows resolve in moving toward the laid path; strong will and drive to accomplish.
Positive attitude	Maintains a positive attitude; represents decisions and policies in a positive manner.
Respect	Demonstrates a high regard for others, regardless of their station in life; treats everyone with dignity.
Service-oriented	Provides extraordinary, "extra mile" assistance to everyone, whether internal to the organization or a customer.
Teamwork	Easily adapts to being a team player; encourages teamwork across the organization.
Work–life balance	Balances time spent at work with other dimensions of one's family, community, and social life.

Danny Kalman
Director Human Resources
Panasonic Europe Ltd.
www.panasonic-europe.com

Panasonic (Matsushita Electric Industrial Co., Ltd.) is one of the largest electronic product manufacturers in the world, manufacturing and marketing products under brands such as Panasonic, National, Technics, and Quasar. Headquartered in Osaka, Japan, the company employs 334,400 people in 122 countries.

Danny Kalman works in the United Kingdom, which is also his country of citizenship. He has held leadership positions for more than four years. In the past two years, Danny has visited 20 countries.

Global Leadership Insights
- Adjust your behaviors to new environments and situations.
- Establish a broad people network.
- Be culturally attuned.
- Embrace change as an opportunity, not as a threat.
- Ensure that you are proactive and respond rapidly when managing, communicating, and adapting to the market.

Companies throughout the world should expect increasing numbers of people to be aware of the type of company for which they are working. Does the organization have good ethics, values, and integrity? People want to be proud of their company, and will increasingly require their organizations to demonstrate social responsibility.

 Global Leadership Viewpoints

This chapter provided information on global leadership characteristics, which include both traits and core values. Along the way, these global leadership viewpoints were shared:

- Leadership traits represent *WHO you are.* They develop over time. We don't know exactly how early our character traits develop, but once formed, they don't change quickly.

- Leadership core values represent *HOW you are*. They are the guiding principles for how everyone in the organization thinks and acts.
- Common traits of world-class leaders include being open to new experiences, curious about the world, enthusiastic and energetic, willing to listen and learn, able to adapt rapidly to change, willing to ask the right questions, innovative and creative, self-assured, and results-oriented.
- It is important that a global leader be willing to share her or his values, and to align them to the company's mission.
- There are 14 key core values of global leaders: conviction, diversity, entrepreneurship, excellence, fairness, humility, integrity, passion, perseverance, positive attitude, respect, service-oriented, teamwork, and work–life balance.
- Trust means moving outside your comfort zone and letting go of always doing things your way, or even the way they've always been done before.
- In terms of work–life balance as a core value, there is a new equilibrium in values, a shifting of priorities away from career toward family, community, and recreation.

Was I born with the right characteristics to be successful as a global leader? I share with successful global leaders the traits discussed in this chapter, so my answer to that question would be "Yes." However, what *made* me a leader was my encounter as a young man with the Cuban émigré, Señor Miguel, at my father's gas station. He was the catalyst that energized me to seek out my global leadership journey. *Gracias*, Señor Miguel.

Luc Bollen
General Manager
Hilton Hefei, China
Hilton Hotels
www.hilton.com

Hilton Hotels Corporation is the leading global hospitality company, owning, managing, or franchising a portfolio of some of the best-known and most highly regarded brands, including Hilton, Conrad, Doubletree, Embassy Suites Hotels, Hampton Inn, Scandic, and The Waldorf-Astoria Collection.

Luc J.J. Bollen works in China, and his country of citizenship is Belgium. He has held leadership positions for more than 12 years. In the past two years, Luc has visited seven countries. His organization's official language is English. He speaks fluent English, Dutch, French, and German. Luc has lived and worked in Belgium, China, Egypt, Madagascar, South Africa, and the United Arab Emirates.

Global Leadership Insights
- Be resilient in dealing with different cultural environments.
- Avoid the "one jacket fits all" mentality.
- Translate your expertise and experiences into new environments.
- People value their family and leisure time perhaps as much as, if not more than, their work.

Don't spend too much time channeling energy negatively, by constantly making comparisons between countries and finding some lacking; instead, look for the opportunities that arise from the differences between different places. The key is to recognize the strengths and opportunities, rather than the weaknesses and threats.

Hugh Peterken
Chief Information Officer
International Federation of Red Cross and Red Crescent Societies
www.ifrc.org

The International Federation of Red Cross and Red Crescent Societies is the world's largest humanitarian organization, providing assistance without discrimination as to nationality, race, religious beliefs, class, or political opinions. Headquartered in Geneva, it has more than 60 delegations strategically located to support activities around the world.

Hugh Peterken works in Switzerland, and his country of citizenship is Australia. He has held leadership positions for more than four years. In the past two years, Hugh has visited 20 countries. His organization's official languages are Arabic, English, French, and Spanish. He speaks fluent English and French. Hugh has lived and worked in Australia, Switzerland, and the United Kingdom.

Global Leadership Insights
- Ensure that people are convinced of your genuineness when introducing requirements into the change process.
- Find ways to get the best out of your people, and to truly develop their potential.
- Have a shared strategic vision.
- Have an understanding of and ability to use consultation, taking into account facts and inputs from a variety of global sources.

Enjoy meeting and dealing with people from different backgrounds. Build the organization around the right people. Create a balance by bringing people with different strengths and backgrounds together. Integrity and diversity are critical behaviors to practice. Having experiences across industries can provide a broader perspective and result in your being a more interesting candidate. Gain international perspectives.

Endnotes

1　J. Stewart Black and Hal B. Gregersen, "High Impact Training: Forging Leaders for the Global Frontier," *Human Resource Management*, Summer/Fall 2000, pp. 173–4.

2　F. Hesselbein and M. Goldsmith (eds), *The Leader of the Future 2* (San Francisco: Jossey-Bass, 2006), pp. 41–42.

3　Ibid., p. 170.

4　Dave Pollard's "How to Save the World" blog, How Knowledge Drives Innovation (http://blogs.salon.com/0002007/), accessed November 27, 2006.

5　Leigh Duncan, "Innovative Leadership – A Definition and Roll Call," The Fast Company Weblog, August 2005 (http://blog.fastcompany.com/archives/2005/08/08/innovative_leadership_a_definition_and_roll_call.html), accessed November 27, 2006.

6　Stephen Rhinesmith, "Global Mindsets for Global Managers," *Training & Development*, 1992, p. 66.

7　James Collins and Jerry Porras, "Building Your Company's Vision," *Harvard Business Review*, September/October 1996, pp. 65–77.

8　J. Kouzes and B. Posner, *A Leader's Legacy* (San Francisco: Jossey-Bass, 2006), pp. 74–75.

9　Chris Silva, "Work–life Concerns Impede Senior Executive Promotions," *Employee Benefit News*, October 2006 (www.benefitnews.com/detail.cfm?id=9581).

Chapter 3

Global Business Acumen

INTRODUCTION

In 1994, I began working for Seer Technologies in Cary, North Carolina. I made my first business trip outside the United States later that year, when I was given the opportunity to fly to London to meet with my counterparts on the Seer training team. The internet was very new, and I didn't have access, so my research comprised reading the standard tourist books that I purchased from my local bookstore. I arrived in London after taking an overnight flight from the States. I had been advised to get myself on local time as quickly as possible, so I went directly to the office. My two weeks in London taught me much about the culture and work environment in the United Kingdom. Most importantly, I realized I had much to learn if I was to become a successful global leader.

Twelve years later, I speak on a regular basis to groups of leaders from varied backgrounds. I always ask them, "How many of you are experts in IT; experts in HR; experts in engineering?" and so on. A lot of hands go up. However, when I ask, "How many of you are experts in the business of business?" I usually see puzzled looks on faces and only one or two hands raised. Successful global leaders recognize the need to become experts in the business of business.

A global leader interviewed for this book was a contact through my godson, John Ballantine, who is a student at the University of Minnesota.

Dr. Oern Stuge
President
Cardiac Surgery
Medtronic, Inc.
www.medtronic.com

Medtronic is the world leader in medical technology, providing life-long solutions for people with chronic disease. Headquartered in the United States, Medtronic employs 36,000 people in 120 countries around the globe. In 2006, revenue was US$11.3 billion.

Oern Stuge works in the United States, and his country of citizenship is Norway. He has held leadership positions for more than 21 years. In the past two years, Oern has visited 15 countries. His organization's official language is English. He speaks fluent Danish, Dutch, English, French, German, Norwegian, and Swedish. Oern has lived and worked in Denmark, the Netherlands, Norway, Switzerland, and the United States.

Global Leadership Insights
- Develop an understanding of cultural differences and the dynamics of the different markets.
- Travel and meet people in their own environment.
- Know what you know and what you don't know.
- Be authentic and transparent.

It is essential that you are accessible for the people and the market. Technology facilitates accessibility. When you have a global responsibility, you can make a greater impact on people's lives. Understand the cultural differences: what works, how people think, and by what criteria they make decisions. Be open, curious, ask questions, listen, and learn.

John introduced me to his roommate's father, Dr. Oern Stuge. Currently, Oern is senior vice president and president of Medtronic Cardiac Surgery, serving as a member of both the Medtronic executive and operating committees. He started his career as a medical doctor, but after three years he took on the additional role of medical director for a start-up. When interviewed by the International Institute for Management Development (IMD), Oern said: "As I became more involved in the business side of things, I realized that I needed another leg to stand on and decided to acquire a deeper business understanding." His search focused on the top European MBA programs, before settling on IMD's MBA. "I learned a lot from both the different educational and cultural backgrounds of my colleagues as well as from the length and diversity of their work experience."

Oern believes that the international perspective and the global business acumen that he acquired contributed significantly to the steady progression of his career. "The program gave me the 'toolbox' to understand and handle profit and loss responsibility, finance, manufacturing, and strategic topics that I didn't learn in medical school. It also gave me confidence in terms of handling these topics," he said.

The Hay Group has teamed up with *Fortune* magazine since 1997 to identify and rank the "World's Most Admired Companies." In 2006, "effectiveness in conducting business globally" was added as a measurement attribute. According to The Hay Group, "It is a timely topic, as operating across geographic boundaries is becoming more and more essential for companies competing in an economy that is increasingly global."[1] The most admired companies in the world are those that understand the importance of developing global business acumen.

Experts define the business of business – or business acumen – in multiple ways. I recently read an article in *Strategy & Business Magazine*, a quarterly publication put out by Booz Allen Hamilton. Ram Charan, in a piece entitled "Sharpening Your Business Acumen," states: "This is the art of business acumen: linking an insightful assessment of the external business landscape with the keen awareness of how money can be made – and then executing the strategy to deliver the desired results."[2] He goes on to present a six-step guide for incorporating external trends into your internal strategies. One simple way to begin is by asking yourself a series of six questions, and then exploring your responses with colleagues and peers:

1. What is happening in the world today?
2. What does it mean for others?
3. What does it mean for us?

Fernán R. Cepero
Vice President of Human Resources
YMCA of Greater Rochester
www.rochesterymca.org

The YMCA of Greater Rochester, New York is a charitable association of members. YMCA of Greater Rochester has been providing human service programs as part of an international organization since 1844.

Fernán Cepero works in the United States, which is also his country of citizenship. He has held leadership positions for more than 14 years. In the past two years, Fernán has visited one country. His organization's official language is English. He speaks fluent English and Spanish. Fernán has lived and worked in Austria, Canada, Germany, Luxembourg, Mexico, Panama, and the United States.

Global Leadership Insights
• Consistently mentor and teach others.
• Gain breadth and depth of experience in your career.
• Study and understand the differences between cultures.
• Don't "hide behind" technology; connect with people individually.

A key leadership challenge for me involved the emerging markets, especially in China. I am going to China as part of a delegation to meet with the government to address their growing economy, market, and presence in the world of business. We hope to identify the challenges they will face in the global market. The major challenge for us is to understand how best to integrate this new major player into the global market.

4.   What would have to happen first (for the results we want to occur)?
5.   What do we have to do to play a role?
6.   What do we do next?

In an article that appeared in *T&D Magazine*, "Build Your Business Acumen," Barry Stern and Bob Walters provide their definition for workplace learning professions: "Understanding the organization's business model and financial goals; utilizing economic, financial, and organizational data to build and document the business case for investing in workplace learning and performance solutions; using business terminology when communicating with others."[3]

Fernán Cepero, vice president of human resources with the YMCA of Greater Rochester, New York, says: "Global responsibility involves understanding political issues, foreign affairs, world trade agreements, and other issues more broadly than managing domestically." This is the essence of the value proposition for why global leaders need to enhance their global business acumen.

So, how *can* you enhance your global business acumen? An MBA degree with an emphasis on International Business would be ideal, but not everyone has the time, inclination, or opportunity to take on further study. (In order to expand the global business acumen of its leaders, Satyam has instituted a Certificate of Global Business Leadership – see Table 3.1.) It is recommended that you hone your skills, focusing on those that are the most critical for your specific business and industry. From the perspective of our world-class leaders, the following are the most critical global business acumen areas:

- business terminology;
- regional and global economics;
- global financial awareness;
- strategic marketing;
- organizational behavior;
- enterprise knowledge management;
- operations management; and
- business innovation.

Let's look at each of the most critical global business acumen areas.

CRITICAL GLOBAL BUSINESS ACUMEN AREAS

Business Terminology

Ramalinga Raju, Satyam's chairman, says: "The best leaders are those who can demystify knowledge, who can explain concepts in

Table 3.1   Building global business acumen at Satyam

The *Certificate of Global Business Leadership* is the result of a close collaboration among three partners. The program equips leaders with best-in-class skills taught in world-class MBA programs. The *Certificate of Global Business Leadership* is a 28-week program, delivered through a partnership with U21Global, covering the essentials of global business acumen. Practice is supported by the use of Harvard Business School Publishing cases, articles, and other supporting material, including Harvard Manage Mentor.

Regional and Global Economics
- The Global Economy
- Strategies for Economic Growth and Development
- Asian Financial Crisis and Subsequent Challenges
- International Trade and Role of Government
- Theories of Foreign Investment
- Impact of Foreign Investment and Role of Government
- Regional Economic Integration
- Internationalization Theories
- Country Analysis for Business Expansion

Organizational Behavior and Leadership
- Decision Making
- Managing People across the Globe
- Managing Groups

The International Business Environment
- Global Environments
- The Employee in the International Business Environment
- Cultural, Political, and Economic Environments
- International Human Resources Management
- Management of Expatriates
- Compensation, Motivation, and Performance Management in an International Setting

Marketing Management
- Customer Needs and Market Orientation
- Positioning and Perceptual Mapping
- Branding of Products and Services
- Services Marketing and Management
- Marketing Mix Elements – Product, Price, Place (distribution channels), and Promotion
- Consumer Behavior
- Customer Relationship Management

Finance and Financial Statements
- Components of Financial Reports
- Financial Statements
- Cash Flow View
- Capital Markets
- Time Value of Money
- Financial Decision Making – Investments, Capital Budgeting, Dividends
- Risk and Return
- Mergers and Acquisitions
- Data Analysis for Decision Makers

Enterprise Knowledge Management
- The Knowledge Economy
- Fundamental Processes of Knowledge Management – Knowledge Creation, Knowledge Sharing, and Knowledge Utilization

Operations Management
- Operations Management – Design, Operation, and Improvement of the Transformation Process to Convert Various Inputs into Output of Desired Goods and Services
- Just-in-time and Lean Manufacturing
- Value Chain Management
- Materials Requirement Planning (MRP) and Enterprise Resource Planning (ERP)
- Quality as a Major Distinguishing Feature in the International Marketplace

Strategic Management for Innovative Businesses
- Strategic Thinking
- Business-level Strategy
- Managing Change
- Global Entrepreneurial Strategies
- 21st-century Competitive Landscape – Globalization and Technological Changes

Tom Rath
Global Practice Leader, Workplace and Leadership Consulting
The Gallup Organization
www.gallup.com

The Gallup Organization employs many of the world's leading scientists in management, economics, psychology, and sociology. Gallup's 2,000 professionals deliver services at client organizations, through the web, at Gallup University's campuses, and in 40 offices around the world.

Tom Rath works in the United States, which is also his country of citizenship. He has held leadership positions for more than eight years. In the past two years, Tom has visited seven countries. His organization's official language is English. He speaks fluent English and Spanish.

Global Leadership Insights
- Open your mind to all perspectives.
- Understand your strengths and blind spots.
- Care about people.
- Become the leading expert in your talent or passion.
- Step back and listen; resist the urge to jump to conclusions.

The collaboration that exists today wouldn't have occurred 10 years back. The people at our company with the best ideas, whether they are in Beijing, Budapest, or London, can quickly proliferate their ideas to a raft of people and eventually to our clients. Technology will continue to dramatically affect leadership in the next five years, because the best opinions out there will have a broader and even more global forum.

their simplest form and make them understandable by all people." All the leaders we interviewed agreed.

Tom Rath of The Gallup Organization and bestselling author of *How Full is Your Bucket?* provides this advice for building your global business vocabulary. "In discussions with executives on a global scale, simply knowing what is going on in your corner of the world will not cut it. Stay in-tune with the leading publications in order to know your business, know your industry, and know how business works."

Regional and Global Economics

All leaders, whatever their industry or market, need to understand how economies impact one another in our global society. The world's economies are so tightly interwoven that a slight fluctuation in the currency of one country can set off a chain reaction around the world. V. Shankar illustrates this in Chapter 9: "As demonstrated by the Asian financial crisis of 1997, the financial circuits of most markets are interlinked and connected. What started as a simple devaluation of the Thai baht turned into a full-scale contagion in Korea, Indonesia, Malaysia, and many other countries in the region."

This interconnectedness affects not only the stability of emerging economies, but also the competitiveness of a company's products produced in one country and exported to another. For example, when the Brazilian real devalued against the US dollar and the Argentine peso, the Argentinean manufactured car export market lost its competitiveness and slumped 20%. Consequently, Italy's Fiat, America's Ford, and France's Renault had to lay off workers in their Argentinean factories.[4]

Global leaders understand the economic environment by studying local, regional, and global economic indicators. Keeping abreast of these indicators by reading the business press and journals, watching or listening to business news programs, and doing original research ensures your ability to understand the circumstances in which you are working and provides an edge over your competitors. As an example of how events in one country can affect the broader business world, let's consider the rapid growth of business in India and China. Accelerated growth has resulted in increased travel, for both business and pleasure, to and from these countries. Increased travel has expanded the demand for hotels and supplemental services, driving up prices and enhancing profits in those markets. In fact, I read recently that a business visit to Bangalore now costs more than a visit to London, Paris, or New York. Bangalore is now third on the list of the most expensive cities for hotel rooms, with average room rates 42% higher than a year ago. Margaret Bowler, the general manager of hotel relations at Business Travel International UK, told *The Telegraph*: "Bangalore has become the home for call centres, so lots of companies have moved in to set up operations. Hotels have been able to put up their prices

Elliott Masie
President
The MASIE Center & Learning Consortium
www.masie.com

The MASIE Center is an international e-lab and think tank located in New York and dedicated to exploring the intersection of learning and technology.

Elliott Masie is a futurist and learning industry legend, who works in the United States, which is also his country of citizenship. He has held leadership positions for more than 22 years. In the past two years, Elliott has visited 13 countries. He has lived and worked in Ireland and the United States.

Global Leadership Insights
- Understand trends globally.
- Be an overt and passionate learner.
- Get multiple perspectives and use 360-degree news.
- Travel extensively, and out of your comfort zone.
- Make long-term relationships across the globe.
- Learn a second language.

It's easy for me to meet people from other countries my own age, but it's harder for me to find the context to talk to an 18-year-old person in India or Beijing. The global phenomenon is both cultural and generational. It is often where the intersection of culture and generations occurs that the most interesting things happen.

on the back of the increase in demand."[5] With international carriers starting to fly directly to Bangalore, the situation is only likely to worsen. British Airways launched a five-times-weekly service from Heathrow in October 2005, and its success has already prompted the airline to increase the frequency to six flights weekly.[6]

Elliott Masie, president of The MASIE Center, advises: "Do an adjustment of the economics. Run a spreadsheet not just as an exchange value issue, but also look at money framed against the cultural context. Many graduates from business schools zoom abroad with a spreadsheet that includes exchange values, but they don't factor in the second, third, fourth dimension of those spreadsheets." These dimensions include cost of living, human capital elements, and intangibles. People who are good at this question what it means beyond the boundaries of their own country's economics.

There are many more factors to consider. "Globalization of the economy, of finances, can be beneficial to everybody, but it's difficult to prove with disaggregating factors such as civil conflict and terrorism," says Giorgio Sfara of the Ministry of Foreign Affairs in Italy. "These factors create new economic divides, instead of multiplying links and connections among people."

Bill Thoet, Booz Allen Hamilton, suggests another dimension to consider: "It's important to understand the balance between the panache of going global and the business returns based upon strengths. When opening up emerging markets, don't lose your ability to serve existing business. The opportunity cost from local markets is higher when you expand globally." World-class leaders never forget that they are running a business; going global is a means to improve their business, not an end in itself.

Global Financial Awareness

Leaders need to be aware of how financials influence their business. There are thousands of books on this subject on the market. The following is an overview of three key areas: reading annual reports; raising funds in foreign markets; and the impact of currency fluctuations.

Reading Annual Reports

Can you read and understand a company's annual report? Whether one is the leader of a company or an investor in it, it is essential that you are able to interpret financials in order to understand how the company is doing. Considerations include revenue recognitions, measurement of profitability, growth orientation, and the ability to read a balance sheet and profit/loss statement. How profitability is measured will depend upon the economics of a particular marketplace. For example, compensation and benefits in India cost

Giorgio Sfara
Minister Plenipotentiary
Ministry of Foreign Affairs, Italy
www.esteri.it/ita

The Ministry of Foreign Affairs (MFA) in Italy is in charge of implementing the government's foreign policy. The MFA employs 8,500 people in Italy and in embassies and consulates in 120 countries across the globe.

Giorgio Sfara works in Italy, which is also his country of citizenship. He has held leadership positions for more than 10 years. In the past two years, Giorgio has visited six countries. His organization's official language is Italian. He speaks fluent English, French, Italian, and Spanish. Giorgio has lived and worked in Belgium, the Dominican Republic, France, Italy, Russia, South Africa, Syria, Sweden, and Switzerland.

Global Leadership Insights
- Learn about, understand, and adjust your actions to differing cultures.
- Attain strong professional skills in the field in which you lead.
- Make sound and timely decisions.
- Integrity and accountability are necessary if you are to be trusted.
- Don't lose hope; be convinced there is a solution to any business issue.

There are three aspects of managing people globally that cover all cultures internationally: (1) identify a common mission; (2) inject into each individual's psychology the idea of a common mission, in order to mobilize energies; and (3) keep people informed and prove that you will look out for their well-being.

significantly less than in the United States. Because the marketplace is aware of this, the expectation is that products and services of the same quality will cost less when they come from India. Therefore, even though one might think that a company providing a service out of India has a greater profit margin (revenue minus labor costs), the reality when doing business in countries with low-cost labor is that margins are, on average, lower and the volume of business (the amount of goods and services sold) is, on average, higher.

Raising Funds in Foreign Markets

Leaders across industries and countries use their global business acumen to raise funds in foreign financial markets. Look at the number of foreign companies listed on the New York Stock Exchange (NYSE): as of December 2005, 453 of the 2,672 companies traded on the NYSE, or 17%, were non-US businesses. In order to carry out a successful initial public offering of stock, or to launch bonds in foreign financial markets, business leaders must comply with foreign regulations. These may require changes in processes and organization structure, such as the creation of investor relations departments, or consideration of the financial and accounting disclosure requirements of the *Sarbanes-Oxley Act* of 2002 in the United States, or of similar policies in the European Union. In addition, the maturity of a financial market affects the amount and type of financing options available to a leader. While in mature markets a leader can find a wide variety of financial products, his or her options may be quite limited in emerging markets.

Be Current on Currency

When determining what areas to concentrate on in order to expand your global business acumen, a further very important economic indicator is currency fluctuations. Consider this:

- In September 2006, US$1 was worth 46.0281 Rupees (average rate)
- In October 2006, US$1 was worth 45.3582 Rupees (average rate)

The fluctuation equated to a 1.46% decrease in the value of the US dollar. The drivers for this could have been a shift in interest rates, or in consumer confidence, or even politics. If you had traveled to India in October 2006, it meant that your loss on converting US$1,000 in cash at that time, instead of a month earlier, was about US$14.60. Perhaps you are thinking it's not a large enough sum to worry about. Well, you couldn't be more wrong!

Bill Thoet
Vice President
Booz Allen Hamilton
www.boozallen.com

Booz Allen Hamilton, founded in 1914, is a leading global consulting firm. It helps government and commercial clients solve their toughest problems with services in strategy, operations, organization and change, and information technology.

Bill Thoet works in the United States, which is also his country of citizenship. He has held leadership positions for more than 13 years. In the past two years, Bill has visited six countries.

Global Leadership Insights
- Understand and embrace cultural diversity.
- Be flexible, and adapt your style and business approach to local conditions.
- Understand the legal differences and risks of working in different countries.
- Use virtual communications in combination with face-to-face meetings.
- Understand the characteristics of the global as well as domestic marketplaces.

If you are doing business in a country such as India, and go in selling by the hour, it becomes glaringly obvious how expensive you are relative to others. If you offer a fixed price, the organization can compare the cost to value derived. Another example is in launching our global business; we may take some leaders abroad, but it's important that we also hire local professionals. Having the right mix of people from multiple countries enhances businesses internally and externally. You gain credibility as an organization by showing that you are hiring the best people.

Let's say an India-based company earns revenues of US$100 million a year from clients in the United States. Average monthly revenues would be approximately US$8 million. A 1.46% fluctuation equates to an average monthly increase in revenues of

US$116,800 for the local company, and to an equivalent average monthly increase in expenses for the US-based customer.

Does that get your attention? Would knowing this assist you in making more informed decisions about billing cycles, when to buy goods from other countries, capital investments, and so on? Of course, it would. Add tracking currencies to your data-gathering process. The internet is the simplest place to find currency information. There are ways to mitigate currency exchange and volatility risk. Global leaders use simple derivatives such as futures contracts and options, which are widely available in most developed countries and in some of the most important emerging markets.

Strategic Marketing

Jair Ribeiro, chief executive officer of Braxis IT Services in Brazil, advises: "Cultural and customer considerations, as well as the scope and size of the market, are more complex. Determining a strategy of how and where to grow involves having fewer boundaries."

Global business acumen includes being well informed about strategic marketing. As Jair suggests, it requires a much more complex understanding of markets, including how different cultures are motivated to buy. Who you sell to, what your product looks like, when you sell (seasonally), where you sell (bricks-and-mortar, online), why people are motivated to buy, class and cultural variances, people's interests and attitudes, and the maturity of the markets are just some of the issues you face when marketing globally. It really comes down to understanding differences among different people and customizing your approach. John Pepper, of Procter & Gamble, shared his experience of seeing short-term sales of a product fall significantly in China following a change in color on the packaging. "What we had missed," John said, "was that in China the consumer really knows what to buy by the color coding. We had the view that it was much better to have just one color for the whole brand, which in many ways is true. One color creates a block appearance on the shelf. We went to great lengths on the packaging to describe the change, but people weren't reading the words."[7] Equally important is when a marketing campaign is translated from one language to another. Dr. Mukesh Aghi provides

Jair Ribeiro
Chief Executive Officer
Braxis IT Services
www.braxis.com.br

Braxis IT Services is a Brazilian company providing a wide range of services, strategic solutions, and complete information technology products to meet the needs of the most competitive business organizations from all productive sectors.

Jair Ribeiro works in Brazil, which is also his country of citizenship. He has held leadership positions for more than 18 years. In the past two years, Jair has visited 10 countries. His organization's official language is Portuguese. He speaks fluent English and Portuguese. During his career, Jair has lived and worked in Brazil and the United States.

Global Leadership Insights
• Understand how motivators and energizers differ.
• Learn to adapt to economic and cultural scenarios.
• Have knowledge of logistics management in order to be able to deal with complicated global environments.

People all over the world want to be energized by their leaders, and the way you position yourself to create that energy may differ. Make sure your intention matches the perception – find the energizing ability within yourself and then position yourself appropriately to convey the right message in the right way. Develop the ability to listen and to ask the right questions, and don't jump to conclusions based solely on your background.

some excellent and insightful examples of this in Chapter 7, "The Artistry and Science of Global Leadership."

Organizational Behavior

Recruiting, developing, and retaining talent is essential for success in any business. However, the complexities of recruiting, developing, and retaining talent are much greater for global leaders, who need to work within multiple cultural norms. People prefer leaders who influence rather than manage, who help to develop competencies and careers, who grow more leaders, and who are able to listen and learn. Most of the global leaders we interviewed nominated the ability to listen, to be open to the multiple views and feelings of others, as being paramount in having a positive organizational climate. Understanding organizational behavior is more than just knowing how to motivate and develop people to gain maximum performance. It also includes having a working knowledge of, or access to appropriate resources on, labor laws and business norms (written and unwritten, spoken and unspoken). Leaders we spoke to agreed that organizational values, missions, structure, and design decisions, as set out by management, as well as external factors such as social norms, politics, and the economy, influence the culture of organizations. An organization's culture influences its organizational behavior, including individual and group dynamics, such as how well people communicate with one another, how well they collaborate, and how well they make decisions. In Chapter 10, Dr. Ralph Shrader discusses the fractured organizational behavior that took place at Booz Allen prior to implementing what they called "Vision 2000." "Some people were building their own revenue bases and competing against each other with sharp elbows to get their share," he says. "There was little collegiality. We didn't appreciate our collective capabilities because there was too much fragmentation." He goes on to describe how, as a result of this fragmentation, "Our revenues were flat, while some of our competitors' revenues were growing."

Enterprise Knowledge Management

The primary purpose of knowledge management is collaboration and sharing of information across the enterprise. "Knowledge through the internet is global," says Dr. Jean-Pierre Garnier, CEO, GlaxoSmithKline. "You can de-aggregate your company and rebuild it, but clearly you need a culture and your enterprise that allows you to do this. You also need to understand that in the new world, the fast will eat the slow, and responsiveness trumps size every day."[8] Dr. Mukesh Aghi reminds us in Chapter 7 that, "The combined result of globalization and the rapid increases in technology has been the advent of what has been coined the new 'knowledge-based' economy." Today, and into the future, how knowledge is captured, catalogued, disseminated, and facilitated is a necessary component of every corporation's strategy.

Knowledge management programs are typically tied to organizational objectives and are intended to lead to the achievement of specific business outcomes such as shared business intelligence, improved performance, competitive advantage, or higher levels of innovation.[9] Knowledge management isn't a new phenomenon. Companies throughout history have maintained archived records of business transactions, as well as of research and development. Elaborate filing systems and massive storage warehouses have been replaced with rapidly accessible technology tools that can be accessed by everyone or by specific people with specific rights and privileges. Knowledge management is much more than just a technology-enabled storage facility for information; it also includes the processes and practices for sorting through the massive amounts of information and then reusing and distributing it back at the appropriate time through learning and information portals. Tools without processes, concepts without culture, won't lead to the intended purpose of knowledge management, which is sharing and collaboration. McKinsey & Company claim that "Successful companies build a corporate environment that fosters a desire for knowledge among their employees and that ensures its continual application, distribution, and creation ... reward employees for seeking, sharing, and creating knowledge."[10] This means that knowledge management acumen is really about helping *people* to work together better – not only technology. "In a world of greater speed," says Dan Moorhead, head of organizational learning at British Telecom, "firms look to knowledge flows more than knowledge stocks, and therefore more toward linking of people (e.g. employees, customers, and suppliers)."[11]

As I write this, it is just after 2.30 a.m. in India, on November 8, 2006. I am watching a live video-cast from the Learning 2006 Conference being held in Orlando, Florida, where it is four in the afternoon on November 7. Elliott Masie, the conference host and someone I have known for almost 20 years, is discussing with Wayne Hodgins, a strategic futurist and one of the world's leading experts on human performance improvement, the huge amounts of data that are now available, and the difficulty in sorting through it all. They agree that we need to find meaningful, appealing ways to sort information. For example, instead of categorizing his music collection by type – such as jazz, classical, or rock – Wayne describes how he classifies it based on mood. Then, if he is feeling in a mellow mood, for example, he can restrict his search to music that matches that mood. Knowledge management is about organizing information so that it can be found and used when required, rather than about storing information.

Operations Management

Firms operating internationally confront significant challenges in coordinating operations across far-flung business units and subsidiaries.[12] Operations management is the model for how the organization works to develop and distribute value to its customers. It includes quick and accurate information flow and materials flow, enterprise resource planning, and quality management processes such as ISO 9000, CMMi, and COPC-2000, which help companies to distinguish themselves in the marketplace. Should operations management vary from country to country? One senior executive working in the United States, responsible for international strategy in a consumer goods company, told us: "Even in the same industry, you might need a different operating model. We are a consumer electronics retailer in the United States, and we understand how to make money here. In Asia, it's a completely different model. We may want to transform it over time to improve the consumer experience, but presently we need to understand that you can be in the same industry and succeed with a different operating model." Another leader working out of the United Kingdom provides a different perspective: "The key – understand your operating model and what you are trying to be globally. If your operating model is that you are trying to improve your supply chain by looking for efficiencies, fine. If you are trying to understand your marketing base, then you have to understand the value provided to specific customers. It's more important to understand your operating model than to get too focused on country-by-country cultural differences."

Developing consistent standards to guide operations can be challenging, as appropriate business practices may be defined differently in different parts of the world.[13] For one company, how people are motivated to buy, and what prompts a buying decision, could drive the business model for that country. For another company, the operating model might be consistent from one place to another (a Coke is a Coke, no matter where you buy it) with little variation. What is important for us, as global leaders, is that we recognize the need to ask the following questions:

- What is our operating model?
- Is our operating model consistent throughout the world?
- If "yes," then why is it consistent?
- If "no," then where are the differences?
- How do we vary our operating models in different markets and geographies?

Business Innovation

"Innovation" is today's new buzzword. Sam Palmisano, CEO of IBM, pointed out in a recent article in *Foreign Affairs*, "Western firms won't be able to effectively serve their global customer base unless they hire and train employees capable of brokering and financing innovation capabilities that are available worldwide."[14]

Innovation is defined as the development and implementation of new ideas by people who, over time, engage in transactions with others within an institutional order.[15] Ramalinga Raju, in Chapter 8, tells us: "There is as much innovation in business as there is in science." He adds: "Once an environment, whether political or economic, becomes conducive, it provides the right stimulus for innovation." True business innovation involves a substantial shift in how things are done, or the invention of something new and better. As companies go global, they will recognize that people's preferences will vary according to their cultural influences and economic situation. They will have to adjust to local laws and infrastructure conditions, and to changes in the dynamics of their industries.

"One size fits all" products, or so-called "locally responsive ... tailored to fit" approaches, fail to address effectively the real needs of markets around the world. Companies need leaders who are prepared to innovate in order to meet the real needs of customers, wherever they might be.[16] At the global level, innovation is a hugely complex process taking place both within and outside organizations and moving back and forth between economies. In Chapter 9, V. Shankar states: "Innovative developments in the low-cost delivery of ATMs and electronic banking are more likely to emerge in India and South Africa than in the developed world, because a vast majority of the population in those countries cannot afford to pay high fees. Once developed, such a banking model could have ramifications and applications not only in the Third World, but in the developed countries as well." Global leaders understand the dynamics that lead to innovation and encourage an environment where experimentation, risk, and yes, even failure, is rewarded. If an initiative doesn't lead directly to a success, it can be seen as a step along the way. Thomas Edison, the US inventor of electrical devices, among other inventions, explained that his failed experiments weren't "failures" as such; rather, on each such occassion, he had discovered a method that didn't work.[17]

Leaders need to view themselves as students of the business of business. Business acumen is about understanding the organization's business model and financial goals, and about utilizing the available economic, financial, and organizational data. *Global* business acumen adds new layers of complexity for leaders, as we have just seen in this section. Many of the leaders we interviewed agreed that global business acumen is best learned by doing. Bonnie S. Stoufer, vice president of learning and development at The Boeing Corporation, advises: "Have geographic and industry mobility in your career. Be willing to jump out there and take a risk. Put yourself in different cultures or in a different industry. Build experiences across the business. Challenge yourself by going where you don't know the culture and where you don't know how to navigate your way around." Take the time to meet people, and to experience their lives, their cultures, and their customs.

Ask the Right Questions to Get the Right Answers

Successful global leaders know that they don't know everything.

Bonnie S. Stoufer
Vice President, Learning, Training and Development
The Boeing Corporation
www.boeing.com

The Boeing Corporation is the largest manufacturer of commercial jet liners and military aircraft combined, with capabilities in rotocraft, electronic and defence systems, missiles, satellites, launch vehicles, and advanced information and communication systems. Headquartered in the United States, Boeing employs more than 155,000 people in 67 countries.

Bonnie Stoufer works in the United States, which is also her country of citizenship. She has held leadership positions for more than 20 years. In the past two years, Bonnie has visited two countries. She has lived and worked in Australia and the United States.

Global Leadership Insights
- Know that you don't know all the answers, and engage people who can help you to learn them.
- Be inclusive in new territories.
- Design and manage global systems and operating rhythms.
- Think about issues and decisions in broad (global) terms.
- Gain assistance from a local coach to learn to be successful in a new environment.

If you want to be a successful global leader, then you should have geographic and industry mobility in your career. Be willing to jump out there and take a risk. Put yourself in a different culture or a different industry. Build experiences across the business, challenge yourself, go where you don't know how to navigate, and learn how. Learn to make new friends, adjust, and adapt.

What they *do* know is how to ask the right questions. For example, the question "How will something that happens in China impact India?" is too general, and will generate answers that are based largely on opinion. Asking, instead, "How can I draw a correlation between what is happening in China and what is happening in India?" will result in a much more specific analysis of the indicators of each country and their relationship to each other.

In 1994, when I made my first business trip to London, I learned it was better to have people laugh when I asked a question than not to ask and to make a potentially critical mistake. When I ask the right questions, I get the right answers. Many times, I follow up with a simple, "Tell me more," for even greater value and the opportunity to enhance my own global business acumen.

Global Leadership Viewpoints

This chapter examined eight critical global business acumen areas: business terminology, regional and global economics, global finance awareness, strategic marketing, organizational behavior, enterprise knowledge management, operations management, and business innovation. Along the way, these global leadership viewpoints were shared:

- The market is recognizing the need for enhanced global business acumen.
- Ram Charan's definition of global business acumen is "linking an insightful assessment of the external business landscape with the keen awareness of how money can be made — and then executing the strategy to deliver the desired results."
- Knowing standard business terminology and being able to articulate it simply is necessary for success in the global frontier. To enhance your understanding of business terminology, read the leading publications in your field in order to know your industry and know how business works.
- Regional and global economics are so tightly interwoven that a slight fluctuation in the currency of one country sets off a chain reaction around the world.
- Leaders need to be aware of how financials influence their business. Three key areas include reading annual reports, raising funds in foreign markets, and understanding the impact of currency fluctuations.
- Being well informed about strategic marketing comes down to understanding differences among people and customizing your approach.
- Global leaders, who need to work within multiple cultural

norms, nominate the ability to listen, to be open to the multiple views and feelings of others, as being paramount in having a positive organizational climate.

- An organization's culture influences its organizational behavior, including individual and group dynamics, such as how well people communicate with one another, how well they collaborate, and how well they make decisions.
- The primary purposes of knowledge management are collaboration and sharing of information across the enterprise. How knowledge is captured, catalogued, disseminated, and facilitated is a necessary component of every corporation's strategy.
- Operations management is the model for how the organization works to develop and distribute value to its customers. Developing consistent standards to guide operations can be challenging, as appropriate business practices may be defined differently in different parts of the world.
- "Innovation" is today's new buzzword. Innovation is defined as the development and implementation of new ideas by people who, over time, engage in transactions with others within an institutional order.
- Ramalinga Raju says, "Once an environment, whether political or economic, becomes conducive, it provides the right stimulus for innovation."
- Successful global leaders know that they don't know everything. What they *do* know is how to ask the right questions.

So, are *you* an expert in the business of business? World-class leaders recognize the need to become experts in the business of global business.

Endnotes

1   Mark A. Royal and Melvyn J. Stark, "Why Companies Excel at Conducting Business Globally," *Journal of Organizational Excellence*, September 2006, pp. 3–10.

2   Ram Charan, "Sharpening Your Business Acumen," *Strategy & Business Magazine*, March 2006, pp. 2–3.

3   Barry Stern and Bob Walters, "Build Your Business Acumen," *T & D Magazine*, June 2005, p. 30.

4   "Brazil's Deepening Crisis," *BusinessWeek Online*, March 22, 1999 (www. businessweek.com/1999/99_12/b3621032.htm), accessed November 11, 2006.

5   Deccan Herald, *Business Travel International (BTI) Report*, October 16, 2005 (www.deccanherald.com), accessed November 27, 2006.

6   Supply Management.com, *Business Travel Supplement*, April 27, 2006 (www.supplymanagement.co.uk/Edit/newsmail_article.asp?id= 14780), accessed November 27, 2006.

7   Christopher B. Bingham, Teppo Felin, and Stewart J. Black, "An Interview with John Pepper: What it Takes to Be a Global Leader," *Human Resource Management*, Summer/Fall 2000, pp. 287–92.

8   Dr. Jean-Pierre Garnier, CEO, GlaxoSmithKline, presented at Advancing Enterprise, February 2005 (www.hm-treasury.gov.uk/media/30C/C2/Dr_JP_ Garnier.pdf), accessed November 27, 2006.

9   Wikipedia, the free encyclopedia (www.wikipedia.org), accessed November 27, 2006.

10 Susanne Hauschild, Thomas Licht, and Wolfram Stein, "Creating a Knowledge Culture," *The McKinsey Quarterly*. January 2001, pp. 74–81.

11 Brian Hackett, "Beyond Knowledge Management: New Ways to Work and Learn," *The Conference Board*, March 2000, p. 11.

12 "Leading the Global Organization: Structure, Process, and People as the Keys to Success," *Hay Group Insight*, Selection 11, April 2006, p. 1.

13 Ibid., p. 2.

14 Navi Radjou, "Innovation Networks: Global Progress Report 2006," *Forrester*, June 14, 2006, p. 20.

15 Andrew Van De Ven, "Central Problems in the Management of Innovation," *Management Science*, May 1986, p. 590.

16 Stuart L. Hart, "Capitalism at the Crossroads: The Unlimited Business Opportunities in Solving the World's Most Difficult Problems," *Wharton School Publishing*, February 15, 2005, p. 21.

17 Paul Sloane, "Failure is the Mother of Innovation," October 13, 2004 (www. innovationtools.com), accessed November 27, 2006.

Chapter 4

Worldview

INTRODUCTION

During the 12 weeks from the time my wife Priscilla (now head of the executive coaching, mentoring, and development programs at Satyam) and I accepted our positions to the day we left northern Virginia, people asked us: "What's it like in India?" We always gave the same answer: "We'll let you know when we get there." We had decided that the opportunity to have a broad impact within a global company based in Asia, at a time when Asia is rapidly emerging into economic prominence, was an adventure we couldn't pass up. We spent hundreds of hours reading books about India's history and culture, and searching the internet for information on everything from schools, to movie theaters, to restaurants and shopping. We enrolled our daughter in school, followed up on suggestions about where to live, and even checked out the satellite images of Hyderabad at Google Earth.

Finally, we took off from Dulles Airport in northern Virginia, had a layover in Amsterdam, and then it was on to our new home in Hyderabad. Twenty-three hours after leaving our old home, we arrived at our new one. With a nine-and-a-half-hour time difference, it was around two in the morning, two days after we had begun our journey. That morning, November 23, 2005, after less than four hours' sleep, we reported to work.

Any time you make a move – whether it is to a new job, or a new city, or a new country – you can expect initially to be out of

Dr. Siow Choon Neo
Managing Director, Training & Performance Enhancement
Federal Express, Asia Pacific, Inc.
www.fedex.com

FedEx provides access to a growing global marketplace through a network of supply chain, transportation, business, and related information services. Headquartered in the United States, FedEx employs over 275,000 people in 220 countries and territories.

Dr. Siow Choon Neo works in Singapore, which is also her country of citizenship. She has held leadership positions for more than 13 years. In the past two years, Siow has visited 10 countries.

Global Leadership Insights
- Be sensitive to cultural norms.
- Balance organizational norms with cultural norms.
- Trust and empower those who work for you.
- Take ownership of your own development and adaptability.

Be personable. Being personable allows you to be sensitive and cuts across all borders. Everyone has the potential to build rapport by being sincerely interested in individuals. Reading widely about the trends of the world from a global perspective is essential. Reading widely means doing so with discretion and a questioning nature, not simply believing everything you read.

your comfort zone. A change of environment requires us to accept that we don't know everything, and challenges us to broaden our perspective. We no longer have our old relationships to rely on, so we have to build new ones. I would advise anyone moving into the global leadership sphere to acknowledge first that they probably don't know quite how they are going to make it work, and then to enjoy the adventure of engaging with the local people and forming a view that combines what you have learned in the past with what you are learning in the unfamiliar present.

Bonnie S. Stoufer advises, "Collaborate more with the local people; they are the ones who know and understand the norms. But,

Jeanette K. Harrison
Vice President, American Express Learning Network
American Express Company
www.americanexpress.com

American Express Company is a leading global payments, network, and travel company. The company is headquartered in the United States, with 65,800 employees located in 130 countries. American Express was founded in 1850.

Jeanette Harrison works in the United States, which is also her country of citizenship. She has held leadership positions for more than 22 years. In the past two years, Jeanette has visited four countries.

Global Leadership Insights
• Think more broadly and outside your cultural box.
• Volunteer for international assignments.
• Don't expect things to work the same way in each new place.

Have true sensitivity toward differences, and an action plan to deal with them. There is a stated way things work, and then the social way things are done. Dealing with difference requires you to be culturally and politically aware. Be able to translate issues for the company; it's not something for the faint-of-heart or that can be taken lightly. If you think you can manage in the same way you have done in the past, you will create problems for the local management as well as for your own reputation as a leader.

don't go over to another country and expect to hear locals say, 'This is how everything works here.'" The longer I live and work in India, the more I identify with these words of Mahatma Gandhi: "I do not want my house to be walled in on all sides and my windows to be stuffed. I want the cultures of all the lands to be blown about my house as freely as possible. But I refuse to be blown off my feet by any."

Leaders with a worldview are constantly in touch with themselves and their environment. They look at the world from every possible angle, intuitively synchronizing themselves to the prevailing culture, social trends, levels of technology, and the dynamics of the local political–economic realities. In effect, they become world citizens, because they are never perceived as being "foreign," wherever they might be. How does a leader develop this global frame of mind?

DEVELOPING A GLOBAL FRAME OF MIND

There's "No Place" Like Home

Many business people who travel regularly to or live in many different countries try to stay within their comfort zones; they arrive in a foreign city, check into a hotel operated by a chain they are familiar with from home, and eat at restaurants frequented by tourists and expatriates, rather than in places patronized by the locals. By cocooning executives on their frequent international business trips, companies in effect isolate them from the very opportunities that would help them develop into global leaders.[1]

Many expatriates also choose to live in neighborhoods favored by other expatriates. They send their children to international schools and spend their leisure hours with others from "home." This narrow perspective affects a global leader's ability to immerse him- or herself in, and to learn as much as possible about, their new environment. I have found from my own experience, and our successful global leader interviewees concur with me, that it is more beneficial and fulfilling to become acquainted with local people, to participate in their customs and rituals, and to be willing to listen and learn from everyone. Marty Seldman says, "There is no replacement for living and working in other parts of the world. Traveling can help, but not when you stay in hotels and eat food that isn't indigenous to the area." Immersion means "watch their television, listen to their music, read their news," says Elizabeth Haraldsdottir Thomas. "You have to want to do this." When you travel to another country, whether for a short-term or long-term stay, immerse yourself in the lives of the local residents as a way of opening up your imagination and spirit. You will be a better person, and a more successful global leader, as a result.

Dr. Steve Hoke
Vice President
Church Resources Ministries
www.crmleaders.org

Church Resources Ministries is a coaching and mentoring organization working to develop leaders who will strengthen and start churches worldwide. It is based in the United States and has 325 staff in 22 countries.

Steve Hokes works in the United States, which is also his country of citizenship. He has held leadership positions for more than 30 years. In the past two years, Steve has visited 15 countries. His organization's official language is English. He speaks fluent English, Japanese, and Spanish. Steve has lived and worked in Japan, Kenya, Singapore, and the United States.

Global Leadership Insights
- Build your intercultural, interpersonal sensitivity.
- Master one or two languages other than your native language.
- Live in another culture for one to three years, and continue to travel.
- Be aware of your cultural baggage and biases.

We are facing a key leadership challenge: how to continue to cross-train across continents, learn from each other, stay in close communication, and develop a sense of camaraderie and community while working on opposite sides of the world. It was one thing when we had North Americans in a few countries, and now in 23 countries, but we also now have national staff in 23 countries.

Assembling a 360-degree Worldview

Three-hundred-and-sixty degrees gives you a view in all directions. World-class leaders have insights and gain knowledge by gathering information and resources from all around them and connecting a multitude of viewpoints. Open and continuous "access to an exploding base of online information and telecommunications is transforming most human activities everywhere."[2] Advances in digitization and connectivity are transforming entire regions of the world and changing the way business is being done in all industries, of all sizes, on all continents. Political issues such as terrorism, and social issues such as rapidly changing consumer attitudes, are also impacting how we carry on business. A 360-degree worldview produces the panoramic vision that is essential if we are to seize the opportunities that become available in our complex and diverse environments, and to lead our organization's response to change.

For the first time in history, every country in the world (with the possible exception of the very poorest African nations) is able to engage in our emerging global economy. Countries everywhere are benefiting from the movement of goods, people, and capital. However, while it is perceived as beneficial by most countries, global growth may mean different things in different places.

A few months after joining Satyam, I was flying to the United States for a series of meetings. Ram Mynampati, president of Satyam, who has spent many years living and working in the United States, was returning there after a visit to Hyderabad. Our flight departed at 3.15 a.m., in time to make our connection in Europe. I wanted to seek some advice from Ram, but decided the middle of the night wasn't the appropriate time. I settled into my seat and quickly fell asleep. Seven hours later, I awoke, washed the sleep from my eyes, brushed my teeth, combed my hair, and then approached Ram. After an exchange of pleasantries, I asked him if I could take a few moments of his time. He gestured for me to take a seat. I sat down and asked the question that had been puzzling me. "Why is it, in India, that Satyam's leaders are always talking about how many people work for the company?"

As an American, I was used to chief financial officers focusing on reporting on the quarterly revenues their companies had earned. Ram explained: "For so long, India has had great unemployment. So, when we speak about Satyam in India, we come from the context of: 'This is how many jobs we have created.' When young people graduate from college, their parents will tell them to apply for a position at Satyam, because we have created so many jobs. Indian people are loyal to companies who employ many people and who contribute to society. When we speak about Satyam in other parts of the world, we vary our message based on what is appropriate for that audience. This could mean talking about how many jobs we have created, or about the company's financials." Before I moved

Alicia Goodman
Vice President – Senior Learning & Development Consultant
Taylor Nelson Sofres PLC
www.tns-global.com

Taylor Nelson Sofres PLC (TNS) provides customer research and analysis, political and social polling, and consumer panel, media intelligence, and TV and radio audience measurement services. TNS is based in the United Kingdom, and employs 13,000 people operating in 74 countries.

Alicia Goodman works in the United Kingdom, and her country of citizenship is the United States. She has held leadership positions for more than 10 years. In the past two years, Alicia has visited 10 countries. She has lived and worked in the United Kingdom and the United States.

Global Leadership Insights
- Be open to different opportunities.
- Understand business challenges with a world perspective.
- Be flexible, and take cultural differences into account in your actions.
- Get out of your comfort zone.

Think about the impact of your decisions, particularly culturally. Working only in your country of origin is easier because it is mostly one culture and, from a human resources perspective, you don't have to worry about legal implications that might arise. As a leader who enjoys getting things done, it's more difficult than working domestically to take yourself out of the achiever role in order to maintain some kind of work–life balance.

to India, I had only experienced the Wall Street way of viewing the value of a company. Ram helped me to understand that "value" depends on where you are and who is perceiving it.

Exposure through 360-degree News

The world is a complex and dynamic environment made up of a wide range of stakeholders and influencing factors. Every day, all over the world, important events occur that are perceived differently by different people. Local and regional media will always have a local or regional bias or point of view. A worldview comes from broadening your perspective, by expanding your sources of information and reviewing how different people in different places react to different events. "Most of us are immersed in our own culturally-specific news feeds," says Elliott Masie. "As soon as you start to operate from multiple points of view, you expand your awareness. When I watch CNN International, instead of CNN out of Atlanta, I see cricket scores. We need to seek out expanded views, because we are increasingly getting a narrow cast of news from specific sources. Multicasting and plugging into 360-degree news has tremendous benefits for global leaders."

On Wednesday, July 12, 2006, headlines around the world brought news of terrorist bombings in Mumbai, India's financial center. Below is a sample of those headlines:

- *Asia Times Online,* China Headquarters: **Mumbai Attacks: A New Spiral of Violence**
- *Bahrain Tribune,* Bahrain Headquarters: **Mubai Derailed; "Rain" of Terror in City**
- *BBC World,* UK Headquarters: **Experts Puzzle Over Mumbai Blasts**
- *CNN.com,* US Headquarters: **Multiple Blasts Kill and Injure Hundreds**
- *International Herald Tribune,* Paris Headquarters: **Train Bombs in Mumbai Kill 147**
- *Mail and Guardian Online,* South African Edition, UK Headquarters: **Train Blasts Rock Mumbai**
- *Washington Post,* US Headquarters: **Bombers Strike Bombay at Rush Hour**

The next day, Thursday, July 13, the headlines began to diversify. Some quoted countries that had condemned the attacks; some analyzed the "who" and the "why"; some offered assistance; some discussed India's business resilience; and some consisted only of a short update.

- *Asia Pulse,* Manila: **Philippine Government Condemns Mumbai Blasts**

Avery Duff
Director Human Resources, International
Rolls-Royce
www.rolls-royce.com

Rolls-Royce is the world's leading provider of power systems and services for the civil aerospace, defense aerospace, marine, and energy industries. Headquartered in the United Kingdom, the company employs 36,000 people in 50 countries.

Avery Duff works in the United Kingdom, which is also his country of citizenship. He has held leadership positions for more than 25 years. In the past two years, Avery has visited 25 countries. He has lived and worked in Australia, Germany, the Netherlands, the United Kingdom, and the United States.

Global Leadership Insights
- Judgment is similar, but breadth of thinking, knowledge, and experience differ globally.
- Have an academic awareness of how the world looks and how it is changing.
- Design a plan for integrating individual and corporate cultures.
- It is a mistake to simply stay with what you know.

Our greatest global leadership challenge is finding sufficient people of quality on a global basis in an increasingly competitive environment who are right for the time and location. For example, there is a population shift in engineering skills, so we need to find a way to go into India and China for knowledge resources, although historically we have had little market presence there.

- *China Daily*: **India is Resilient in Wake of Blasts**
- *CNN.com*: **Mumbai Bombings: 400 Detained**
- *Hong Kong Standard* (in reference to the Bombay Stock Exchange): **Mumbai Shares Resilient After Attacks**
- *London Telegraph* – Telegraph.co.uk: **Bombay Rises in Defiance from Bomb Carnage**
- *New York Times*: **Bombers Targeted India's Upper Class**
- *PTI India*: **Give Proof of Those Behind Mumbai Blasts, We'll (Pakistan) Cooperate**

- *The Age*, Melbourne: **Suspect Linked to Mumbai Blasts**
- *The Nation*, Pakistan: **Pakistan Offers Help in Mumbai Blasts Probe**

To gain a worldview perspective, it is imperative to gain a 360-degree view of the world news. Each news agency, each country, will have its own particular views on the news of the day. Don't assume that each is covering the events in full or taking the same perspective. The world wide web has made this vast array of viewpoints accessible to all. There are literally thousands of quality news media websites to choose from, including the BBC, CNN, CNBC, *The International Herald*, *The London Times*, *The Financial Times*, *Al Jazeera*, *The Australian*, and *The Far Eastern Economic Review*, to name just a few. A website dedicated to "Today's Front Page" is located at www.newseum.org/todaysfrontpages/.

Getting your news from only one source will inevitably bias your thinking. "Being constantly updated about the trends of the world globally is essential," advises Dr. Siow Choon Neo of Federal Express Pacific. "This makes reading widely very important. Reading widely means doing so with discretion and an enquiring mind – not simply believing everything you read."

Developing 360-degree Awareness

Black and Gregersen state, "A global leader must stretch his/her mind to encompass the entire world with hundreds of countries, cultures, and business contexts."[3] Jeanette Harrison, from American Express Company, cautions that leaders should be aware of "cultural aspects, such as religion, heritage, days of national recognition, as well as the laws."

Jeanette believes that "you cannot lead with an ethnocentric mindset without doing serious damage to your own credibility as a leader."

In order to make complex information more digestible, leaders often make assumptions about people based on superficial characteristics. For example, Nishi, a colleague with whom I have worked for many years, is of Indian origin. She looks Indian, and she has an Indian-sounding name; so, one could easily assume her

Angela Hyde
Vice President
AstraZeneca
www.astrazeneca.com

Headquartered in the United Kingdom, AstraZeneca is a leading pharmaceutical company manufacturing medicines to combat cancer, cardiovascular and gastrointestinal diseases, infections, respiratory ailments, and inflammation. The company employs 65,000 people in approximately 50 countries.

Angela Hyde works in the United Kingdom, which is also her country of citizenship. She has held leadership positions for more than seven years. In the past two years, Angela has visited 10 countries.

Global Leadership Insights
- Know yourself and how you impact other people.
- Be flexible and develop trusting relationships quickly.
- Understand how to build a highly effective and successful virtual structure.
- Respect diversity, and the fact that there are multiple ways of arriving at an outcome.
- Ask for extensive feedback to gain self-awareness.

Global information systems, although challenging to implement, can end up driving globalization (global standardization). Technology decisions should be driven by required functionality, but increasingly global systems determine the processes, because it is difficult to meet all parties' needs effectively.

to be Indian, complete with all the cultural reference points and traditions that go with it. However, it would be a false assumption. Nishi's great-grandparents left India in the early 1800s. Her mother's family settled in Guyana, in South America; and her father's family settled in South Africa. As young adults, Nishi's parents studied in Dublin, Ireland, where they met and married. Nishi was born and raised in Ireland until the age of 10. Her family then moved to Mauritius and a few years later relocated to South Africa. Years later, Nishi moved to the United States. The irony in Nishi's story is that she now lives in India, where she works for Satyam. People whom she encounters in India automatically assume that she understands, and is able to navigate, the local culture both personally and professionally. But, as Nishi's story illustrates, one cannot make assumptions based on looks alone. As discussed in previous chapters, in a global environment a successful leader knows to ask the right questions and not to take anyone or anything at face value.

Steve Hoke from Church Resources Ministries can relate. He spent 15 years growing up in Japan. "It's more difficult for me to live and work in America," he says. "Because I don't consider it my home culture."

Mary Capozzi tells a story about how she became aware of the different perception of time in Italy, compared with what she was used to in the United States. "After three weeks in Italy, my boss took me aside and asked me for my watch. I thought it was a weird question, but I took my watch off and gave it to him. He said, 'Can I keep this?' I said, 'What?' He responded, 'I want you to work without your watch for a little while.' The lesson was loud and clear: I had to learn to feel and appreciate the rhythm and flow of time in Italy."

As a leader, it is important to be aware of the prevailing social structure and value system, wherever you are in the world. These values may not be the same as your own values. One of the best ways to gain a new perspective is to "get out of your comfort zone," says Alicia Goodman of Taylor Nelson Sofres PLC. "In order to understand the cultural differences, you have to work in other locations. It doesn't have to be for a year a two; even six to eight weeks can help you understand how other people, in other places, work on a day-to-day basis. Talking to people on the phone or emailing them won't give you that connection. You need to push yourself out of that comfort zone in order to learn."

Avery Duff, from Rolls-Royce International, shares another perspective on awareness. "Leaders need to be aware of where to find the right people of quality on a global basis in an increasingly competitive environment. For example, there was a population shift in engineering skills, so we realized we needed to find a way to go into India and China for knowledge resources, although historically we have had little market presence there."

Find external ways to expand your awareness. Business

Thomas Czaplicki
Vice President, Information Technology, Japan and Asia Pacific
Johnson Controls, Inc.
www.johnsoncontrols.com

Johnson Controls provides innovative automotive interiors that help make driving more comfortable, safe, and enjoyable. The company is headquartered in Milwaukee, Wisconsin, in the United States. It has over 150,000 employees in 58 countries.

Thomas Czaplicki works in Singapore, and his country of citizenship is the United States. He has held leadership positions for more than 16 years. In the past two years, Thomas has visited 12 countries. He has lived and worked in China, Germany, Mexico, Singapore, the United Kingdom, and the United States.

Global Leadership Insights
- Seek to understand, rather than to be understood.
- Travel, and meet people where they live.
- Be patient and develop solid relationships.
- Be an extrovert and proactive with people.
- Ask intelligent questions, and make communication transparent.

One of the perils of our current technology orientation is the belief that email is effective communication. It's actually one of the worst forms of communication for getting content across. Live, face-to-face communication is best. If it has to be long distance, video- and audio-conferencing are 100% better than email communication. Without a foundation of understanding for each individual, the situation they are in, the dynamics with which they are dealing, your interactions with them won't be effective. Adjust your approach to each person.

schools and professional associations can help. Watch out for trends, ask questions, and learn from other people's experiences. The next time you find yourself scheduled to go to a new country, or to a country where you haven't been in a while, go to the Geert Hofstede™ Cultural Dimensions website: www.geerthofstede.com (see Box 4.1). Once there, look up the country you are interested in learning more about and you will find some extremely useful information.

Pursuing 360-degree Understanding

Angela Hyde, from AstraZeneca in the UK, told us: "The challenge companies increasingly face is how to manage externalization – outsourcing – and then how to work effectively as a virtual company. The notions of 'what is a business' and 'what is a company', and then therefore 'what is the role of leadership,' are changing."

Leadership is evolving to a state of such complexity that it extends well beyond one's own area of expertise and training. By studying different business models, cultures, and socio-economic systems, you will expand your understanding of the world we live in, resulting in a greater ability to learn from others and to vary your behavior appropriately. Karl-Heinz Lensing, from Kathrein Mobilcom Brasil LTDA, advises that there is great value to be derived from combining commonalities and differences. "It's important to understand different mentalities and different ways of seeing the

BOX 4.1   GEERT HOFSTEDE™ CULTURAL DIMENSIONS

Geert Hofstede has conducted extensive research on the interactions between national cultures and organizational cultures. He is the author of several books, including *Culture's Consequences* (2nd, fully revised edition, 2001) and *Cultures and Organizations, Software of the Mind* (2nd, revised edition, 2005, with Gert Jan Hofstede).

The site (www.geerthofstede.com), which includes excellent descriptions and explanations, identifies five dimensions for each culture:

- power distance;
- individualism vs. collectivism;
- masculinity vs. femininity;
- uncertainty avoidance; and
- long-term vs. short-term orientation.

Karl-Heinz Lensing
General Manager
Kathrein Mobilcom Brasil LTDA
www.kathrein.de

Kathrein Mobilcom Brasil LTDA is the world's largest antenna-producing enterprise, with the longest-standing tradition of all marketing competitors, and a leading high-tech telecommunications company. Headquartered in Germany, it employs more than 6,300 people, with more than 50% of sales generated internationally.

Karl-Heinz Lensing works in Brazil, and his country of citizenship is Germany. He has held leadership positions for more than 29 years. In the past two years, Karl has visited 14 countries. His organization's official language is English. He speaks fluent English, German, and Portuguese. Karl has lived and worked in Brazil and Germany.

Global Leadership Insights
• Always have solid, professional preparation.
• Transparent leadership – discuss not only your ideas, but also those of everyone involved.
• Motivate through inclusion.
• Deliberately provoke opinions.
• Constantly observe local behavior and perceptions.
• Don't overemphasize your home country.

Try to learn the language of the country where you live. Language is the key to another mentality and way of thinking. I have seen people come from a foreign country for many years and not learn to speak even a sentence of the local language; this kind of arrogance is a mistake.

same problem. In considering both sides' thinking throughout, you can get to the same solution while avoiding unnecessary conflict."

Thomas Czaplicki of Johnson Controls works in Singapore. "In my opinion it's a challenge because, without knowing, we [all people] are guilty of lumping all of Asia into one category called 'Asia.' We fail to understand the unique differences between all of the different countries. Each one is so unique in itself, that it takes time to understand the differences." For this reason, Thomas recommends that leaders take assignments overseas where they are in the minority. "Unless you spend time living abroad, not just visiting, in a foreign country where you are a minority, it is very difficult to be effective globally."

Women, who remain in the minority in the global workplace, have additional complexities to deal with as a result of local socio-economic and cultural values. Mary Capozzi of Best Buy says, "As a global leader and a woman, it was different for me. Not only did I need to lead people from other cultures, I also needed to lead people from other genders. I had to learn the cultural rules around gender – which were often more difficult than other differences." Priscilla Nelson moved from the United States to India to lead executive coaching and mentoring programs for Satyam. In Box 4.2 she describes some of the challenges that senior-level women face.

Understanding how people with whom you will be working live (including the laws and traditions by which they regulate their lives), and having some knowledge of what interests them, will significantly increase your chances of building successful relationships. "The most important thing is that you are aware that everybody is different and that if you have different opinions you have to put yourself in their shoes and try to understand their point of view."[8]

Many global leaders recognize the need to have a coach when they work overseas – a professional, not necessarily a local, who knows not only how to navigate the local landscape, but also how to work with executives and provide appropriate guidance. Others believe that it's important to have assistance from a local person who can provide useful introductions and assist with communicating effectively. Stephen Heathcote, from the Association of Chartered Certified Accountants (ACCA) in the United Kingdom, explains: "A local professional who comes with me can brief and guide me on the culture, sensitivities, and business protocol. It's key to have a supporter or sponsor who understands the local market." Elliott Masie agrees. "There is an incredible role for global leaders to look for and develop scouts. We recently went to Dubai, Bahrain, and Saudi Arabia, and I spent a fair amount of time talking to people who could provide, on an ongoing basis, information about the environment, perceptions, and other areas of importance."

BOX 4.2   GLOBAL OPPORTUNITIES AND CHALLENGES FOR WOMEN IN LEADERSHIP

Priscilla D. Nelson

A man can freely move throughout the world, accepting employment wherever he wishes, with pretty much the same rules. Yet, women face varying labor laws, norms, and traditions that change from country to country.

"Indra Nooyi's (CEO Pepsico) climb from last year's number 11 to the top of Fortune's 2006 list of powerful women has been breathtaking. The list of brand-name firms with women chief executives is longer and more impressive than ever, after a year of stunning breakthroughs in corner-office hiring. Added to this, is a recent study by *Catalyst*, that shows Fortune 500 companies with the highest percentages of women corporate officers yielded, on an average, 35.1 percent higher return on equity than those with the lowest percentages."[4] ICICI Bank, HSBC, and Biocon, as well as a few other organizations such as Satyam, recently chosen as one of India's top three organizations to work for, have targets for women in leadership roles as part of their strategic goals.

In 2000, IBM had no women as country managers; today, women are country general managers in Peru, France, Spain, Hong Kong, Indonesia, Singapore, Thailand, and New Zealand, and a woman heads operations in northeast Europe.[5] Having traveled extensively across the globe completing short- and long-term assignments in many cultures, I have lived in the United Kingdom, the United States, and now India. I was often a consultant, sometimes a consumer, and for many years an employee. I moved up the career ladder and today I am the global lead for executive coaching, mentoring, and development for Satyam in Hyderabad. I work with an amazing group of leaders from around the world who make a concerted effort to include me; still, many times, I feel like an "afterthought" in a male-dominated culture. Dedicated as the number of qualified women leaders are, many dynamics, culture among others, come into play. Women have to work harder to compete for the same positions held by men.

A report on the *May 2006 Symposium on Diversity and Inclusion* shows interesting findings. Although Japan is nearly racially homogeneous, it has a long history of segregation of people from equal rights in the workforce. Japan falls far behind other developed nations, even other Asian countries, when it comes to diversity, and Japanese businesses and leaders are starting to realize that competing in today's economy will require full utilization of all its talent. By 2007, the population of Japan will begin a steady decline. Japan's baby boomers will begin to turn 60 and retire. This will compound the world's much-acknowledged knowledge worker shortage. Japan will face a huge labor shortage and, because there is much discomfort regarding foreigners, the Japanese will turn their focus to women.[6] Perhaps Japan, China, or India will realize they are sitting on a competitive gold mine of untapped and highly educated talent. Sheer volumes of both men and women, properly trained, developed and allowed to advance in their careers, could resolve the crises for qualified knowledge workers and put their countries in the driver's seat of the world's economy.

The "missing gender" in leadership is a global concern. A controversial approach was unveiled in January 2006, in Norway, when the government imposed a quota system for its top 500 publicly traded firms. By 2008, boardrooms in Norway must achieve a 40% woman executive population or face the possibility of being de-listed. France announced a 20% quota, and Spain has stated it will give preferential treatment to any company that appoints more women to its board.[7] While the quota system is controversial, and no doubt faces many challenges, statistics bear out that quotas can and do work. In Scandinavia, the number of women on boards grew significantly when quotas were introduced. Norway's success is a blueprint other countries are considering. Up from 22% in 2004, women now claim 29% of director-level roles in the largest Norwegian companies. In Sweden, Finland, and Denmark, this approach has increased women in boardroom positions from 18% to 23%!

With the emergence of emotional intelligence, appreciative inquiry, strengths-based leadership, as well as executive coaching and mentoring programs, we are learning more and more about the benefits of multifaceted teams. Women in leadership positions balance the delicate conversations of cultural differences with the ever-present demands of a dynamically changing world.

Stephen Heathcote
Director, Education and Learning Development
Association of Chartered Certified Accountants (ACCA)
www.accaglobal.com

ACCA (the Association of Chartered Certified Accountants) is the world's largest and fastest-growing international accountancy body, with 260,000 students and 110,000 members in 170 countries.

Stephen Heathcote works in the United Kingdom, which is also his country of citizenship. He has held leadership positions for more than seven years. In the past two years, Stephen has visited 13 countries. He has lived and worked in the United Kingdom and the United States.

Global Leadership Insights
- Be open-minded, not presumptuous.
- Build credentials in global leadership by showing that you can lead.

Take local residents (we call them sponsors) with you to provide guidance on culture and sensitivities, and to ensure that you follow protocol. You have to start with the assumption that you don't know everything, and understand your limitations. You may not know the market you are leading, which means you require education on everything from general business practices to the local culture.

Understand your business model, and what you are trying to do globally. Are you trying to improve your supply chain or increase your marketing base? Either way, it's most important to understand your customer and not get overly focused on country-by-country or cultural differences.

Marty Seldman, an executive coach, says: "I have coached more than 1,500 leaders and at least half were international, working in countries other than their own, or managing global teams and organizations. It's important to understand how each culture defines leadership. The same behavior received positively in one culture might be received negatively in another culture."

In summary, use local resources such as executive coaches and colleagues who can assist you in gaining a broader understanding of your new surroundings so that you can properly interpret what you hear and see, and then adjust your response accordingly.

BEING A GLOBAL BUSINESS AMBASSADOR

Armed with 360-degree views gained from global news sources, and with greater awareness and understanding of other people and places, you will be prepared not only to become a successful global leader, but also a global ambassador for business. You have the serendipitous opportunity to give back to society. Increasingly, the business sector is being called on to provide leadership and to use its enormous reach, knowledge, problem-solving skills, and access to capital in the service of solving society's greatest dilemmas.[9] Corporate social responsibility, on a global scale, is becoming an integral part of multinational organizations' global strategies. Navi Radjou, at Forrester Research, understands that a truly world-class leader engages with all parts of society.

"A leader can become socially engaged, and make the company socially active. Rather than only thinking about shareholder value, leaders also need to think about stakeholder value management, and that includes society. For example, instead of going to India and seeing one billion arms waiting for soap, see one billion souls with multiple and complicated aspirations. We have a moral responsibility to participate in the development of society, and not just to view people as consumers." Personally, I find it enlightening and satisfying each time I engage with the local society (see Box 4.3).

BOX 4.3   THE CHILDREN OF SRI MAHESHWARI VIDYALAY

There is a small school I have visited twice, called Sri Maheshwari Vidyalay. Located in Hyderabad's "Old City," the school, which started in 1999 purely with the intention of serving the poor and the lower-middle class, has 350 students ranging from three years in age to class 10. It is an English-medium school that also teaches lessons in Telegu and Hindi, so that the children won't lose their native language.

My first encounter with the children was their first encounter with a foreigner. I was amazed by their curiosity. Each child came up to me and politely extended his or her hand and with a large smile said, "Hello, Sir" or "Nice to meet you, Sir." While at the school, I asked how I might help. The principal told me, "With the fast-changing world scenario, our children need to learn to use computers. This isn't possible without computers, which we cannot afford." My second visit took place three months later, after the Satyam Foundation donated four computers to the school. The principal asked me to inaugurate the computers, in a ceremony that was held on a Sunday morning. When I arrived, I was humbled to see that hundreds of children and their parents had turned out.

It was a wonderful experience to meet and speak with everyone. I left the ceremony with three thoughts:

1. Leaders are the ambassadors of global business. When we take time to engage with society, to give back, and to share our knowledge, it really does make a difference.
2. Desktop computers have been around for 25 years. This encompasses most of my career. We must remember that the tools available to us, and the access to the world that we enjoy, are not yet available to everyone.
3. The children refreshed my desire to keep listening, learning, and being curious about this wonderful world.

I think next month I shall go and visit with the children again. Who knows, maybe one day I will be blessed to hire a graduate of Sri Maheshwari Vidyalay.

The author with the children and parents of Sri Maheshwari Vidyalay school, Hyderabad

Global Leadership Viewpoints

This chapter discussed how to maintain and enhance your broad worldview. Along the way, these global leadership viewpoints were shared:

- Any time you make a move – whether it is to a new job, or a new city, or a new country – you can expect initially to be out of your comfort zone. A change of environment requires us to accept that we don't know everything, and challenges us to broaden our perspective.
- When you travel to another country, whether for a short-term or long-term stay, immerse yourself in the lives of the local residents as a way of opening up your imagination and spirit.
- World-class leaders have insights and gain knowledge by gathering information and resources from all around them and connecting a multitude of viewpoints.
- For the first time in history, every country in the world (with the possible exception of the very poorest African nations) is able to engage in our emerging global economy.
- While it is perceived as beneficial by most countries, global growth may mean different things in different places.
- A worldview comes from broadening your perspective, by expanding your sources of information and reviewing how different people in different places react to different events.
- Leadership is evolving to a state of such complexity that it extends well beyond one's own area of expertise and training.
- Women have additional complexities to deal with when leading globally, as a result of local socio-economic and cultural values.
- Understanding how people with whom you will be working live (including the laws and traditions by which they regulate their lives), and having some knowledge of what interests them, will significantly increase your chances of building successful relationships.
- Many global leaders recognize the need to have a coach when they work overseas – a professional, not necessarily a local, who knows not only how to navigate the local landscape, but also how to work with executives and provide appropriate guidance.

Navi Radjou
Vice President
Forrester Research, Inc.
www.forrester.com

Forrester Research (Nasdaq: FORR) is an independent technology and market research company that for 23 years has provided pragmatic and forward-thinking advice about technology's impact on business and consumers.

Navi Radjou works in the United States, and his country of citizenship is France. In the past two years, Navi has visited 15 countries. His organization's official language is English. He speaks fluent English, French, and Tamil. Navi has lived and worked in Canada, France, India, Singapore, Thailand, and the United States.

Global Leadership Insights
- Understand how to manage partners, and provide each with appropriate roles.
- To reduce the complexity of the global environment, employ empowerment and avoid micro-managing.
- Don't succumb to short-term needs by sacrificing long-term vision.
- Be aware of the risk that you may run counter to a "flat world."
- Think about your company's role in society.

The days of the charismatic, zealous, Superman-like leader are dying. In the era of globalization, leadership is being refined into a more diffused, collective leadership. We will have increasing numbers of stakeholders involved and influencing business decisions. Leadership will be more participatory, collective, and democratic. The new global model is flatter hierarchies for leadership, with people improvising their way forward by taking cues from their partners.

Others believe that it's important to have assistance from a local person who can provide useful introductions and assist with communicating effectively.
- Increasingly, the business sector is being called on to provide leadership and to use its enormous reach, knowledge, problem-solving skills, and access to capital in the service of solving society's greatest dilemmas.

There is a vast quantity of information available on the internet and in other forms for anyone wishing to broaden their understanding of foreign cultures. But however much you have read, it will only really be when you have your first encounter with the local people, the company culture in the local office, the roads and shopping precincts, and the "way they do things there" that you will begin to realize just how different the place is from your home country.

Endnotes

1   G. Oddou, M. E. Mendenhall, and J. B. Ritchie, " Leveraging Travel as a Tool for Global Leadership Development," *Human Resource Management*, Summer/Fall 2000, pp. 159–72.

2   Frederick W. Smith, "Access: Changing What's Possible". FedEx Corporation, Washington, DC, May 23, 2006, p. 4 (www.fedex.com/us/about/today/access/mediacenter.html?link=4), accessed October 30, 2006.

3   J. Stewart Black and Hal B. Gregersen, "High Impact Training: Forging Leaders for the Global Frontier," *Human Resource Management*, Summer/Fall 2000, p. 174.

4   C. Hymowitz, "Diversity in a Global Economy – Ways Some Firms Get it Right," *The Wall Street Journal Online* (www.careerjournal.com/myc/diversity/20051117-hymowitz.html), accessed November 27, 2006.

5   Ibid.

6   *Global Diversity, Diversity in Japan? Report on the May 2006 Symposium on Diversity and Inclusion in Japan* (www.diversitycentral.com/learning/global_diversity_06_10.html), accessed November 27, 2006.

7   Shyamal Majumadar, "Why There Are So Few Women Managers in India," Rediff.com, reprint from *Business Standard*, October 6, 2006 (www.rediff.com///money/2006/oct/06guest.htm), accessed November 27, 2006.

8   Cristina Moro Bueno and Stewart L. Tubbs, "Identifying Global Leadership Competencies," *The Journal of American Academy of Business*, Cambridge, September 2004, p. 85.

9   Nicholas A. Andreadis, "Leadership for Civil Society: Implications for Global Corporate Leadership Development," *Human Resource Development International*, June 2002, pp. 143–9.

Chapter 5

Global People Leadership

INTRODUCTION

Having observed leadership in North America, Europe, Africa, Asia, and the Pacific Rim, I have determined that many, if not most, people leadership competencies and behaviors are consistent, wherever in the world the leader is based. However, the enhanced complexities – the demonstration and prioritization of these competencies and behaviors in different parts of the world – exemplify global people leadership.

As an experienced leader now living in India, I recognize that my colleagues and those I lead have different contextual experiences. When I first arrived at Satyam, my team and other new colleagues had to adjust to my constantly asking about their geographic, religious, social, and company cultures. Additionally, they had to adjust to my more direct "American" style of leadership. That is, until I realized that the responsibility for adjusting primarily belonged with me, the leader. Leaders who are willing to adjust their style, expectations, and timelines will have greater success in harnessing the strengths of the team's background, experiences, cultures, and traditions within the context of what will work in each situation and each world market.

How is Leading People Globally Different from Leading People Domestically?

Leading people globally means you are leading a more diversified population with varied backgrounds in a totally different environment with completely different challenges. The scale and complexity complicates communications and relationships, and this requires more interpersonal and intercultural sensitivity.

- Emotional intelligence differs among cultures. The leader will need to observe cultural clues very carefully in order to vary his or her style and lead others appropriately.
- Labor laws differ from one country to the next. The leader must know which questions to ask, in order to have the requisite knowledge.
- Local, regional, and global business teams require sensitivity to diverse cultures. People's viewpoints will differ from one place to another. It's much harder to create a collaborative multicultural team than one that is more culturally homogeneous.
- Cultural and language differences are challenging.

As we continue to integrate teams across the globe, people leadership is at the forefront of our minds. And, while many of the people leadership principles you have learned will serve you well, being aware of the complexities and the nuances will aid you on your journey toward global success.

ATTRACTING AND RETAINING WORLD-CLASS TALENT

Gone are the days when physical and financial assets were the primary strengths of nations and organizations. We have entered an era in which intellectual capital constitutes the new wealth of nations and corporations.[1] There is a storm brewing that is threatening to disrupt the global marketplace: the impending retirements of the baby boom generation in the developed countries, aging populations worldwide because of declining birth rates and longer average life spans, a widening skills gap, and insufficient numbers of people entering the workforce are all factors that, when combined, could create a "perfect storm" that will threaten every type of industry and employee group. Here are a few of the storm warnings already out there.

With the United Kingdom predicting that it will be facing a shortage of up to 500,000 professionals with top-end networking skills within the next three years, South Africa can brace itself for some serious headhunting from UK companies – a situation that could exacerbate a local shortage.[2] "The looming talent war is a topic of great importance," says Neil S. Lebovits, president and chief operating officer of Ajilon Finance. "All companies large and small will be affected. As the market for talent becomes increasingly global and the economy continues to recover, smart, focused, productive people will be the most important currency businesses have."[3]

It is estimated that by 2010, the number of 35 to 44-year-olds, those normally expected to move into senior management ranks, will have declined by 10%. The pool of workers aged 35–44 is expected to shrink by 19% in the United Kingdom, by 27% in Germany, and by 9% in Italy.[4] By 2010, India will need approximately 250,000 leaders at different levels, but it is expected there will be a shortfall of one-third of that number. Leadership development is going to be a challenge in India.[5] *The Economist* reported that an international study by the Corporate Executive Board found that 62% of all senior human resource managers worry about company-wide talent shortages. Three-quarters of them made attracting and retaining talent their number one priority.[6]

We are receiving many such storm warnings from all over the world. The question is, will global leaders heed these warnings, or will they ignore them in the same way the officials in New Orleans did prior to Hurricane Katrina?

The need to attract and retain talent is on every global leader's mind. Luc Bollen of Hilton Hefei, China, told us: "We are experiencing a shortage of skilled labor globally. The economic growth of China surpasses even the rate at which China graduates people through its universities. There is still a serious shortage of skilled labor and management in the labor-intensive hospitality industry." Clive J. Pegg, from Bayer CropSciences AG, believes that "Recruiting, retaining, and managing personnel is more important than it was historically. There appears to be less loyalty to particular

Clive J. Pegg
Managing Director
Bayer CropSciences AG
www.bayer.com

Bayer is a research-based, growth-oriented global enterprise with core competencies in the fields of health care, nutrition, and high-tech materials. Headquartered in Germany, Bayer has 110,200 employees in 120 countries.

Clive Pegg works in Germany, and his country of citizenship is the United Kingdom. He has held leadership positions for more than 23 years. In the past two years, Clive has visited seven countries. His organization's official language is English. He speaks fluent English, French, and German. Clive has lived and worked in Belgium, Germany, India, Malaysia, the Philippines, and the United Kingdom.

Global Leadership Insights
- Have a positive attitude toward new challenges.
- Maintain strong personal core values
- Have a will to succeed in diverse cultures.
- Speak other languages, to help learn the culture.

Give people the necessary amount of time. If you try to move too quickly, issues may not be understood by all due to language differences or because they are outside the context of others' experiences. Don't think that you know best. You need an overall business framework and you must adapt local models within that framework. It's a mistake to assume that every concept is transferable.

companies than there has been in the past. Even though you have succession plans in place, turnover can dislocate the business."

Human Resource Management found in a 2003 survey that "83% of workers were 'extremely' or 'somewhat' likely to search for a new job when the economy recovered."[7] Dominique de Boisseson, chairman and CEO of Alcatel China Investment Company, says: "It is important to find, retain, and develop the right people so that they will be unique contributors. This is especially important for the young, fast-growing markets such as India and China."

So, how does a leader attract and retain the best talent? Here are eight methods used by world-class leaders.

1. Help your organization to be an "employer of choice."
2. Hire the right talent.
3. Don't view talent as yours alone.
4. Demonstrate an interest in others.
5. Listen to others, and be sure that everyone is heard.
6. Empower and motivate people.
7. Establish clear goals and roles.
8. Celebrate every success.

Help Your Organization to be an "Employer of Choice"

Being an "employer of choice" means that your organization will be preferred by those seeking positions. Characteristics of an "employer of choice" include: high visibility and name recognition; the approachability of senior leaders, especially the CEO; a reputation for being successful; a high number of applications received for each opening; and a corporate culture that is held in high regard (for example, values-based leadership, family-friendly policies). People also want to work for companies where the existing employees are content, turnover is low, and job security is considered high.

Many publications rank organizations on how well they are rated by their employees. Take a look at www.greatplacetowork.com to find a comprehensive list of companies that meet their criteria. They define a great place to work as somewhere where employees "trust the people they work for, have pride in what they do, and enjoy the people they work with." They measure employee satisfaction based on the interactions between employees and management, between employees and their jobs/company, and between employees and other employees.[8]

As competition for talent increases, organizations that offer family-friendly policies and services will emerge the winners. Some of the friendly policies and services that contribute to an organization being an "employer of choice" include:

**Dominique de Boisseson
Chairman & Chief Executive Officer
Alcatel China Investment Co., Ltd.
www.alcatel.com.cn/alcatel_china**

Alcatel, headquartered in France, provides communications solutions to telecommunication carriers, internet service providers, and enterprises for delivery of voice, data, and video applications to their customers or employees. The company operates in more than 130 countries.

Dominique de Boisseson works in China, and his country of citizenship is France. He has held leadership positions for more than 25 years. In the past two years, Dominique has visited 20 countries. His organization's official language is French. He speaks fluent English, French, and Spanish. Dominique has lived and worked in China, Denmark, France, and the United States.

Global Leadership Insights
- Respect that you can't change people or culture. As leader, it is up to you to adapt.
- Motivate people with different backgrounds to work together.

Our greatest global leadership challenge is finding, retaining, and developing the right people to reveal their unique contributions. This is very important for the young, fast-growing markets such as India and China.

Travel is the best way to be prepared for the world of tomorrow. We will need "global leaders" who can succeed in diverse cultures. We see many young people, especially Europeans right out of business school, coming to China for work because they want to learn and gain know-how as soon as possible.

- flexible work schedules, including flexitime, telecommuting, part-time work options, and job sharing;
- employee services such as onsite day care, banking and financial advice, convenience store, fitness center, cafeteria, and concierge services for dry cleaning and personal travel;
- excellent medical, dental, and vision plans;
- retirement programs;

- health and wellness programs, including onsite nurses, fitness facilities, and health club discounts;
- personal leave packages, including dependent care and sabbaticals;
- educational assistance opportunities, including tuition reimbursement; and
- personal computers and laptops for employee use at home and during business travel.

Companies wishing to attract and retain talent should assess how they currently treat their employees. Those that treat their employees poorly, or believe that increasing compensation alone retains talent, will lose their best people to other companies offering a better "package" of benefits.

Hire the Right Talent

Stephen Green, group CEO of HSBC, has been quoted as saying, "We don't look so much at what or where people have studied but rather at their drive, initiative, cultural sensitivity, and readiness to see the world as their oyster."[9] I learned from Frank DeVita how to hire the right talent. Frank hired me, in 1994, to work for him at Seer Technologies in North Carolina, in the United States. During our first meeting, Frank explained why he had hired me. He said, "I always hire SWANs." Puzzled, I thought to myself, "Swans are graceful, swans are beautiful ..." Sensing my confusion, Frank explained: "*S* stands for Smart, *W* for Winner, *A* for Attitude, and *N* for the most important trait of all, Nice." It has been more than 13 years since that meeting, and I have always applied Frank's advice when hiring people. With only a few exceptions, I have been blessed in selecting and bringing together incredible global teams.

Don't View Talent as Yours Alone

Talent belongs to the organization. Many leaders don't recognize this and create environments where employees feel it is easier to leave the organization than to transfer within it. That kind of possessive

Phillip R. Styrlund
President
The Summit Group
www.summitvalue.com

The Summit Group works with Fortune 1000 companies to achieve sales force superiority and to transform managers into exemplary leaders.

Phillip Styrlund works throughout the world, and his country of citizenship is the United States. He has held leadership positions for more than 21 years. In the past two years, Phillip has visited 30 countries. During his career, he has lived and worked in the United Kingdom and the United States.

Global Leadership Insights
- Focus on others.
- Paint a clear picture of the future; reduce uncertainty and ambiguity.
- Be tenacious and resilient.
- Learn from adversity.
- Be passionate about diversity.
- Experience as much of the world as possible.

To lead globally, it takes patience and maturity to move beyond your own needs and focus on the needs of others. It is essential to understand the motivators that drive individuals around the world. All people want to feel a sense of personal worth and value; all want a better future for themselves; and all seek to understand where their organization is going and where they fit within it.

behavior diminishes employee attraction and retention. When I was at Booz Allen, the chairman, Dr. Ralph Shrader, repeatedly said, "I would rather see 'Booz Allen' on your business card than on your resume." Booz Allen established a career mobility program that allowed employees to apply for internal positions. At Satyam, movement isn't only encouraged, it is rewarded. Those who have the greatest variety of experiences are the ones who move up the career ladder the fastest.

Demonstrate an Interest in Others

Phillip R. Styrlund of The Summit Group has a simple piece of advice: "My father always told me that the key to any relationship, whether it be with customers, employees, or other relationships, is that it's better to be 'interested' than 'interesting.' If you are deeply interested in the other person, you can identify their needs and expectations in a way that transcends cultures."

When you take the time to get to know someone, such as an employee, on a personal level, trust is enhanced, it is easier to gain their buy-in, and they will feel more satisfied in their work. I demonstrate interest in each person on my team by asking them about their history, their families, and their goals. I also share with them information about who I am and about my life. The more I know about what motivates a person on multiple levels, the more able I am to make decisions that impact positively on them. Dr. Siow Choon Neo of Federal Express Pacific, Inc. agrees: "Be personable. It allows you to be sensitive and cuts across all countries. Everyone has the potential to build rapport if they show they are sincerely interested in others."

Being personable and showing an interest in others allows people to feel safe in letting you know how to succeed in each new environment. David J. Gee, from Eli Lilly Japan K.K., says: "Most of the people I work with have been to my home. If you consistently maintain a forthright, honest, and well-intentioned attitude in your relationships, your people will trust you." World-class leaders understand that it is crucial to take the time to get to know the family situations, career goals, and motivations of their employees, if they are to develop holistic relationships that benefit all those involved.

Listen to Others, and Be Sure that Everyone is Heard

Have you ever been in a meeting where the leader tells those present what he or she is thinking, and then asks for their opinions? I have observed that, in most cultures, if the leader speaks first, then the leader will be the only one to speak. Most people don't want to contradict their leader publicly. So, ask people what they think

Lisa Earnhardt
Director of Human Resources Latin America
Royal & SunAlliance
www.royalsunalliance.com

Royal & SunAlliance is one of the world's leading insurance groups. It has business in 130 countries, providing general insurance products to over 20 million customers worldwide.

Lisa Earnhardt works in the United States, which is also her country of citizenship. She has held leadership positions for more than 20 years. In the past two years, Lisa has visited 10 countries. Her organization's official language is English. She speaks fluent English and Portuguese. Lisa has lived and worked in Brazil and the United States.

Global Leadership Insights
- Always do what you love.
- Have a purpose and passion, in order to realize your potential and develop it in others.
- Curiosity is key to learning.
- Achieve results by working across the organization through a complex matrix of relationships.
- Share knowledge and best practices broadly and deeply.
- Create work environments that foster learning and innovation.
- Empower and energize others.

My approach is to interact with leaders as a business partner and to be accountable to add value to the top and bottom line. Encourage personal accountability and personal development by measuring, rewarding, and recognizing success. As a global leader, ask yourself what legacy you wish to leave.

first, listen to what they have to say, and then incorporate their thoughts into your carefully thought-through summation. "Do a lot of listening," advises Tom Rath of The Gallup Organization. "Try not to make assumptions. This takes discipline when you are used to working with people you know well. Try to suppress voicing your own opinion, in order to listen to others and learn about what's happening in each different scenario."

Davide Arpili of AlixPartners LLP advises, "Always make sure everyone is heard. This is especially important when the first language of the individual is different than the business language of the organization." You could say, "Let's go back for a second and listen to such-and-such a person." Allowing one culture to dominate others could impact the morale of the team. The leader is responsible for listening and for balancing relationships. Jair Ribeiro agrees: "Develop within yourself, and your team, the ability to listen. Leaders need to pay respect to cultural differences, and never underestimate the human factor. Hear several points of view before taking action. In an international scope, when environments are broader and more complex, you should rely more on listening and on feedback."

Empower and Motivate People

It takes patience and maturity to motivate and empower others. In *The Leader of the Future 2*, Usman A. Ghani refers to leaders as "leader integrators." He says, "Leader integrators eagerly invite a wide variety of experiences, visions, and skill sets into the task of forming and then expanding the corporate vision. As a result, the leader integrator not only increases the passions of every worker for his or her contribution to the corporation's direction but also amplifies the workers' personal commitments to the organization."[10] Motivators that drive people, regardless of culture, include their leader's ability to instill in them a sense of worth and value, so that people feel they are important and that they are making a difference. Once his or her team is motivated, the leader's main responsibility is to influence them through coaching, mentoring, and teaching, as well as by breaking down the barriers to success.

Lisa Earnhardt, human resources director, Latin America Region for Royal & SunAlliance, is someone I have known for more than a decade. We worked together at an earlier company and I always marveled at her creativity and ability to create a highly engaged team. Lisa says, "Creating a high-performance culture promotes a positive and challenging work environment." She advises, "You have to constantly encourage teamwork – empower and energize others to bring out the best in people. Create work environments that foster learning and innovation. As a leader, be energizing, engaging, and motivating to others in order to create future success." Navi Radjou, from Forrester Research, agrees: "You need to empower employees. Fire up the imagination and energize employees to contribute to the major cause of the company. They will feel like their ideas are being listened to, and will want to contribute to the organization's success."

When leading globally, there is the added complexity of knowing how to motivate people from different cultures. Jair Ribeiro, CEO of Braxis IT Services, advises: "Let your people help set the strategy, sell that strategy to the team, and energize them to act with a sense of urgency. A major quality of a leader is the ability to energize people. People all over the world want to be energized, but the way you position yourself to create that energy may differ. From India to Chile, people want leaders who can energize and motivate them to action." In fact, leaders with global responsibility all agree that one has to adapt one's style in order to determine what works in different cultures and for different individuals. "Be sensitive and take into account cultural differences," advises Dominique de Boisseson. "Recognize that everyone is part of the group. Rather than arguing about differences, motivate people of different cultural backgrounds to work together and complement each other. Make sure they know they are better together than alone, and they will learn from each other." Spending time with your people can enhance team trust and provide a greater sense of security for everyone. "If you believe your employees are trustworthy and professional, then managing remotely isn't an issue," says Dr. Siow Choon Neo of Federal Express Pacific. "Trusting and empowering them is important. To do this, you need to have enough contact with them. One-to-one and team contact is important."

Establish Clear Goals and Roles

A leader needs to communicate explicit goals and roles for each team member. Davide Arpili of AlixPartners, LLP advises, "Identify the needs of team members up front. Tell them what you want to do, provide the opportunity for them to ask questions and to get a feel for your approach. Make sure each individual has a clear understanding of what is needed." Mary Capozzi, from Best Buy, learned that partnering people with complementary skills is an effective way to build teams. "In Turkey we had many skilled engineers, but the managerial competencies were underdeveloped. So, we had to find local people who were good at managing, and partner them with the great engineering staff. If you assess local people that you know and trust, utilizing their feedback, you can make better choices for the team as a whole."

Celebrate Every Success

Every success is an opportunity to celebrate! When I get an email from someone with great feedback about something the team has accomplished, I send it to the entire team and others to let everyone know. Many organizations have "spot bonuses," which leaders can use to reward successes. Added to this, is what I call "Catch Someone Doing Something Great" acknowledgments. A short hand-written note or a quick phone call can go a long way in lifting someone's spirits.

Does your organization have a culture of celebrations? If not, then you can still create one within your own area. Develop a plan; don't expect it just to happen. And make sure that you and your leaders have similar rewards in mind. For example, I used to have my leaders carry around tickets to the local movie theater, so that when they heard of or caught someone doing something great, they could acknowledge them by handing them a couple of tickets. It was a small price to pay for a large return! Every quarter, I take my entire team, with their families, for a team day. I tell them, "We work hard for three months to deliver world-class service, so today we will stop and take the time to celebrate our accomplishments." At the end of every year, Satyam has an evening of entertainment for all its associates and their families. It takes place at the company's offices around the world and allows people to get together to celebrate their hard work and contributions to the company's success.

The competition for talent offers many benefits – from boosting productivity to increasing opportunities, from promoting job satisfaction to supercharging scientific advances. The more countries and companies compete for talent, the better the chances that geniuses will be raked up from obscurity.[11]

MANAGING MULTIFACETED DIVERSITY

In the time that I have spent in India, I have truly come to appreciate the multifaceted possibilities afforded by an exceptionally inclusive environment. This experience has unquestionably extended my awareness. A multifaceted workforce is more prepared to take full advantage of opportunities that result in mega-innovation and limitless creativity (see Figure 5.1). Diverse ecosystems promote enhanced relationships, resulting in continuous organizational benefits. Broad diversity emerges from the multiplicity of cultures, designations, demographics, economic standings, education levels, gender, geographies, industries, personality types, and leadership priorities. "Multi-cultural societies with their diversities can be looked at as a source of strength and an engine of innovation," says Ahmad A. Ajarimah, of the Saudi Arabian Oil Company, in his article entitled "Major Challenges of Global Leadership in the Twenty-First Century." "Diversity brings different perspectives, which, if employed effectively, can lead to breakthrough thinking

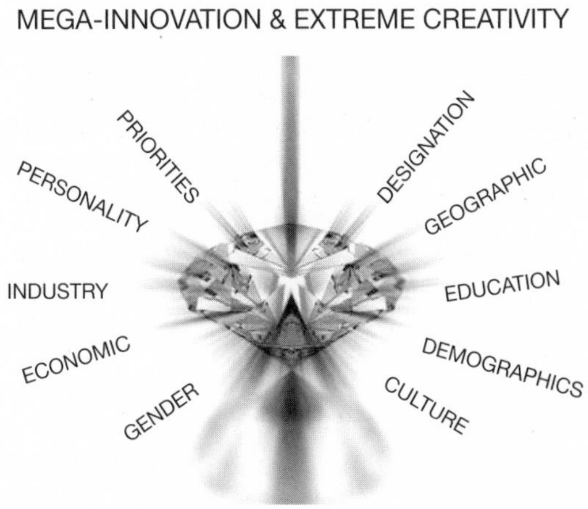

MEGA-INNOVATION & EXTREME CREATIVITY

Figure 5.1 **Multifaceted diversity results in mega-innovation and extreme creativity**

Mahesh Pratapneni
Senior Vice President
IT & Sourcing
Indymac Bancorp, Inc.
www.indymacbank.com

Indymac Bancorp is the largest savings and loan in Los Angeles and the seventh-largest mortgage originator in the United States. It employs 9,000 people worldwide.

Mahesh Pratapneni works in the United States, which is also his country of citizenship. He has held leadership positions for more than 11 years. In the past two years, Mahesh has visited seven countries. His organization's official language is English. He speaks fluent English, Hindi, and Telugu. Mahesh has lived and worked in India and the United States.

Global Leadership Insights
- Be aggressive without being abrasive.
- Have a deep working knowledge of your workforce.
- Understand cross-border, cultural business trends.
- Link priorities to business goals.
- Communicate continuously.

If a leader creates a team that is too close to him/her geographically or ideologically, he/she won't be able to see other points of view in relation to the team, the positioning of information, and the market. It's very easy to work in that mode, and this is a tremendous leadership mistake. A leader must create diversity in the team, sources of information, and approaches to the market.

and advancement in all human endeavours. Living in a multi-cultural society requires a heightened awareness and respect for human rights."[12]

Managing diversity is a process by which people employ the full potential of the talent available in the organization or community. The demographic and cultural shifts taking place throughout the world have profound implications for managing diversity, especially in the areas of public policy, workforce management, and education. Many voices need to be heard, and the potential for fragmentation is real. The challenge is to nurture and respect diversity while finding common ground and a sense of responsibility to one another.[13]

Multifaceted diversity really comes down to selecting a team that is built on more than skills alone. "I make sure that the organization is built around the right people," says Hugh Peterken, from the International Federation of Red Cross and Red Crescent Societies. "I create a balance by bringing people with different strengths and backgrounds together. When building a team I try to balance out the weaknesses and capitalize on strengths that allow people to be successful in the organization."

Mahesh Pratapneni, from Indymac Bancorp, agrees and adds: "If a leader creates a team that is too close to him/her geographically or ideologically, he/she won't be able to see other points of view. It's very easy to work in that mode, and this is a tremendous leadership mistake. A leader must create diversity in the team, sources of information, and approaches to the market."

Kent O. Jonasen of A.P. Moller – Maersk shares his perspective: "A global company has the opportunity to look to different countries for leadership potential. For example, India is a base where we recruit significant finance talent. Also, in Denmark we only have structural unemployment, so finding talent locally isn't easy, which means we have to turn to other countries to recruit other people."

The concept of multifaceted diversity isn't new to me; it's just more real. Something that I used to take for granted, I now look forward to with each new encounter. I am not trying to imply that multifaceted diversity is working everywhere. In fact, in India, women still make up less than 25% of the total workforce, and there are very few women at the top of the Indian corporate ladder. Moreover, there is still a tremendous economic divide. That said, India – and "India, Inc.," as the aggregate of all business is referred to – has evolved rapidly over the past decade. Just 10 years ago, close to half of the more than one billion people in India were living below the poverty line. Today, the number stands in the low 20th percentile. With the possible exception of China, no other country has achieved this magnitude of change so rapidly. The ability to lead multicultural and cross-functional teams effectively

Kent O. Jonasen
Group Vice President and Deputy Head
Corporate Human Resources
A.P. Moller – Maersk A/S
www.maersk.com/en

A.P. Moller – Maersk A/S is an international company of Danish origin widely recognized for its activities within shipping, energy, offshore, retail, and industry. It has more than 110,000 employees in over 125 countries.

Kent Jonasen works in Denmark, which is also his country of citizenship. He has held leadership positions for more than 11 years. In the past two years, Kent has visited nine countries. His organization's official language is English. He speaks fluent English and Danish.

Global Leadership Insights
- Acknowledge the worldwide talent pool and recruit globally.
- As you move up, identify what you need to stop doing, start doing, or continue doing.
- Confront all the facts, including cultural implications, when making decisions.
- Renew yourself and your perspectives regularly.
- Learn to lead virtually; it's the way of the future.

Recruit people for international assignments who are sensitive to cultural differences. For local work, allow people to handle issues in a manner appropriate to their local context and culture. Work and live in other countries; however, we have found that people are sometimes more nationally focused abroad, rather than being open to experiencing and learning about new places and people.

is becoming a critical differentiator between winners and losers in the global marketplace.[14]

MORE ON COMMUNICATION

Communication is defined by one's ability to transmit ideas, receive information, and interact with the environment around

BOX 5.1 SARINA'S STORY

Sarina Pasricha

Today's technology and the human ability to network have made it possible for a half-Filipino, half-Indian woman who stands just four feet two inches (127 centimeters) tall to move from Manila, in the Philippines, to Hyderabad, India, to be of productive use to the information technology community. I am part of the minority and the "differently abled" sector of society that hasn't been afforded equal treatment, affirmation, and professionalism in the workplace. My life before relocating to India had been a series of painful and hurtful experiences perpetrated by work colleagues in the Philippines.

I was a college and graduate schoolteacher – an excellent one, according to my students, and my reviews reflected this – but my peers wondered why groups listened to, much less respected, someone half their size. It's simple – *knowledge cannot be measured by one's size or looks*. I was also a newspaper columnist, who shocked my editor when he met me in person. The shift in his behavior was obvious. Sitting before me, he turned cold and distant, the reverse of the warm personality that I had been used to interacting with on the phone and in faxes and emails.

In Manila, I am a dwarf who just happens to have a Master's degree. In Manila, dwarfs are found in freak shows and lunchtime variety shows for ridiculous entertainment. Hence, the solution was to get out of Manila, to find a place where people would see beyond my small stature, and value me for my skills, my craft, and my mind.

When I applied for and was offered a job with Satyam, I dropped everything and moved to Hyderabad. I left home (for the first time in my life), family, friends, dogs, comfort food, and cable television that ran English programming. I had never been to Hyderabad and had no clue about what was in store for me. Change was difficult to manage. It brought on an emotional roller-coaster ride. There were many occasions when I questioned my decision to move to India. Initially, there was no one to interact with on a personal and intellectual level. There was no one to bond with. My only sources of connection were the calls and emails from my parents. However, my initial sense of isolation meant there were no distractions to prevent me from coming face to face with myself. There is a lot I would change in order to be treated normally, like everybody else. But I am also proud of my unique attributes.

Enter my current boss, Shailesh Shah, whose attitude was: "I don't care what she looks like, as long as she can get the job done." This was the dealmaker that guaranteed that I would be treated just like everybody else – even be fired, if I didn't deliver. I accepted this opportunity, which was too beautiful, too ideal, to pass up.

Since beginning work at Satyam in October 2005, I haven't been the object of stares, of finger-pointing, of laughter, or of cruel jokes by colleagues at work or by the citizens of Hyderabad. I ride on public transportation by myself, with drivers who are decent and respectful. I interact with colleagues – no politics, no hidden agendas, nothing mean or malicious. I get praised when I churn out good work, and I get told if otherwise. Life is good. Moreover, it's not only for me, but also for others who are in similar situations. I have seen fellow associates (Satyam calls its employees "associates") who are "differently abled" welcomed into the group.

"Diversity" refers to the variety of human experience and achievement and to tolerance of and respect for that variety. Diversity manifests so many positive outcomes, yet only few embrace and profit from it. A characteristic trait of diversity is that it doesn't limit ideas, access and participation, and freedom of expression and choice. Diversity drives innovation and progress. Tolerance for diversity is a sign of successful economic development.

one. In global teams, where time zones, and cultural and language differences have the potential to disrupt communication, leaders need to communicate clearly and precisely, and adapt to local variables, while remaining authentic.

Elizabeth Haraldsdottir Thomas has been working internationally almost her entire career, having spent time in Canada, Denmark, France, Germany, Sweden, the United Kingdom, and now Switzerland. She explains: "You have to be yourself, while at the same time realizing that the way you speak, the way you do things, and the way you make requests may be received differently depending upon where you are. If you understand the differences, you can communicate effectively. You could be surprised by others' behavior, but if you can work out what is happening, you'll have a much greater chance of leading effectively. You need to be able to deal simultaneously with different rhythms in different parts

Elizabeth Haraldsdottir Thomas
Director
Global Management System
World Health Organization
www.who.int/en

The World Health Organization (WHO) is the United Nations' specialized agency for health. WHO is headquartered in Geneva, Switzerland and is governed by 192 Member States through the World Health Assembly. It has locations in 146 countries.

Elizabeth Haraldsdottir Thomas works in Switzerland, and her countries of citizenship are Iceland and the United Kingdom. She has held leadership positions for more than 18 years. In the past two years, Elizabeth has visited 13 countries. Her organization has six official languages, with English and French spoken at the global headquarters. Elizabeth speaks fluent Danish, English, French, and Swedish. She has lived and worked in Canada, Denmark, France, Germany, Sweden, Switzerland, and the United Kingdom.

Global Leadership Insights
- Learn about, understand, and adjust your actions to differing cultures.
- Understand the complexities of your environment.
- Create a shared vision.
- Motivate others to act in a way compatible with the culture and where the organization is going.
- Allow people to be innovative wherever possible.

Be open to the feedback you receive. You have to be yourself, while at the same time realizing that the way you speak, the way you do things, and the way you make requests may be received differently depending upon where you are.

of the world, and with people in different environments and with differing cultures."

Some of our global leader interviewees felt it was very important to know the local language. Karl-Heinz Lensing, from Kathrein Mobilcom Brasil LTDA, says: "Language is the key to another mentality and way of thinking." While it isn't always feasible to become proficient, even learning a few words and phrases of the local language can go a long way when trying to understand and build relationships with those whose first language differs from yours. Again, it goes back to demonstrating interest in others, being willing to listen, and allowing everyone to be heard.

When working in another country, advises Elliott Masie, "even with people fluent in your language, slow down. People process language differently, and so do you." Avoid using irony or figurative language, and always keep in mind that humor may not translate well from culture to culture. Having others paraphrase or repeat back what they think they have heard is a very useful technique for making sure you are being understood. It also works well in reverse: paraphrase or repeat back to others what you think you have heard, to make sure you have correctly understood them. There is no point in rushing to conclude a meeting if there are people present who don't understand exactly what has been agreed or decided.

It isn't possible to have every meeting, or even the majority of meetings, face-to-face. Regular teleconference or video-conference calls can assist in maintaining communication – and a sense of connectedness – between far-flung team members. Just remember to slow things down to aid comprehension and minimize misunderstandings when conducting such meetings. Clive J. Pegg says, "It's important to communicate in a way that everyone understands. Even though English is the primary language for our business, some fundamental misunderstandings occur because English isn't the first language for everyone. In many places, you face the challenge of people who don't understand but would rather not say they don't understand."

In global environments, and especially with new teams, the extra time you take to understand and be understood will enhance the chances of a successful outcome. Try to be realistic in terms of your expectations, or people may become frustrated. Bonnie Stoufer of The Boeing Company agrees: "You don't know what you don't know, so be inclusive in your approach. When I showed up in a global leadership scenario, I assumed I didn't know for sure what would work and I asked people for their advice and coaching. When things began moving, I included those participants in the formulation process. Be inclusive and democratic, by asking for feedback and questions."

DEVELOPING LEADERS

There are two types of leaders. The first waits for talented people to show up and then recruits those people onto his or her team. The second type develops talent by nurturing potential leaders, guiding their growth by broadening their experiences, and mentoring and coaching them along the way. According to David J. Gee, "There will always be a shortage of the right kind of people. You need the ability to create a supply of talented people who can eventually grow into your role." Are you a user of talent or a developer of talent? Navi Radjou believes the era of globalization will redefine leadership into a more diffused, collective leadership. "We will have increasing amounts of stakeholders involved and influencing business decisions. Leadership will be more participatory, collective, and democratic."

World-class leaders continuously identify and develop their stars. They are more interested in growing leaders than they are in increasing the number of people following them. Whether you are leading domestically or globally, Tom Rath from Gallup advises, "Make sure your emerging and existing leaders have a real opportunity to learn every day. Allow them time to learn about the latest developments and research."

Leaders should look across their entire organization to identify and nurture future leaders, who must then be given opportunities to lead. Only a CEO can ensure that global leadership succession planning is drilled down so far into the very heart of the company that it touches how even bright young graduates with high potential global talent are being recruited for future top global leadership positions. The problem, however, is that many CEOs may be reluctant to develop a global leadership succession plan.[15]

BUILDING SUSTAINABLE RELATIONSHIPS

Kal Patel, from Best Buy, provides an interesting perspective on building relationships regardless of where people are physically located. "Ninety per cent of the activities could happen through intuitive video-teleconference and collaboration technology, using big screens so that faces and body language are visible.

Then take all the money saved to have more get-togethers in cool places everyone enjoys. This results in building communities and strengthening relationships between people. Today, in order to do business in India, you travel to India for a few days – maybe a week – and then return. This includes the hotel cost, fares, etc. Let's assume you could do all of that through some other platform, but for one week the people in India and in the United States all go to Shanghai for a massive learning session on the business of the future. You save the travel time to create space for collaboration and innovation. You take people from where they are and expose them to new places, new cultures, and new people."

Global leaders agree that once people have met and spent time together, virtual contact can be effective in enhancing and solidifying their relationships. Today, we are only beginning to understand the potential of building relationships in a blended way. Elliott Masie says, "Establish sustainable colleagueships with people of different cultures that extend over time. This is helped by technology. Be intentional about this; it takes time, but it helps." I have known some of my colleagues for nearly 30 years; others I've known for less than an hour. Cultivating relationships around the world isn't only important, it is extremely fulfilling.

The essence of global people leadership comes down to this: you cannot understand every nuance of every culture. Even if you have worked in many different countries and consider yourself to be a global citizen, you still need the help of professionals who have a deeper understanding of the local culture. Develop, utilize, and believe in each individual in your global team. Erna Adelson of Sony Corporation puts it best: "You have vision and the ability to manage change and to communicate well. Then you take that ability globally, beyond what you have accomplished in all your life, to new areas. Global leadership is about being on a bigger stage with much more complexity." That comes back to listening, learning, being inclusive, and demonstrating that you are interested in others.

Global Leadership Viewpoints

This chapter discussed people leadership and the complexities that are encountered on the global frontier. Along the way, these global leadership viewpoints were shared:

- Even though many, if not most, people leadership competencies and behaviors are constant, enhanced complexities – the demonstration and prioritization of these competencies and behaviors in different parts of the world – exemplify global people leadership.
- World-class leaders adjust their style, expectations, and timelines to achieve the same outcomes as they would in their country of origin.
- To attract and retain talent, companies should assess how they currently treat their employees. There are eight key areas that assist in attracting and retaining top talent: (1) help your organization to be an "employer of choice"; (2) hire the right talent; (3) don't view talent as yours alone; (4) demonstrate an interest in others; (5) listen to others, and be sure that everyone is heard; (6) empower and motivate people; (7) establish clear goals and roles; and, finally, (8) celebrate every success.
- Being personable and showing an interest in others transcend cultures and allow people to feel safe in letting you know how to succeed in each new environment.
- Try not to make assumptions. This takes discipline when you are used to working with people you know well.
- It takes patience and maturity to motivate and empower others. Motivators that drive people, regardless of culture, include their leader's ability to instill in them a sense of worth and value, so that people feel they are important and that they are making a difference. People are motivated when they see that their career is progressing and that someone is working with them to make that happen.
- Multifaceted diversity emerges from the multiplicity of cultures, designations, demographics, economic standings, education levels, gender, geographies, industries, personality types, and leadership priorities.

- As a leader in a diverse environment, you have to be yourself while at the same time recognizing that the way you speak, the way you do things, and the way you make requests may be perceived differently depending upon where you are.
- When working in another country, even with people fluent in your language, slow down to make sure everyone understands and is correctly processing information.
- Understand the value of developing more leaders.
- Once people have met and spent time together, virtual contact can be effective in enhancing and solidifying their relationships. Today we are only beginning to understand the potential of building relationships in a blended way.
- The essence of global people leadership is recognizing the power that comes from harnessing the team's background, experiences, culture, and traditions within the context of what will work in any particular situation or market.
- Global leadership isn't about control; it's about influence. It's about creating a motivating environment that empowers decisions to be made at the lowest level, encourages innovation, and helps people to fulfill their potential.

As an experienced leader, now living in a country that isn't my country of origin, I realized that before I could teach others about leadership, I first had to become the student, to discover and learn, to adjust and adapt my style of leadership to what works in the environments where I find myself.

Endnotes

1   Ahmad A. Ajarimah, Saudi Arabian Oil Company (Saudi Aramco), "Major Challenges of Global Leadership in the Twenty-first Century," *Human Resource Development International*, March 2001, pp. 9–19.

2   Org Geldenhuys, "Networking Skills Shortage Could Hit South Africa" (www.itworldcanada.com/topic/84d5c492-7517-4093-b449-3521f0e6353f/pg9.htm), accessed November 27, 2006.

3   Neil S. Lebovits, "The Next Decade's Talent War," Report, Ajilon Finance, June 2005 (www.ajilonfinance.com/articles/Talent%20War-ext%205-26-05.pdf).

4   Lynne Morton, "Managing the Mature Workforce," *The Conference Board, 2004*, July 2005, p. 2.

5   Mike R. Jay, Founder, Leadership University, "India will need 250,000 leaders in next 3 years," The Rediff Interview, May 13, 2006 (http://inhome.rediff.com/money/2006/may/13inter.htm), accessed November 27, 2006.

6   Adrian Wooldridge, "A Survey on Talent – The Battle for Brainpower," *The Economist* print edition, October 5, 2006 (www.economist.com/surveys/displayStory.cfm?story_id=7961894), accessed November 27, 2006.

7   Ibid.

8   www.greatplacetowork.com/great/.

9   Stephen Green, Fred Hassan, Jeffrey Immelt, Michael Marks, and Daniel Meiland, "In Search of Global Leaders," *Harvard Business Review*, August 2003, p. 40.

10 Usman A. Ghani, "The Leader Integrator," in Marshall Goldsmith and Frances Hesselbein (eds.), *The Leader of the Future 2* (San Francisco: Jossey-Bass Publishing, 2006), p. 244.

11 Wooldridge, op. cit.

12 Ahmad A. Ajarimah, op. cit.

13 Nicholas A. Andreadis, "Leadership for Civil Society: Implications for Global Corporate Leadership Development," *Human Resources Development International*, June 2002, pp. 143–9.

14 J. S. Black and H. B. Gregersen, "High Impact Training: Forging Leaders for the Global Frontier," *Human Resources Management*, Summer/Fall 2000, pp. 173–84.

15 Trevor O'Hara, "Making the Case for Global Leadership Succession Planning," www.leader-values.com, 2005 (www.leader-values.com/Content/detail.asp?ContentDetailID=1073), accessed November 27, 2006.

Chapter 6

Global Business Leadership

INTRODUCTION

I have had the opportunity to visit many places in Asia, including parts of India, Japan, Singapore, Thailand, and Vietnam. In the coming year I will make a long-anticipated visit to China. Asia is unique in its range of cultures, traditions, political systems, and levels of economic development. My experiences in Asia have taught me many things about business leadership, but perhaps the most important thing I have learned is: allow things to happen when the timing is right. The flow of time is different in Asia than it is in the United States, say. An example of this is the way the widespread use of mobile phones in India has affected the way leaders manage their time.

In India, the mobile phone and email are the principal communication tools. When I moved to Hyderabad, I wasn't surprised by the widespread take-up of email, but I hadn't expected that my mobile phone would become my primary communication device. I had come from a culture where my calls were screened by my assistants, which allowed me to manage my time in a way that I considered efficient. On encountering the culture at Satyam, where everyone answered their own mobile phone and was at the beck and call, as I saw it, of anyone who had their number, my first thought was to try and change that culture. My goal was to convince leaders to abandon their mobile phones so that their assistants would take and screen their calls. However, I quickly learned two important lessons.

First, leaders in India prioritize being accessible to stakeholders. Even our family doctor provides his patients with his mobile phone number. When we call him, he either answers straight away or returns our missed call. Time management in India means being accessible. Second, an assistant handles travel and other arrangements, manages schedules, writes reports, and, most importantly, conducts extensive research with which to brief the leader. Assistants are usually recently graduated MBAs who learn the ropes by working alongside a leader for a couple of years, in a form of apprenticeship. In Chapter 1, we discussed how competencies are the same for leaders throughout the world; the key difference is in how they are prioritized and demonstrated in each culture. Learning about the use of mobile phones in India, and their importance in managing time, was a true wake-up call for me.

I don't mean to imply that business moves more slowly in Asia than in other parts of the world. In fact, companies in the IT and pharmaceutical industries are experiencing 30–40% annual growth. In 2006 alone, Satyam hired 12,000 new associates, representing a more than 30% increase in size. It is building new premises at more than a dozen sites across India. And this growth has been sustained for several years. What I find significant about the different rhythms of time in different parts of the world – let's call them "time zones" – is the challenge this poses to a global leader, who must "straddle" those many different time zones and still be attuned to the "right time" to make a move or take a decision.

Business leadership is much more complex on the global frontier. Here is an overview of the magnitude of global business leadership.

Globalization has been creeping into every aspect of modern life. Think computerization, the Internet, e-commerce, multinational corporations, and satellite TV channels beaming their programs to different regions 24 hours per day. Look at the global economy, which responds in London and New York to events that occur in China and Japan only a few hours after their occurrence. Think of international travel and transportation by air and sea and how it reduced cycle time and strengthened the interconnectedness of the world's regions and cultures. Think of distance learning degree programs offered by various institutions of higher education. Think of the billions of dollars that can be transferred across national borders in fractions of a second. Finally, do not forget the major instruments of globalization such as the World Bank, the United Nations, the World Trade Organization, and the regional coalitions such as the European Union, ASEAN and the Gulf Cooperation Council.[1]

Satyam's Global Leadership Survey identified decision-making and problem-solving abilities, aligning and utilizing complex networks, vision and strategy skills, and change leadership skills as primary competencies for global leaders. In that context, we will now provide an overview of some of the business complexities faced by global leaders: vision and strategy, organizational structure, organizational economics, the role of technology, and the value of having broad networks.

GLOBAL VISION AND STRATEGY

In their book, *A Leader's Legacy*, Jim Kouzes and Barry Posner write: "What people really want to hear is not about the leader's vision. They want to hear about their own aspirations. They want to hear how their dreams will come true and their hopes will be fulfilled. They want to see themselves in the picture of the future that the leader is painting. The very best leaders understand that their key task is inspiring a shared vision, not selling their own idiosyncratic view of the world."[2]

Inspiring a shared vision in a world filled with so many differences isn't an easy task. Leaders have to make sure they know and understand what motivates people in all the different locations where they operate. "I consider one of the attributes of a world-class leader is helping the organization change," says Bill Vincek of MGI PHARMA. "It's difficult to get people to accept change, get management to be an example of change, and move forward. If you want to move toward being a number one company, people need to share the vision and then develop a shared strategy."

Bill Vincek
Senior Vice President
Technical Operations and Manufacturing
MGI PHARMA, Inc.
www.mgipharma.com

MGI Pharmaceuticals, Inc. is a biopharmaceutical company focused in oncology and acute care that acquires, researches, develops, and commercializes proprietary products that address the unmet needs of patients.

Bill Vincek works in the United States, which is also his country of citizenship. He has held leadership positions for more than 18 years. In the past two years, Bill has visited five countries. He has lived and worked in the United Kingdom and the United States.

Global Leadership Insights
- Observe and emulate (within your own scope) those who lead well.
- Listen in the context of where in the world you are working.
- Recognize people's unique traits.
- Focus on the benefits of differences.
- Be accessible.
- Have a vision.

Read and learn about, and show respect for, the local culture. A leader needs to show that he/she cares about the people in the organization. Don't underestimate the power of employees knowing that their leader cares about what happens to them.

When developing a global vision and strategy, the vision should be concrete and apply across the enterprise. The strategy and its implementation should be flexible enough to adapt to different parts of the world.

Dr. Siow Choon Neo of FedEx Asia Pacific says, "You need the ability to articulate a shared vision, aligned to the business goals, and adjusted towards communicating with different cultures." Culture isn't the only implication to keep in mind. Context is necessary when laying out a shared vision and strategy, to help others understand what you and your organization are trying to accomplish. The educational and experience levels of people in different countries can also vary greatly.

I was the first person in my family to enter the corporate business world. When I joined the world of business, I had many mentors and colleagues to observe and from whom I could learn. Fifteen years ago, relatively few people worked in corporations in India. However, since the economic liberalization of the 1990s and the advent of outsourcing, their number has increased dramatically.[3] Because the corporate scene in India is young, first-generation business people there tend to have few people they can turn to for mentoring and guidance. This means they may not have the context for the strategy you are trying to set. For example, I wanted everyone on my team to understand the concept of "world-class service," so I asked them to tell me the best hotel they had ever stayed at in the world. Of the 20 people on my team, three said they had never stayed in a hotel, and most had never traveled outside India. While I had expected the latter, I was surprised by the former. I quickly realized the need for a different context, and so I took those team members who hadn't stayed in a hotel to a five-star establishment so that they could observe the service and see how things worked. This experience enabled them to see what I meant by "world-class."

Elizabeth Haraldsdottir Thomas, from the World Health Organization, puts context to how a vision should be: "Create a shared vision on what the future should be and plot out how we would get there. But, like sailing, you don't get there in a straight line, and it may take longer to get there than you would like." The wind fills the sails, taking the boat in a preferred direction. The crew are responsible for getting to the final destination. How they get there will depend on many different variables.

A shared vision is essential when you lead globally. Stefan Mahrdt lives in Sri Lanka, where he is CEO of a major international bank headquartered in Europe. "Backgrounds and development stages of people vary," he says. "When you are working in one country, you have to deal with different issues than you might in another country. You have to lead with a widely diversified population of backgrounds. The challenges are being able to adjust to degrees of exposure, knowledge, and experiences that people have in each particular field."

Stefan Mahrdt
CEO of a major international bank in Sri Lanka

A leading global investment bank in Germany and Europe that is continuing to grow in North America, Asia, and key emerging markets.

Stefan Mahrdt works in Sri Lanka, and his country of citizenship is Germany. He has held leadership positions for more than 18 years. In the past two years, Stefan has visited 15 countries. His organization's official language is English. He speaks fluent English and German. Stefan has lived and worked in Germany, Malaysia, Pakistan, Singapore, and Sri Lanka.

Global Leadership Insights
- Being a successful global leader is mostly about how you interact with people.
- Listen to, digest, and try to understand the views, feelings, and thinking of the people with whom you work.
- Communicate a vision, and be flexible enough to adjust it as necessary without losing sight of the end goal.
- Create an environment of enthusiasm and team spirit.

Lead from the front – what you expect from others, you have to be willing and able to do first. Create an environment of enthusiasm and team spirit.

Combine excellence in your particular field's hard skills, while gaining the necessary leadership skills. Take advantage of both formal and informal opportunities to learn about leadership.

Ideval Munhoz of Satyam is responsible for Latin America. "It's sometimes a challenge," he says, "to understand others' cultures and to manage your team with emotional intelligence in such a way that they will activate your strategy. Study the different particularities of each country, focus on your objectives, and set the right context for people to understand what the results should look like." Dealing with the complexities of developing a shared vision is both a great challenge and a great opportunity.

All of our leader interviewees agreed that, as Usman A. Ghani states in his chapter in *The Leader of the Future 2*, the complex, multifaceted challenge of diversity allows leaders to "escape the bonds of tradition to incorporate many levels and many domains within their vision. They have the ability to translate challenges into opportunities and the future into present reality as they move the organization forward."[4]

ORGANIZATIONAL STRUCTURE

Organizational structure is impacted both by internal factors and external factors. Internal factors include business goals, the type of industry one is in, the availability of skilled workers, and finances. External factors include politics and economics, which will vary from one region to the next. Sam Sahana, from International Air Transportation Association, advises: "We should understand that organizational structure must lend itself to functioning in a global environment. Along with that, the skills you put into an organization enable that organization to function."

But what functions should exist where, and how do we develop the right leaders in the right places? Three perspectives on organizational structure are presented in this book:

- Ramalinga Raju discusses Satyam's structure in Chapter 8, "Satyam: The Creation of a Global Company."
- Dr. Ralph Shrader discusses the structure of Booz Allen Hamilton in Chapter 10, "Booz Allen Hamilton's Global People Strategy."
- Antonio Alemán discusses Vodafone's structure in Chapter 12, "Vodafone Change Leadership."

Global organizational structures need to have the right people, processes, and technologies, complemented by an organizational culture of openness and empowerment. A flexible, agile organization allows its people to make decisions based on local information, while at the same time aligning itself with the global foundations of the organization. Successful organizations are shifting to flatter, less hierarchical structures, using fewer people, and allowing for greater efficiencies and responsiveness in order to enhance their competitive edge. Kal Patel of Best Buy says that while his company encourages innovation and experimentation among his employees,

Ideval Munhoz
Country Manager, Brazil & Latin America
Satyam Computer Services, Ltd.
www.satyam.com

Satyam Computer Services Ltd. is a global consulting and IT services company, spanning 55 countries, across six continents.

Ideval Munhoz works in Brazil, which is also his country of citizenship. He has held leadership positions for more than 10 years. In the past two years, Ideval has visited 10 countries. His organization's official language is English. He speaks fluent English, Portuguese, and Spanish.

Global Leadership Insights
- Have a detailed knowledge of your business and role.
- Hire the right people for the right positions.
- Open your mind to new ideas from your team.
- Present a strong vision that integrates your team's ideas.
- Focus on your main objectives.

Study the different cultures and particularities of each country. Collaborate across different cultures and countries. Collaboration is key for global leaders.

their ideas will have no value unless they can be shared effectively across the entire firm. The infrastructure boundary requires specific steps to be taken in order to build a cohesive global structure. Global leaders require a new view of structure to meet the new demands of global business leadership.

ORGANIZATIONAL ECONOMICS

Organizational structure influences organizational economics. Differentials come from multiple factors that include the market value of the services offered, the actual work performed, and the differences in costs for a company headquartered in a high-cost

BOX 6.1   THE EFFECT OF ECONOMIC DIFFERENCES ON DECISION-MAKING

Prior to joining Satyam, I spent eight years as a senior leader with Booz Allen Hamilton, the global strategy and technology consulting firm. As an example of economic differences, let's look at revenue per employee for both companies.

Booz Allen Hamilton
For the most recent financial year ending March 31, 2006, Booz Allen's revenues were US$3.7 billion. With 18,000 employees worldwide, the average revenue per employee was approximately US$205,000.

Satyam Computer Services
For the most recent financial year ending on March 31, 2006, Satyam surpassed the US$1 billion mark. With 23,500 employees worldwide at the time, the average revenue was approximately US$45,500 per employee.

country as opposed to one headquartered in a low-cost country. A broad understanding of the economics of markets around the world is essential when developing business plans that aim to maximize the firm's efficiencies and profitability. Economic differences influence the decisions a leader needs to make in order to maximize outcomes. For example, the fact that the cost of labor varies from country to country will affect the amount of investment available for learning programs. This entails negotiation of pricing that accounts for regional differences or, in some cases, the decision to buy local (see Box 6.1).

THE ROLE OF TECHNOLOGY

This morning, while doing my usual online search for useful news from across the globe (I must admit I have become obsessed with seeing how different countries report the big news items of the day), I came across an interesting article in *The Middle East Times*, published in Egypt, on the importance of gaining access to technology. The

Sam Sahana
Chief Information Officer
International Air Transportation Association
www.iata.org

The International Air Transportation Association (IATA) is the global trade organization for air transport. In operation for over 60 years, the IATA has developed commercial standards for the industry. Headquartered in Montreal, Canada with executive offices in Switzerland, it has around 83 offices worldwide.

Sam Sahana works in Switzerland, and his country of citizenship is the United Kingdom. He has held leadership positions for more than seven years. In the past two years, Sam has visited 35 countries. He has lived and worked in Hong Kong, India, Ireland, Switzerland, the United Kingdom, and the United States.

Global Leadership Insights
- Design organizations with a foot in the past, a grasp on today, and a vision for the future.
- Listen to and learn from the leaders in your own life.
- Utilize and draw from differences to create the best organizational strategy.
- Understand the strengths of each culture, and then bring them together while continuously discovering and learning.

Be aware of and learn from trends; the world is changing faster than ever. Observe where things are going with cultures, markets, goods and services, and emerging markets throughout the world. Whatever is valuable in the market today will become commoditized somewhere in the world tomorrow, so you constantly have to reinvent.

article stated, "Broadband Internet access is becoming so vital for businesses that it can be seen as a new utility comparable to water and electricity, the United Nations Conference on Trade and Development (UNCTAD) said in a report Thursday."[5]

Technological advances have revolutionized global business along with the way we live. Dr. Mukesh Aghi provides a timeline and history of technological advances in Chapter 7, "The Artistry and Science of Global Leadership."

Umesh Kumar Dhoot, from the Indian Oil Corporation, says: "Continuous use of technology is helping us to grow in a very systematic manner." A search of the internet for "business technology" will turn up more than a million references. Practically everything, today, is dependent on technology. In the course of the week, I respond to at least a hundred emails a day; I participate in teleconferences and video-conferences; I instant message people all over the world; and I use a variety of accounting, human resource, travel, and other systems to enhance my efficiency.

In today's world, one can do business from almost anywhere. "Businesses [are] no longer tied down by their locations, or even by the size of their enterprise," says Dr. Mukesh Aghi in the next chapter. Phillip Styrlund of The Summit Group describes the potential for using technology to do business differently, as follows: "I have participated in conference calls from the middle of Tanzania, to beaches in Thailand. We are an ultimate virtual business model. We have no physical offices. We assemble talent based on specific engagements. Specific needs can be native language differences, specializations required, in-culture availability. Delivery of our training changes, based on the engagement. I have a laptop and mobile telephone on which I run my entire business. It doesn't matter where I am; I can run the business from anywhere, at any time. With wireless portable technology, business is truly unplugged."

Danny Kalman describes how Ely Lilly keeps its people connected: "We use a global human resources system for information sharing. Knowledge management helps to avoid redeveloping the same systems and programs. From an educational and learning perspective, we use webcasts and e-learning. We also have weekly webcasts on the industry that introduce people to thought leaders." Technology is allowing people to share ideas, make collaborative decisions, and run large-scale operations without the borders that used to confine us. Dominique de Boisseson, from Alcatel China Investment Company, agrees: "From email to meetings, we use technology daily. We have a worldwide network; we use video-conferencing and net meetings. When we have manager meetings, we all meet online, and everyone can see the speaker and slides." Mary Capozzi, from Best Buy, says: "We use technology in every possible way to alleviate travel. I have had teams in Asia, Europe,

Umesh Kumar Dhoot
Senior Manager
Indian Oil Corporation, Ltd.
www.iocl.com

Indian Oil Corporation Ltd. is currently India's largest company by sales, with US$41 billion in revenues in 2005. Indian Oil employs 31,000 people in four countries, and is in the process of expanding its global presence to Europe and the Middle East.

Umesh Kumar Dhoot works in India, which is also his country of citizenship. He has held leadership positions for more than seven years. In the past two years, Umesh has visited three countries. His organization's official language is English. He speaks fluent English, Hindi, and Malayalam.

Global Leadership Insights
- Read the fine print of the culture.
- Involve locals in the decision-making process.
- Adopt a positive, resilient attitude.
- Be open to feedback.
- Develop strong communication skills.

The retention and management of talent is a major challenge. Finding the right people in a global market is difficult, and retention is becoming a problem as the competition for labor, especially in India, continues to rise. As deregulation continues to take place, that competition will only increase.

South America, and the United States. We rotate timings, setting up teleconferences at a time convenient for the European teams, the next time when it's convenient for Asia, and others are up early or late. Being attentive to and flexible in terms of the needs of others helps with buy-in."

Technology, as a tool for increasing efficiency and aiding communication, can enhance relationships that are already established, but most of our interviewees agree that technology also has its limitations. We use technology for "email, chat, video-conferencing, and shared folders," says Oliver Huegli of UBS (Union Bank of Switzerland) Service Centre, India.

"However, there is only so much you can do with technology. Today, most relationships still require some face-to-face interaction." Vladimir Raschupkin of Rolls-Royce International in Russia agrees: "You have to use whatever technology is available. Many communications require personal comfort, where knowing the person on the other end is best. For that reason, I prefer to meet face-to-face from time to time to help understand 'who is' this person that I work with."

Srinivas Prasad, from GlaxoSmithKline, Consumer Health Care, advises: "Technology should aid business decisions. Technology should help leaders to get an overall perspective of what is happening in the business and support business decisions. Technology is good for reducing and eliminating non-value-added roles through automation. Sometimes new technology adds to the complexities we already face on a daily basis. Technology should reduce or eliminate complexities, enhance relationships, and boost, not hinder, work–life balance."

Another reason technology-based communication can be a challenge is that "the internet is really one huge melting pot of people, ideas, and culture." It's not just the technology, but the global environment, that creates a challenge. However, as Kit Lum describes, this challenge of greater complexity comes with one major benefit. By using communication and collaboration tools, most notably the internet, one can be open for business worldwide. "You are going to be serving customers from the West Coast to the Far East, and everywhere in between."[6] Navi Radjou, from Forrester Research, describes how a major aerospace company deals with its many partners all over the world when building a new plane. Using project management software, they can rapidly prototype the plane virtually. Putting it together in the virtual world improves speed and delivery, and helps the company to avoid physical-world mistakes.

However, with so much technology available, it is becoming increasingly complex to determine what works best within a particular organization. Most organizations today have experts responsible for enhancing, upgrading, and maintaining technology. "Focus on the technologies that work for the organization," advises Hugh Peterken of the International Federation of Red Cross and Red Crescent Societies. "For example, because we have

Oliver Huegli
Head Legal & Compliance/Head of Operational Risk
UBS Service Centre (India) Pvt. Ltd.
www.ubs.com

UBS is the world's largest wealth manager, investment banking and securities firm, and a key global asset manager. UBS is headquartered in Zurich and Basel. It has offices in 50 countries and employs more than 69,500 people.

Oliver Huegli works in India, and his country of citizenship is Switzerland. He has held a leadership position for just over a year. In the past two years, Oliver has visited five countries. His organization's official language is English. He speaks fluent English and German. Oliver has lived and worked in India, Switzerland, and the United States.

Global Leadership Insights
- Over-organize; be very clear and precise.
- Have no expectations coming in.
- Go abroad, and look and learn.

Be open in approaching others and asking questions about their culture and language. Be curious and honest in your dealings with others. Be able to speak the language of business. Broaden your horizons by breaking out of your comfort zone and living somewhere new.

poor connectivity in many places, we use an email system that is particularly strong on replications with extensive offline capability. Another example: in certain countries it is very expensive to make a telephone call, so we introduced collaboration tools that are suitable for those countries. With our international business, we have problems with time zones and connectivity; and establishing criteria helps to meet those requirements."

Raymond Tamayo of Citigroup adds: "You can't design a system for one country and then expect to push it out to other countries without taking their needs into account; it just never works. By reaching out to people and understanding what their technical or business issues are, you can consider those when you build or buy your next group of systems. It helps to look globally before you act."

The emergence of new technologies can clearly be disruptive and challenging, as well as beneficial. Clive Pegg, from Bayer CropSciences AG, told us: "New technologies can be a game changer. Sometimes how fast you adopt technology can drive you out of the market or allow you to become a market leader." Today, access to technology is expanding economies that historically were stalled. Thomas Donahue, president and CEO of the US Chamber of Commerce, was in Vietnam in late 2006 for the APEC CEO Summit. During a roundtable talk with *VietNamNet*'s editor-in-chief Nguyen Anh Tuan, he said: "With an educated workforce, you will get a lot of technology – computer chip, computer business, telecommunication, biotechnology, medical science, etc. All of these things have a future here in Vietnam. I also think there is a future for consumer finance here because the middle class is expanding."[7]

Looking to the future, Tom Rath from Gallup says: "Technology will dramatically impact leadership in the next five years, because the best opinions out there will have a broader global forum. The people at our company with the best ideas, whether they are in Beijing, Budapest, or London, can proliferate their ideas quickly to hundreds of people and eventually to our clients. The collaboration that exists today wouldn't have occurred 10 years back."

When it comes to business leadership, "You don't have to be a technical expert," says Elizabeth Haraldsdottir Thomas. "Understanding technology is about understanding the external environment. From a leadership point of view, one should understand how it influences the world, as well as how one can use it."

COLLABORATIVE BUSINESS NETWORKS

The successful global leader must be able to manage and align many different types of business partnerships, spread across many countries, cultures, time zones, and industries. Author and academic Srikumar Rao describes the issue as "interdependence ... becoming greater and much more complex. The interdependence goes beyond business relationships to encompass governments, nongovernmental organizations, and other parts of the citizen sector."[8]

Vladimir Raschupkin
Regional Director, Russia
Rolls-Royce International
www.rolls-royce.com

Rolls-Royce is the world's leading producer of power systems and services for the civil aerospace, defense aerospace, marine, and energy industries. The company is headquartered in the United Kingdom and employs 36,000 people in 50 countries.

Vladimir Raschumpkin works in Russia, which is also his country of citizenship. He has held leadership positions for more than 20 years. In the past two years, Vladimir has visited seven countries. His organization's official language is English. He speaks fluent English and Russian.

Global Leadership Insights
• Get to know the people with whom you are dealing.
• Treat people fairly regardless of their background.
• Avoid cultural narrow-mindedness.
• Be willing to listen to people in the field.

Take cultural differences into account, and consider varying how you communicate to ensure you are understood. There are new angles to global leadership. Within a country there is usually a single culture and language. Operating globally is much more complex with respect to communication and operations. Develop trust and relationships with people in order to communicate with them successfully and gain their confidence.

Having experience of dealing with complex networks at Boeing, Bonnie Stoufer says: "[The most] perceptive leaders look at the broadest possible view of issues, are willing to look at many different scenarios, and acknowledge that a situation could evolve in many different ways. When you are coming up with a solution, if you become too parochial the solution will only work in a couple of places and get rejected elsewhere." Clearly, world-class leaders use their complicated stakeholder networks in business decisions precisely because they help leaders to manage diversity and complexity better. "People don't like diversity and complexity, because it's confusing and costly to manage," says Navi Radjou from Forrester. "If you only have one type of customer, it's simple enough to satisfy their needs efficiently ... the more guests you invite to a dinner, the more difficult it will be to meet all their tastes effectively." Collaborative business networks help you to satisfy seemingly endless special requests. They allow you to react to markets and to innovate faster; they give you cultural insight and the ability to solve complex problems. In short, collaborative business networks are about utilizing your business relationships to do things you could never do on your own. And the potential for collaborative business networks is greatest on a global level.

Our global leader interviewees identified two important strategies for successfully leading networks: asking questions, and empowering one's partners. Hugh Peterken believes that *consultation* is one of the most important skills required of a global leader. Consultation is about asking stakeholders questions, and then discussing their responses in order to improve their ideas. A leader needs to understand the various perspectives involved in an initiative and to convince each party of the leader's genuine interest in their input. Hugh Peterken says, "I came across the power of consultation as part of a team trying to build mobile telephone networks. We were dealing with community outrage over our plans to erect towers and antennas in a certain neighborhood. We spent a lot of time consulting with the community on the key issues surrounding the network. Some people wanted the service, while others couldn't see any benefit in having it. Going through the process of consultation, being able to bring forward a useful solution while at the same time inviting the opinions of the community, improved the entire outcome."

Navi Radjou described for us the second, widely mentioned, strategy: *empowerment of one's partners*. In a collaborative partnership, it is a major challenge to figure out which roles to give to which partners. Navi explains, "Boeing deals with this through trust and empowerment of the members in its networks. They might say, 'Here are the objectives – you figure out how to do it,' or 'I need you to build a part of the wing, and make sure it works well and fits the rest of the wing.' They are able to reduce complexity by *not micromanaging* each aspect of the activity."

Srinivas S. Prasad
General Manager
Leadership and Organizational Development
GlaxoSmithKline, Consumer Health Care
www.gsk.com

GlaxoSmithKline (GSK) is one of the few pharmaceutical companies that is tackling the World Health Organization's three "priority" diseases – HIV/ AIDS, tuberculosis, and malaria. Headquartered in the United Kingdom, with operations in the United States and over 150 offices worldwide, the company has nearly 100,000 employees.

Srinivas Prasad works in India, which is also his country of citizenship. He has held leadership positions for more than nine years. In the past two years, Srinivas has visited three countries. His organization's official language is English. Srinivas is fluent in English, Hindi, and Telugu.

Global Leadership Insights
- Let go of micro-management.
- Have a clear four- to five-year plan that your team can readily implement.
- Learn to spot and develop talented people.
- Choose technologies that reduce, not add, complexity.

It is important to customize solutions to the needs of a particular region. Learn to empower people by letting go of micro-management. Avoid having stereotypes at the back of your mind. We should constantly reassess what we know, and not allow ourselves to be carried away by stereotyping based on media and experiential influences. It is important to be aware of these issues, but don't allow them to drive business decisions.

Broadening Your Networks

Grow your network within the organizations where you work, as well as across industries, geographies, and all dimensions of your life. Become a believer in the value of networks. I have kept in contact – or reconnected – with classmates, professional colleagues, friends, and even distant relatives. My network has people I have known for almost 40 years down to those I met in the last hour. You can never have a large enough network. Your network can open doors you would never have imagined. For example, my wife and I wanted to adopt a baby. We told people we knew of our plan, and one of them happened to know an attorney who specialized in adoptions. Less than a year later, our beautiful MacKenzie, who is now 16, came into our lives.

In doing research for this book, we plotted where the leaders we had spoken with had lived and worked. We discovered that we hadn't talked to anyone from Russia or Brazil. After a simple email to my network, we had access to the global leaders we needed to provide the broadest perspective for this book.

Professional associations, both online and face-to-face, provide the opportunity to network with people from around the world. Over the years, I have expanded my network considerably with those that I refer to as my "conference friends." Conference friends are professionals I have met at various conferences and who I see maybe only a few times a year. The connections we make during conferences are sustained for years through the networking that follows.

The next time you need to contact a particular person, or want to add someone to your network, try this. Ask people you know if any of them knows the person. If no one does, then ask: "Who do you know that might know [the person you want to meet]?" There is a significant chance you will have found someone who can introduce you.

Here is another great example of how powerful networking can be. The other day someone invited me to join her LinkedIn network at www.linkedin.com.[9] Normally I ignore these sorts of messages, but a while back someone who I trust mentioned LinkedIn.com, saying that it is a great way to substantially expand your network. It works on the "degrees of separation" premise. I found it very user-friendly and respectful of my privacy. In order for someone to invite me to join their network, they have to know my email address, or be introduced to me by someone else in my network.

On November 1, 2006, I had 76 connections in my network. My connections had connections that added to more than 3,200

Raymond Tamayo
Director, Development
Citigroup – Commercial Business Group
www.citigroup.com

Citigroup, Inc. is today's pre-eminent financial services company, involved in consumer banking, corporate and investment banking, and global wealth management. Citigroup has nearly 300,000 employees in over 100 countries.

Raymond Tamayo works in the United States, which is also his country of citizenship. He has held leadership positions for more than 25 years. In the past two years, Raymond has visited five countries. He has lived and worked in Switzerland and the United States.

Global Leadership Insights
• Understand the business, and how technology can impact the business in a positive way.
• Provide a clear line of sight and expectations for your team.
• Be a risk taker. Get out and explore different cultural and business environments.
• Don't assume that what works in one place will work in others.

People in one country don't want to feel that they have been relegated to do minor work, or less important work, than those in other countries. If you get out there and show them the big picture – where they fit in, and how important their role is in the ultimate success of a project – then you as a leader will have success working with them.

connections (the second level of separation). Their connections (the third level of separation) had more than 402,400 connections. This meant that through my own connections, I could meet more than 3,000 people; and through my connections' connections, I had access to more than 400,000 people across the globe. I decided to see how quickly I could expand my network, so I went online and started asking other people I know and trust if they would like to join my network, or if they would introduce me to their contacts who might like to join my network. I followed three simple rules: (1) I only asked people I knew to join my network; (2) I only asked

Figure 6.1   Ed Cohen's LinkedIn.com network, November 5, 2006

You are at the center of your network. Your connections can introduce you to 1,420,300+ professionals. Here's how your network breaks down:

① 👪 **Your Connections**
Your trusted friends and colleagues   **105**

② 👪 **Two degrees away**
Friends of friends; each connected to one of your
connections   **36,000+**

③ 👪 **Three degrees away**
Reach these users through a friend and one of
their friends   **1,384,100+**

Total users you can contact through an
Introduction   **1,420,300+**

Source: www.linkedin.com.

my trusted connections to introduce me to one of their trusted connections if I thought there was mutual value to be gained from networking with that person; and (3) I didn't want to incur any costs in expanding my network.

Figure 6.1 shows the status of my LinkedIn.com connections just four days later, on November 5.

Along the way, I reconnected with people with whom I had attended university and with former colleagues, and I made connections with many new people. Just 20 days later, on November 24, I went back to LinkedIn.com and my network had almost doubled again. The chart indicating the size of my network of trusted professionals now read, "You are at the center of your network. Your connections can introduce you to 2,165,500+ professionals." If you were to collect business cards from every one of these contacts, and stack them one on top of the other, the pile would stand more than 550 meters (1,800 feet) high. The stack would be taller than the tallest building in the world, the Petronas Towers in Kuala Lumpur, Malaysia! That is a BIG network!

While building my online network, I met Ron Bates. I was intrigued by his profile, and by the size of his network. I asked him for his views on the value of networking. His response is set out in Box 6.2.

BOX 6.2   RON BATES ON NETWORKING

Ron Bates
Managing Principal
Executive Advantage Group
www.executive-advantage.com

How has networking enhanced your career?
As an executive recruiter, I network to identify and gain access to the most highly qualified and talented business professionals required by my clients to fill mission-critical retained executive searches. Networking has enhanced my career by exposing me to and helping me build relationships with highly accomplished people. Some of these relationships have turned into mentoring relationships and some have turned into friendships.

How do you set up a formal network?
The biggest mistake people make in networking is they attempt to network without any concrete objectives. They just attempt to collect relationships. Everyone has a different networking objective. A large network might be necessary for one individual, while a small network might be sufficient for someone else. Start by networking with people you know. Research the companies, markets, and regions applicable to your objectives, and identify the people you want to connect with. Combine approaching them directly with building relationships with people you know who are connected to the people you want to meet. Persistence and perseverance pays off. The hardest thing for many people to keep in mind when networking is it isn't all about *you*. Invest in understanding how you can add value to each networking relationship. This is the "give before getting" concept of investing in goodwill.

When someone joins an online network, how can they avoid being spammed?
This is going to happen no matter what networking platform you join. I have over 30,000 contacts. I simply delete messages that don't apply directly to me or that obviously aren't directed specifically at me. Ultimately, networking is about giving before getting. By definition, that implies being willing to accept a certain amount of risk when you connect to someone.

Can you provide an example of the value derived from online networking?
Online networking has contributed directly to my establishing a visible internet presence. I had one prospective client I had never heard of send me an email stating they wanted to talk to me about doing a search for a vice president of sales. I responded, telling them when I would be available to speak with them. I also wrote: "If you'd like to know a little more about me, you can Google me." The prospect responded with: "I already did; that's why I'm reaching out to you." Because of my visible internet presence, that connection ended up being worth close to $100,000 for me.

 Global Leadership Viewpoints

This chapter discussed business leadership and the complexities that are encountered on the global frontier. Along the way, these global leadership viewpoints were shared:

- Globalization has been creeping into every aspect of modern life. Think computerization, the internet, e-commerce, multinational corporations, and satellite TV channels beaming their programs around the world, 24 hours a day.
- Decision-making and problem-solving abilities, aligning and utilizing complex networks, vision and strategy skills, and change leadership skills were identified as primary competencies for global leaders.
- World-class leaders are able to inspire a shared vision and strategy.

- A strategy and its implementation should be flexible enough to adapt to different parts of the world.
- Context is necessary when laying out a shared vision and strategy, to help others understand what you and your organization are trying to accomplish.
- Organizational structure is impacted both by internal and external factors.
- Technological advances have revolutionized global business, triggering dramatic changes in the social, economic, natural, and political environments of global civil society.
- Most organizations today have experts responsible for enhancing, upgrading, and maintaining technology. Leaders don't have to be technical experts. However, they should understand how technology influences the world, as well as how it can be used to gain efficiencies and reduce complexity.
- Technology, as a tool for enhancing efficiency and aiding communication, can enhance relationships that are already established.
- Technology will dramatically impact leadership in the next five years, because the best opinions out there will have a broader global forum.
- Networks allow you to have the contacts you need when you need them.
- Professional associations, both online and face-to-face, provide the opportunity to network with people from around the world.
- Connections made during conferences can be sustained for years through the networking that follows.
- The next time you want to connect with someone you don't know, ask your network, "Who do you know that might know [the person you want to meet]?"
- There are many online networks forming. LinkedIn.com provides access to a global network of more than 8 million people.

Endnotes

1   Ahmad A. Ajarimah, *Major Challenges of Global Leadership in the Twenty-first Century* (Human Resource Development International, March 2001), pp. 9–10.

2   Jim Kouzes and Barry Posner, *A Leader's Legacy* (San Francisco: Jossey-Bass, 2006), p. 108.

3   Arvind Panagariya, *India in the 1980's and 1990's: A Triumph of Reforms* (International Monetary Fund, March 2004), pp. 1–38.

4   F. Hesslebein and M. Goldsmith (eds.), *The Leader of the Future 2* (San Francisco: Jossey-Bass, 2006), p. 251.

5   "Developing world lags, broadband dubbed new utility," *The Middle East Times*, November 16, 2006 (www.metimes.com/storyview.php?StoryID=20061116-092218-4650r), accessed November 27, 2006.

6   Kit Lum, "Making Cultural Differences Work in Your Business" (2004) (www.leader-values.com/Content/detail.asp?ContentDetailID=195).

7   "Vietnam is Expanding, Growing and Reaching Out," *VietNamNet Bridge*, November 17, 2006 (www.english.vietnamnet.vn), accessed November 27, 2006.

8   Hesslebein and Goldsmith, op. cit., p. 174.

9   LinkedIn is an online network of more than 8 million experienced professionals from around the world, representing 130 industries.

Part 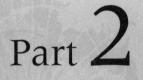 2

Successful Strategies from World-Class Leaders

Chapter 7

The Artistry and Science of Global Leadership

Dr. Mukesh Aghi

Dr. Mukesh Aghi is the first chief executive officer of Universitas 21 Global ("U21Global"), where he combines his considerable leadership skills with a strong entrepreneurial orientation. Mukesh joined U21Global after successfully establishing and leading sales for technology group Ariba Corporation in the Asia-Pacific region. His leadership experience includes managing strategic outsourcing for IBM out of Singapore, and serving as president of IBM India, where he tripled annual revenues. Prior experiences include J. D. Edwards in Japan, Dynamic Applications, and working as a senior fellow in the US House of Representatives.

Dr Aghi has a Ph.D. in International Relations from the Claremont Graduate School and an MBA in International Marketing from Andrews University. He received his Bachelor's degree from Middle East College in Beirut, Lebanon, where he graduated Phi Beta Kappa. He was recognized as an Esquire *magazine "Young Leader of Tomorrow" in 1984, and is a recipient of the Star of India and Asian Leader awards.*

Mukesh Aghi
Chief Executive Officer
Universitas 21 Global
www.u21global.com

U21Global, established as a joint venture between Universitas 21 and Thomson Learning, is a premier online graduate institution, custom-built for today's learning needs. Backed by 19 of the world's best universities, U21Global has students from over 55 countries worldwide and is a pioneer in quality, online graduate education. U21Global is recognized by a number of international accrediting bodies. In 2005 it was awarded the Certificate of eLearning (CEL) accreditation by the European Foundation for Management Development, one of the world's most prestigious accreditation and certification bodies. It is also an international member of the Association of Advanced Collegiate Business Schools.

Dr. Mukesh Aghi works in Singapore, and his country of citizenship is the United States. He has held leadership positions for more than 19 years. In the past two years, Mukesh has visited 10 countries. U21Global's official language is English. Mukesh speaks fluent English, Hindi, and Urdu. He has lived and worked in India, Japan, Singapore, and the United States.

Global Leadership Insights
• Accept and adapt to business changes resulting from globalization.
• Respect and appreciate other cultures and diversity.
• Be quick to adopt new technologies.
• Be able to build, foster, and maintain relationships and alliances.

To lead globally in the next decade, a leader will have to be a global chameleon – someone who can adapt to the various cultural climates with which they have to interact.

The artistry and science of leadership has a complex genealogy, studded with the works and accomplishments of remarkable people. In this chapter, I will address the manner in which globalization has changed the world, coupled with the explosion of technological advances over the last few centuries, and discuss the impact this has had on the global nature of leadership today.

THE WORLD IS NO LONGER AN ISOLATIONIST PHENOMENON

Thomas Friedman wrote, "The world is being flattened. I didn't start it and you can't stop it, except at great cost to human development and your own future. But we can manage it, for better or worse."[1]

A quick glance at our lives will reveal the truth of this statement unambiguously. I live in a city which, although Asian by geographic location, could be a microcosm of the rest of the world today. The cars we drive, the clothes we wear, the people we are in contact with, are all global in nature. "Access" is the key word. We have immediate access to the culture, the produce, the language, and the history of the rest of the world. There is a palpable integration, an irrefutable buzzing and spilling over of borders and boundaries.

Victor K. Fung, the Group chairman at Li & Fung, a global consumer products trading company with its headquarters in Hong Kong, illustrated this clearly when he explained the rationale behind the Group's response to an order from a client for 10,000 shirts. "First, we would consider the best place to source the yarn, perhaps deciding on the Republic of Korea, where we will identify an appropriate factory. For dyeing and weaving the fabric, the client's need, timing, capacity, and the technology requirements may lead us to select China. We ship the yarn from Korea to, say, two factories in China because we have a tight deadline to meet. Next, we would identify the best place to tailor the shirts, the final process in the chain of adding value. In this case, for reasons of labor, skill, and capacity, we may select three different factories in Thailand. The final products delivered to the retailer will look as if they had all come from one single factory, even though they were manufactured in six factories in three different countries!"[2]

As the world becomes smaller and its people become more connected, the manner in which we interact with everything around us is changing dramatically.

Globalization: A Short History

This "flattening of the world" is a reference to the manner in which the boundaries between countries, cultures, and economies are becoming more and more integrated – a process known as globalization. This statement begs the question of what exactly defines globalization. Is it the integration of political, economic, and social systems? Is it an American economic and cultural dominance of the world? Is it a force for overall economic growth and prosperity? Is it an exploitative, destructive force that makes the rich countries even richer, while impoverishing the developing world? The one undeniable thing that can be said is that "since 1950, world trade has increased more than 19-fold, and world output has increased by six times."[3] This prolific increase in world trade has come about as a result of the removal of the boundaries to international trade (or economic boundaries) that were prevalent prior to World War II – under the auspices of globalization.

Anthony Muh, the Citigroup head of investment in Asia, says: "Uncertainty is the only thing to be sure of." When we look back at the progression of the world over the past century, I cannot help but agree. The one thing that we can hold constant is change. In the shadow of two world wars, the Great Depression, and the Space Race, we have seen people striving to adapt to the most stringent adversities, to maintain relevance, and hence to survive, in a constantly changing, often turbulent environment. With the end of World War II, a war during which 2% of the world's population perished,[4] people made a decision aimed at circumventing the possibility of another such terrible disaster. The chosen medicine was liberalism.

It was in this environment of reconciliation and hope that new lines of international trade were drawn. In 1944, the world's major powers came together in the town of Bretton Woods, in the United States, to create an institutional forum for global economic governance. At the conference, they agreed to create three institutions: the World Bank, the International Monetary Fund, and the International Trade Organization, which became the General Agreement on Tariffs and Trade (GATT) and, later, the World Trade Organization (WTO). The idea was simple: having rules in place would discourage the kind of behavior that had provoked world war. GATT and, later, the WTO were the unconscious forerunners of globalization, a phenomenon that has had an incredible impact on various aspects of our lives on a global level. The dramatic increases in global trade have accelerated to the point that, today, the WTO boasts 140 members, up from a dozen at the time of GATT, two-thirds of whom belong to developing countries.

Globalization isn't globalization if it doesn't include the developing world – Africa, Latin America, and Asia. It is an important point to note. "For globalization to be more than merely the increasing economic integration and political harmonization of the rich countries of North America, Western Europe, and East Asia, it is important that the barriers which separate the North and the South, richer and poorer countries, must be overcome."[5] As the overall volume and value of trade increases, it is interesting to see how much both the developing and less-developed countries (LDCs) are benefiting from the breakdown of barriers. In 2004, the WTO listed 50 nations as "least developed countries," and reported that the total trade of all nations was almost US$19 trillion. The LDC share of that total, however, was less than 1%, or just US$133 billion. This raises the question of why countries in the developing world would wish to become a part of the globalization project. Mahathir Mohammad, the former Malaysian prime minister, said: "In reality, this concept was designed by the developed countries on behalf of their companies and financial institutions to overcome the regulations set up by developing countries to promote their domestic economy and local firms."[6] The reason boils down to this: globalization brings opportunity. For an LDC, globalization offers access to a global export market, foreign capital, and advanced technology. Growth and development due to an influx of foreign direct investment leads to faster growth, which, in turn, can promote the reduction of poverty, increase democratization, and lead to an increase in labor and environmental standards. In essence, globalization offers the LDC a chance to share in global business.

Vast Technology Enhancements

Business, leading to the acquisition of material possessions, has long been a key driver of human behavior. The desire to accumulate and multiply wealth has defined the manner in which the world has developed from ancient times, when it manifested itself in the form of crude money and the barter and trade of goods. Since the mid-20th century, a steady stream of inventions has changed the way we conduct business, making us more efficient and business easier to conduct (see Table 7.1). For example, inventions such as the cell phone have allowed us greater mobility and flexibility.

Table 7.1   Key technology inventions

1950	First credit card invented by Ralph Schneider
1956	First computer hard disk developed
1964	BASIC (an early computer language) written by John George Kemeny and Tom Kurtz
1968	First computer with integrated circuits invented
1973	Xerox and Robert Metcalfe invented Ethernet
1979	Cell phones came into being
1981	MS-DOS came into being
1984	Apple Macintosh rolls out to market
1990	World Wide Web and HTML developed by Tim Berners-Lee

The creation of the World Wide Web and WWW language (HTML) in 1990 by Tim Berners-Lee changed the very essence of the way in which we conduct business .[7] The internet completely redefined the way we were able to transmit information, goods, and services, and caused a paradigm shift. The "knowledge economy" was born.

What made the internet so crucial to business was that it "was at once a world-wide broadcasting capability, a mechanism for information dissemination, and a medium for collaboration and interaction between individuals and their computers without regard for geographic location."[8] Businesses were no longer tied down by their location, or even by the size of their enterprise. They were now able to access a huge database of information, contacts, and customers – connected to them through computers. People tapped into the demand for and supply of goods and services with an ease that had never before been possible. The physical boundaries between nations dissolved with the arrival of this new and instant way to disperse a newly important factor of production – knowledge. Today, according to VeriSign estimates, global internet traffic is doubling about every 12–18 months. Currently, there are approximately 900 million internet users worldwide, with 269 million located in Europe, 242 million in North America, 246 million across Asia, and 58 million in Latin America. China has approximately 90 million internet users, and Japan has approximately 82 million.[9] The world has literally shrunk to fit on to the screen of a computer.

The role of creativity and innovation has morphed in this new business climate. In the late 1940s, Edward Land was taking family photographs on a vacation, when his young daughter asked: "Why do we have to wait to see the pictures?" Land thought to himself, "Good question!" Back in his laboratory in Boston, he began thinking of ways to answer his daughter's question. The Polaroid camera and the science of instant photography appeared soon after. However, Kodak's marketing department made the decision not to develop the idea of instant photography at that time, believing that customers would be willing to wait for their pictures as they had always done. Kodak didn't get involved in the business of instant photography until too late, when development costs and patent infringement suits cost them billions of dollars and a lost market.[10]

Innovation is critical. Value comes from the final product and the thinking process behind it. Einstein said that the most important tool he acquired was "figuring out how to think about the problem." Clearly, innovation, creativity, and bravery are crucial to the betterment of a business; yet, in the mid-20th century, innovation was still taking a back seat to the acquisition of assets such as labor and capital. We shall see that, in today's world, this focus has changed rapidly.[11]

THE KNOWLEDGE ECONOMY

The combined result of globalization and the rapid increases in technology has been the advent of what has been coined the new "knowledge-based" economy. For 200 years, labor and capital had been the two most important factors of production, having overtaken land as the primary factor. Today, knowledge and technology are replacing labor and capital as the primary factors of wealth creation. For example, about 70% of the production cost of a new car can be attributed to knowledge-based elements such as styling and software. A modern luxury car includes more computer power than was used aboard Apollo 11! The value-added generated by knowledge industries in the Organisation for Economic Co-operation and Development (OECD) countries increased at an annual average rate of 7% between 1985 and 1994, while the figure for the business sector as a whole was just over 5%.[12] In advanced economies, more than 60% of employees are knowledge workers – that is, workers who manipulate symbols rather than machines. They include designers, teachers, researchers, architects, and various computer-related professionals.

With the access the leaders of today have to a global workforce and the vastly increased mobility of information, a company's comparative advantage will lie in its ability to innovate, to be creative, and to derive the maximum value possible from the information available to it. Therefore, leadership will shift from style, and employing smart and hardworking people, to substance and recognizing the need for smart and hardworking people who have the appropriate skills to manipulate the new knowledge economy. In this new information society, knowledge leadership, with a focus on the diversity available from the global village, is essential. The nature of management and the very definition of leadership are changing.

The enigma we are attempting to unravel is: what really constitutes leadership? What, in essence, is a leader? Political leaders such as Gandhi and Churchill, military leaders such as Hitler and Napoleon, and business leaders such as Jack Welch (of General Electric, or GE) and Anita Roddick (of The Body Shop) all had something in common: a certain charisma that, when combined with a specific set of circumstances, produced something akin to magic. Is this charisma, this set of qualities that sets these people apart from others, innate? Can it be learned? The *American Heritage Dictionary* defines a leader as "someone who leads or guides." To guide another, a leader must have a very clear sense of where they are going and where they eventually want to be. This idea of leadership hasn't changed significantly since prehistory, when the "first caveman whittled himself a spear and gathered together a group of Cro-Magnons to kill a mastodon."[13] But while the essence of leadership may not have changed much, the manner in which it has been organized, demonstrated, and implemented *has* changed.

This can be seen clearly in the development of American business from the 1700s until today.

THE EVOLUTION OF THE BUSINESS LEADER

The evolution of the business leader can be traced back to the 1700s and the birth of American industry. Then, in the 1800s, came the theory that only the strong would survive. Leaders such as Cornelius Vanderbilt built empires on the principle of sheer power. The concept of unity and cooperation in leadership surfaced in the 1930s, when Chester Barnard wrote the bestselling book, *The Functions of the Executive*. In 1950, after World War II, the United States accounted for more than half the world's gross domestic product. It seemed that the "management practices of America were invincible,"[14] given its sheer economic might. American industry was all-powerful in the 1960s, so there was no need for concepts such as creativity, talent, and research. In the 1960s, thinking and planning were the management styles of choice. Big business conglomerations were the norm, where a business could manage anything, as long as it had the finances and the market influence. Employees were small pieces in a larger business machine that were replaceable, replicable, and interchangeable. There was no room for innovation, invention, or creativity, because organization was key and every person had a very specific, preordained role to play. It was truly a "white-collar world," where management was structured tightly and the rule came from top-down. An example of this was Robert McNamara, who espoused the "Harvard Business School way of doing things (the analytic model)."[15] Management was all about numbers, analysis, and profit. There was little or no room for people – employees or the customer.

The failure of the economy in the 1980s, which saw double-digit unemployment, interest rates of over 20%, and a rise in inflation to over 10%, drew attention to the shortcomings of this hierarchical style of leadership. Companies such as IBM, Hewlett-Packard (HP), and 3M were leaders in leadership, bringing to the forefront the need for a new, ground-up style of management that embraced the customer and recognized the importance of every person in the industry. They promoted the idea of innovation in highly decentralized organizations. Jack Welch, the charismatic leader who came to the helm of GE in 1981, embodied this new style of leadership. He eliminated or divested over one-third of the company's workforce over the next five years,[16] clearing out the deadwood and raising the awareness of strong, valuable, and reliable employees. Welch himself said, "Leadership isn't someone on a horse commanding the troops. It's the ability to succeed through other people's successes." He promoted an organization without boundaries within GE, and even started the company's own management school that was so successful *Fortune* magazine called it the "Harvard of Corporate America." The notion that workers could be innovative, and that the spirit of creativity should be celebrated, was born and would have major implications in the coming age of technological advancement and knowledge. Companies moved toward streamlining their management processes and injecting more autonomy into the way things were run.

The Global Leadership Paradigm

The way we live has changed dramatically as a result of the changes that globalization and technology have brought to every aspect of our lives. An example of this is the emergence of a new kind of leadership. Leaders in the global environment face the challenge of navigating an escalating market, an increased product base, and a more aware and empowered consumer. Gone are the days when leadership was a simple figurehead position, a removed presence at the pinnacle of a large company. Mukesh Ambani, the chairman and director of Reliance Industries Limited, said: "The organizational architecture is really that a centipede walks on a hundred legs and one or two don't count. So if I lose one or two legs, the process will go on, the organization will go on, the growth will go on." An organization today is like a centipede; it takes many small parts of the big wheel to make the machine turn. A leader in the new world must be the brain of the organism, providing direction, focus, and clarity to followers. Peter Drucker has stated that even when "the right things are being done" in a company, they are pointless if the focus and assumptions of the leadership are incorrect. He gives the example of General Motors (GM). For half a century,

GM was one of the most successful automobile companies in the world. It subscribed to the theory that consumers would constantly upgrade their current vehicles for a new and improved model; and that by targeting specific income brackets, it could predict what kinds of cars to mass-produce. In the 1970s, as customers became more sophisticated, this theory collapsed – yet GM continued to market its vehicles to consumers according to their income. By the 1980s, GM's inability to adapt to shifting consumer demands saw its market share and profit margins dwindle.

"Leadership" is an elusive term. There is no single definition of the qualities a great leader should possess. A great leader is the equivalent of a hiker's compass. The hiker on his own may be a gifted athlete, but without the aid of navigation, he is sure to get lost. A leader guides and motivates others to follow a path that in her mind is clearly defined. She is able to generate a climate of honesty, trust, and accountability. This positive climate of cooperation, which is essential for a company to succeed in the global environment, is often referred to as the "corporate culture" of an organization.

IBM, under Tom Watson's leadership, had a defined corporate culture of "white shirts and company songs, with service excellence and a blue-chip image."[17] Then, in the 1970s and 1980s, it became excessively rigid and lost the flexibility it needed to adapt to the changing business environment. Sixty percent of respondents to an *InformationWeek* poll of 250 IT executives conducted in September 2001 said that it was "somewhat or very difficult to change their companies' cultures or to encourage knowledge sharing and collaboration instead of knowledge hoarding."[18] The failure to encourage collaboration is a vestige of the old business world where everyone looked after themselves in what was in effect a meritocracy. In the new knowledge- and team-based economy, it is the responsibility of the leader to find the right blend of personal motivation and team-building. In his essay entitled "Trust in People," David Packard contrasts the culture he wanted to imbue into HP with one aspect of the culture at his previous company that he considered flawed. He recalls how "they were especially zealous about guarding its tools and part bins to make sure employees didn't steal anything."[19] This lack of faith made people want to challenge the management, and there was a higher level of theft of tools than may have been prevalent without the strict rules. Packard decided that at HP, "our part bins and storerooms should always be open."[20] To him, this simple act sent the message out to the employees at HP that trust was at the core of the company's culture.

There has been a definite shift in the structure of businesses in the last 20 years. Companies can no longer afford to be hierarchical, power-hungry structures, where employees are simply pawns in a game for profit. Previously, employees would try to climb the corporate ladder to further their own growth. This kind of vertically structured organization encouraged individualism and an unhealthy competition among team members. Leaders were distant, autocratic figures who controlled the business from a dictatorial position.[21] They were a separate entity from the rest of the organization and were difficult to reach. They often didn't know what was happening in the lower levels of management. The competencies that a leader was the most concerned with were honesty, integrity, loyalty, an in-depth knowledge of the local market, and dedication.

In today's organizations, growth is lateral. New and young employees recognize that, in order to succeed, they must acquire skills that will complement those of others in the organization. Young executives are willing to jump from job to job, picking up new skills along the way. Leaders must therefore have the capability to attract and retain the best talent. Leaders need to be more approachable today. They must be able to come down to the level of the least senior member of the team and communicate with him in his language.[22] The competencies that are the most valuable to a leader today are intelligence, talent, innovation, and creativity. A leader must be more than just a manager, as Warren Bennis, distinguished professor of business administration at the University of Southern California, and chairman of the board of directors of the Harvard University Kennedy School of Government's Center for Public Leadership, explains: "The manager administers; the leader innovates. The manager is a copy; the leader is an original. The manager maintains; the leader develops. The manager focuses on systems and structure; the leader focuses on people."[23]

Jack Welch said, "Boundaryless is the language, the behavior definer, the culture, the soul of a true global enterprise. It ignores geography, borders, accents, currencies and unites people of all cultures."[24] This "boundaryless" nature of the world is having the greatest impact on global leadership today. With the boundaries diminishing between countries, companies, and cultures, leaders must have the ability to adapt to a whole range of new cultures, customs, and practices. "According to the U.S. Department of Labor, the number of African, Asian, Native, and Hispanic Americans represented just 7.6% of the workforce 50 years ago. In 2000, that number more than doubled to 16%, and, according to the Hudson Institute, is projected to surpass 30% by 2020."[25] This figure demonstrates the meshing of cultures within North America, yet this phenomenon is taking place the world over. For example, Thomas J. Watson, Jr., the CEO of IBM, said in 1957: "It is the policy of IBM to hire people who have the personality, talent, and background necessary to fill a given job, regardless of race, color, or creed." Today, IBM employees come from nearly every country in the world, from Austria to Zimbabwe. IBM Australia is so aware of the multicultural nature of the workforce, as a result of the diverse ethnic make-up of Australia today, that it implemented a Diversity Council in 2003. The council is responsible for "heightening employee awareness, increasing management awareness, and encouraging the effective use of IBM's diverse workforce."[26] IBM has implemented policies such as a floating holiday program, where employees can exchange a public holiday for a cultural holiday of significance, such as Chinese New Year. This awareness and acceptance of, and adaptation to, the cultural diversity that is widespread in the global marketplace is crucial to companies' success today.

Success is More about Behavior than Technology

Today's leaders must have the ability to adapt to the challenges arising from cultural diversity. By understanding the needs and beliefs of different cultures, leaders can create a conducive environment in which to conduct business and ensure the healthy and smooth transition to global enterprises. They must be able to communicate clearly their goals and desires, while adapting to new markets and unfamiliar scenarios. There are many examples of failures to communicate, whether verbally or non-verbally, across cultures. For example, in China, communication between two parties may be more indirect and subtle than the direct and overt style of communication favored by Americans. Another difference is that the Chinese hold *guanxi*, or relationships, in very high esteem. They value the building of relationships for the purpose of business, and see certain alliances as long lasting. Americans don't tend to hold the development of personal relationships in such esteem and would prefer to have terms and agreements formalized on paper, regardless of the seniority of the person they are dealing with in a company. Differences such as these can be frustrating and confusing for a leader who isn't well versed in differences in culture. The same applies to advertising in another culture. Without a firm grasp of the language and customs of the market you are entering, mistakes are easily made. When Coke first entered the China market, the company translated the name "Coca-Cola" as "Ke-Kou-Ke-La." Only after thousands of advertising signs had been printed was it discovered that the phrase meant, "Bite the wax tadpole" or "Female horse stuffed with wax" (depending on the dialect spoken). Pepsi made a similar mistake in Taiwan when it translated its famous tagline "Come alive with Pepsi" as "Pepsi will bring your ancestors back from the dead." In a culture where the dead are revered, this was seen as an unforgivable mistake.

THE NEW GLOBAL LEADERS WITHOUT BORDERS

As markets have become global, the resources needed to serve them must also be global. However, companies that are reaching out to global markets must be able to satisfy the unique, local requirements of specific markets if they are to stay competitive. In other words, companies must be able to "think globally and act locally." According to Professor Ian Mitroff, "For all practical purposes, all business today is global. Those individual businesses, firms, industries, and whole societies that clearly understand the new rules of doing business in a world economy will prosper; those that don't will perish."[27]

The new global leader without borders must adopt certain strategies if they are to be capable of handling the pressures and demands of a new kind of workplace, where knowledge, talent, and skill are of primary importance. Global leaders must:

- have the experience of foreign travel;
- be able to form teams with individuals of diverse backgrounds who are able to work together seamlessly;
- incorporate training that involves classroom and action learning projects;
- have taken on overseas assignments; and
- apply traits revered in leaders of the past, such as vision, integrity, and focus on results and enduring customer satisfaction, while also creating a shared vision, developing and empowering people, achieving personal mastery, encouraging constructive dialogue, demonstrating integrity, and maintaining a competitive advantage.

Jack Welch once said, "I learned years ago that most organizations are too large to be run from one office or through the sheer dynamism of a few individuals. I also learned that if we do not listen to our people, encourage them to participate, and recognize the immense talent they have, we shall fall short of our growth expectations and our obligation to provide our constituencies the performance they expect."

Global trade has created access to new markets of highly skilled and talented workers, who are crucial to the knowledge-based economy. The combination of global trade, and global communication through English as the language of business, has given rise to a prevalent global business culture. There is a famous old saying: "To lead yourself, use your head; to lead others, use your heart." The importance of building strong, relational bridges between yourself and the people you are leading should not be underestimated. In the new global world, with employees from a gamut of countries and religions, it is important to be able to communicate not only your ideas and goals, but also your cares and concerns openly and clearly. If the people you are leading know that you care, they will follow you willingly, rather than by compulsion. Norman Schwarzkopf, commander of the Coalition Forces in the Gulf War of 1991, shook hands with thousands of his troops on Christmas Day 1991 to wish them a happy holiday. "I must have shaken four thousand hands in four hours," he later said. Such actions strengthen the organization and put everyone on the same page, enabling them to work together toward a common goal. To be able to do business in specific markets such as Asia, Mexico, and Argentina, for example, leaders must be aware of the importance of relationships and alliances with local businesspeople. An ability to foster these alliances will lead to more open communication and shared aspirations among the two parties.

Today's global leader is dealing with a global marketplace and a global workforce. The new face of global leadership is one of trust, cooperation, learning, and integration. The true success of a global leader lies not in the number of talented people they can attract to their fold, nor in the clever strategies they can implement to manipulate the raw material of the knowledge-based economy. True success is about embracing the people and knowledge that are defining the new world of business.

Global Leadership Viewpoints

In this chapter, Mukesh Aghi, CEO of U21Global, discussed the history of and context for the emergence of the new paradigm for global leadership. Along the way, he shared several global leadership viewpoints:

- There is a palpable integration, an irrefutable buzzing and spilling over of borders and boundaries.
- Globalization isn't globalization if it doesn't include the developing world. For less-developed countries, globalization offers access to a global export market, foreign capital, and advanced technology.
- The very essence of the way in which we conduct business has evolved as a result of globalization and the vast enhancements in technology.
- The knowledge economy was born because of the paradigm shift caused by the internet, which completely redefined the way we are able to transmit information, goods, and services.
- Knowledge and technology are replacing labor and capital as the primary wealth-creating assets.
- Today, a company's comparative advantage lies in its ability to innovate, be creative, and derive the maximum value possible from the information available to it.

- Global leaders face the challenge of navigating an escalating market, an increased product base, and a more aware and empowered consumer.
- A great leader is the equivalent of a hiker's compass.
- In the knowledge-based economy, it is the leader's responsibility to find the right blend of personal motivation and team-building.
- Knowledge leadership, with a focus on the diversity available from the global village, is essential.
- Companies must be able to "think globally and act locally," meaning that products must be able to satisfy the unique, local requirements of a specific market.
- With the boundaries diminishing between countries, companies, and cultures, leaders must have the ability to adapt to a whole range of new cultures, customs, and practices.
- Global leaders must:
  - have the experience of foreign travel;
  - be able to form teams with individuals of diverse backgrounds who are able to work together seamlessly;
  - incorporate training that involves classroom and action learning projects;
  - have taken on overseas assignments; and
  - achieve personal mastery, encourage constructive dialogue, demonstrate integrity, and maintain a competitive advantage.
- To be able to do business in specific markets such as Asia, Mexico, and Argentina, for example, leaders must be aware of the importance of relationships and alliances with the local business people.

Endnotes

1   Thomas L. Friedman, *The World Is Flat: A Brief History of the Twenty-First Century* (New York: Farrar, Straus, and Giroux, 2005), p. 469.

2   United Nations Economic and Social Commission for Asia and the Pacific, "High-level Government–Business Dialogue for Development in Macao, China in October 2005."

3   www.tradewatchoz.org/guide/econ_glob.html.

4   http://en.wikipedia.org/wiki/World_War_II.

5   Frank-Jürgen Richter and Pamela Mar (eds.), *Recreating Asia: Visions for a New Century* (Singapore: John Wiley & Sons, 2002), p. 17.

6   Ibid., p. 5.

7   http://inventors.about.com/library/weekly/aa010500a.htm.

8   www.isoc.org/internet/history/brief.shtml.

9   www.verisign.com/verisign-inc/news-and-events/news-archive/us-news-2005/page_029135.html.

10   www.quantumbooks.com/Creativity.html.

11   Ibid.

12   Y. Bakos, "The Emerging Role of Electronic Marketplaces on the Internet," *Communications of the ACM*, 41(8), 1999, pp. 35–42.

13   P. Krass (ed.), *The Book of Leadership Wisdom: Classic Writings by Legendary Business Leaders* (New York: John Wiley & Sons, Inc., 1998), p. xiii.

14   Tom Peters, *Re-Imagine! Business Excellence in a Disruptive Age* (New York: Dorling Kindersley Limited, 2003), p. 306.

15   Ibid., p. 313.

16   Krass, op. cit., p. 76.

17   www.optimizemag.com/article/showArticle.jhtml?articleId=17700582.

18   Ibid.

19   Krass, op. cit., p. 230.

20   Ibid., p. 231.

21   HBS Global Study on Leadership.

22   Captain Michael D. Abrashoff, *It's Your Ship* (New York: Warner Books, Inc., 2002), p. 53.

23   W. G. Bennis, *An Invented Life: Reflections on Leadership and Change* (Reading, MA: Addison-Wesley, 1994), pp. 264–7.

24   Krass, op. cit., p. 85.

25   www.culturosity.com/articles/CulturalDifferences.htm.

26   www.ibm.com.

27   www.culturosity.com/articles/CulturalDifferences.htm.

Chapter 8

Satyam: The Creation of a Global Company

B. Ramalinga Raju

B. Ramaliga Raju ("Raju") has been described by the media and various eminent people as a visionary, a global business leader, and a thinker. Raju uses his own simple, yet extensive management model for value creation ("network of value-creating entities"), which creates and promotes leadership, innovation, entrepreneurship, customer orientation, and the pursuit of excellence. Raju received an MBA degree from Ohio University and is also an alumnus of Harvard Business School. He is an ongoing contributor to policy formulation in India. He is the 2007 chairman of NASSCOM, member of the National Executive Councils of Confederation of Indian Industry and the Federation of Indian Chambers of Commerce and Industry, and member of the International Advisory Panel of Malaysia's Multimedia Super-Corridor. Raju also serves on the boards of several educational, research, and not-for-profit institutions, including Harvard Business School (Regional Advisory Board), Indian School of Business, and Administrative Staff College of India.

Raju has given shape to his social vision of aiding greater social equity and providing opportunities to the underprivileged by setting up three institutions: Satyam Foundation, providing urban transformation; Byrraju Foundation, providing rural transformation; and Emergency Management & Research Institute (EMRI), providing emergency response services across India in line with similar services (911) and standards in the United States.

B. Ramalinga Raju
Founder and Chairman
Satyam Computer Services Limited
www.satyam.com

Satyam Computer Services Ltd. (NYSE: SAY) is a global consulting and IT services company with corporate headquarters located in Hyderabad, India. As of December 31, 2006, Satyam's network spans 55 countries, across six continents, and has nearly 40,000 dedicated and highly skilled IT professionals operating out of development centers in India, the United States, the United Kingdom, the United Arab Emirates, Canada, Hungary, Singapore, Malaysia, China, Japan, and Australia, and serving over 500 global companies, including over 157 Fortune 500 corporations. Satyam has strategic technology and marketing alliances with over 50 top-notch companies.

B. Ramalinga Raju works in India, which is also his country of citizenship. He has held leadership positions for more than 25 years. In the past two years, Raju has visited 15 countries. Satyam's official language is English. Raju speaks fluent English and Telugu. During his career, Raju has lived and worked in India and the United States.

Global Leadership Insights
- The first language of a successful global leader should be metrics.
- Adjust the message you are delivering to the audience.
- Your customers will teach you a lot, provided you are willing to listen.
- Global leadership is an acquired trait.

Every successful company, wherever in the world, should create its own "one firm" way of working and creating value as it captures business opportunities. At Satyam, our own way, our own path to value creation, is called the SatyamWay. It is the unique way in which we create value for our stakeholders.

INTRODUCTION

According to Gartner, a market research firm, the global business process outsourcing (BPO) market will be valued at US$173 billion in 2007, of which US$24.23 billion will be outsourced to offshore contractors. Of this, India has the potential to generate US$13.8

billion in revenue. The projection includes revenues of pure-play Indian BPO service providers, captive operations of multinational corporations operating in India, third-party service providers, and BPO subsidiaries of IT services firms.[1] The internet economy has enabled companies such as Satyam – and economies such as India, China, Russia, and Brazil, to name just a few – to grow and prosper. Global delivery of services provides increased opportunities to countries with high unemployment, while other countries with low unemployment and talent shortages benefit from outsourcing critical services.

While most companies grow primarily on domestic revenues, Satyam has emerged as a global company, with most of its revenues coming from outside India. The genesis of Satyam is traceable to a group of companies that had operated prior to Satyam becoming associated with information technology (IT) services. The motivation for getting into IT was the wish to do something that would excite *us*, and not because of any great commercial opportunities. At that time, we operated with the mindset that creativity and innovation have more to do with science and technology than with business. Our views changed quite dramatically when we realized that there is as much innovation in business as there is in science. However, we were convinced that we had to do things our way. We were willing to experiment. For example, when we started our business with Satyam, we didn't focus on the domestic market, as others did, but took any opportunities that came along. That helped us to gain access to international markets more quickly and slowed down the competition.

The Indian IT industry in the early 1990s delivered critical services to support some of the largest corporations in the world. One direct benefit was the exposure that Satyam gained from doing business globally at a very early stage. Everyone who works at Satyam is a leader and collaborator in the growth of the organization, so we call ourselves "associates" rather than "employees." This exposure made it easy to teach our associates to adopt a global mindset. In turn, this expanded Satyam's ability to handle critical issues, deliver on promises, hire diverse talent, build processes, and compete against companies that were many times larger. This culture of continuous learning quickly became part of Satyam's DNA. Satyam's global emergence and success can be divided into six orbits, each with a specific emphasis, focus, and growth goals (see Figure 8.1).

- Orbit 1: Onsite
- Orbit 2: Offshore
- Orbit 3: Process
- Orbit 4: Global
- Orbit 5: Competency
- Orbit 6: Business Transformation

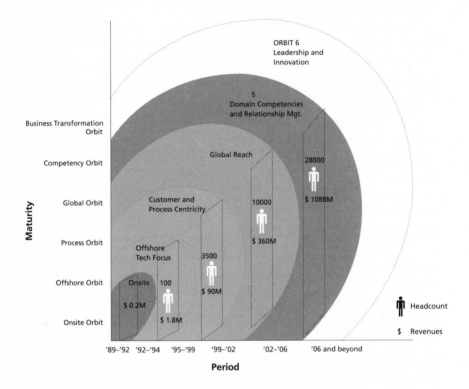

Figure 8.1   Orbits in Satyam's evolution

ORBITS IN SATYAM'S EVOLUTION

Orbit 1: Onsite – From Across the Road to Across the Sea (1987–92)

Capitalizing on the IT sector's fast-growing demand for human resources, Satyam's journey began in 1987. The first four years were spent deploying associates to customer premises to deliver IT services in the United States and the United Kingdom. Soon, as our associates demonstrated their superior skills, Satyam began to co-manage software development projects with our customers.

Once an environment, whether political or economic, becomes conducive, it provides the right stimulus for innovation. In 1991, the external environment changed when the Indian government commenced economic reforms. Satellite communications and telecommunications benefited enormously from this reform. Satyam, which had fewer than 100 people, developed an enhanced way to deliver IT services to customers globally. This increased Satyam's potential to recruit excellent talent and to scale up, while making possible 24/7 operations with dramatic productivity improvements and the resultant cost savings.

We proposed this new business model to our customers, but they were reticent. Sending a core operation thousands of miles away wasn't immediately an appealing option. There was a great deal of trepidation, and rightfully so, as IT services are core not only to the success of every company, but also to survival in the global market. The Illinois-based John Deere & Company, where we already had associates providing services onsite, seemed interested, but we knew we had to convince them beyond any doubt. In 1991, we rented premises across the road from the software development center of our first Fortune 500 customer – John Deere – and named it "Little India."

Staffed by 10 path-breaking engineers, "Little India" connected to John Deere through a 64 kbps satellite link. The engineers were prohibited from interacting directly with any of their customers at John Deere, and they worked only during the night to simulate the way offshore engineers would have to do their jobs. The experiment was so successful that the team actually performed better than they had under their onsite manager. John Deere was convinced, and the global delivery model was born. We extended the telephone lines by 10,000 miles, shifted our people to India, and became the first Indian software company to deliver commercial software through satellite communication links. Within months, others followed. *We added entrepreneurial enthusiasm and the ability to think outside of the box to Satyam's DNA.* Nothing that the customer demanded was too much trouble, and we left no stone unturned in our quest to delight the customer. *With the vast majority of our business coming from outside India, Satyam was a company walking the global passage along with the likes of IBM, Microsoft, and Accenture.*

Orbit 2: Offshore – from Outsourcing to Rightsourcing™ (1992–94)

Beginning in 1992, Satyam focused on the global delivery model piloted with John Deere and developed superior process management systems and technology to ensure success on a wider scale, forming the foundation for rapid corporate growth. Satyam pioneered Rightsourcing™, a global delivery model that offers customers the right mix of global delivery and onsite delivery and development services. At the same time, we realized the need to demonstrate to customers that Satyam could consistently conform to the highest quality standards. We sought and received ISO 9000 certification and earned the 9001/TickIT certification from the UK's Bureau Veritas Quality International (BVQI).

Soon after our success with John Deere, we had our first brush with global IT competitors. Dunn & Bradstreet (D & B) was looking for a partner that provided IT services from India. With a shortened list of approximately 25 companies as potential candidates, there were several rounds of elimination. Finally, D & B selected Satyam as its partner and in January 1994, DBSS (Dun & Bradstreet Satyam Software) started its operations. Today, DBSS is known by a different name – Cognizant Technology Solutions Corporation (NasdaqGS: CTSH). DBSS shifted Satyam into the major leagues. Soon after the D & B deal, Satyam was selected by Selective Insurance and another large insurance company, as well as by Caterpillar. All three remain our customers today.

Orbit 3: Customer and Process Centricity, Building Internal Systems to Prepare for Growth (1995–99)

Much of Satyam's early success came from keeping our focus on our customers' needs. The highly entrepreneurial ability, within a culturally adaptive environment, of the initial set of associates who joined Satyam allowed associates a lot of elbow room in which to operate and generated interest from people working for competitors. Satyam had its mission statement and operating principles, but there was no hand-holding. We didn't tell anyone, "Here, this is your job. Do this by the end of this week." This allowed us to hire outstanding associates who were high on energy, enthusiasm, and creativity, without sacrificing quality.

To become excellent and expand globally we needed to adopt some of the practices that the best in the business followed. One of the most efficient ways to learn this is through a business partnership with a company that one thinks is best in its class. At Satyam, we admired the ability of General Electric (GE) to empower its managers with an entrepreneurial drive within a large company structure. GE has a sworn allegiance to the quality and cost improvement toolkit of Six Sigma. The company constantly raises the performance bar and gets its managers striving ever harder. *Customers actually teach you many things, provided you are willing to learn,* is an oft-repeated phrase. In addition, Satyam wanted to learn the process-centric way of doing business. In 1995, we got our opportunity when GE conducted its periodic review of IT vendors and invited Satyam to participate. GE had a system where it evaluated partners in terms of quality standards and pricing. It was to select four vendors out of the short-listed eight. Each partner was evaluated on a number of parameters. GE was outsourcing two different pieces of work: one was application development, while the other related to engineering services. Despite Satyam's lack of experience in engineering services, GE management gave us the opportunity to work in that area. They felt that, with learning, entrepreneurial spirit, and innovation in our DNA, Satyam could *hire and train the right people* to meet their needs. They cited our campus at Satyam Technology Center – a 35-minute drive from Hyderabad's airport, with its dormitories for housing associates – as being ahead of the market. With GE as our role model, Satyam became one of the first companies to be certified SEI-CMMI level 5 (the highest level of maturity attainable) in its first attempt. Developed by Carnegie Mellon, Software Engineering Institute, Capability Maturity Model® Integration (CMMI) is a process improvement approach that provides organizations with the essential elements of effective processes. It guides process improvement across a project, a division, or an entire organization.

CMMI helps to integrate traditionally separate organizational functions, set process improvement goals and priorities, provide guidance for quality processes, and provide a point of reference for appraising current processes.[2] During this orbit, we constructed our Satyam Technology Center just outside Hyderabad.

In 1996, Satyam realized that business consulting would be one of the competitive drivers of the future and set up Satren. A year later, we set up another subsidiary, Satyam Enterprise Solutions, to focus on package implementation work. In 2001, both these companies merged into the parent company. Our judgment has been borne out by the fact that close to 40% of Satyam's revenues accrue from these two units.

Orbit 4: Global Reach (1999–2004)

By 1999, Satyam had established its presence in 30 countries across North America, Europe, and Asia-Pacific, and started expanding its footprint. With customers throughout the world, Satyam was now a global company with a new focus on adapting to the needs and cultures of the countries where we deliver services and live. Satyam listed on the New York Stock Exchange in 1999.

Orbit 5: Domain Competencies and Relationship Management

The deep, domain-specific needs of our customers required Satyam to set up strategic business units to serve the needs of industries such as insurance, banking and financial services, telecommunications, manufacturing, transportation, and healthcare from top to bottom, pioneering the "virtualization" of India's IT consulting and services sector.

Orbit 6: Leadership and Innovation

We focus on leadership and innovation achieved through enhanced decision-making, partnership, collaboration, entrepreneurship, and operational excellence. A traditional hierarchical organization simply cannot grow fast enough to meet the demands of the market. Instead, Satyam needs to be an organization where leaders can work independently, with speed and agility. Our central focus, beginning in 2005, has been to transform our own company by creating such leaders. We now say that we are in the business of growing leaders. Connected products and technology is innovation in the traditional perspective. Indeed, human society has invented many, many products, services, and beliefs. However, this isn't the only way to look at it. Innovation can also be the way you conduct business itself.

The concept of full life-cycle leadership is a case in point, among the many other inventions by Satyamites over the years. It enables us to manage our businesses as separate entities but to deliver value to our customers as one company. The organization strives to channel our associates' entrepreneurial energies effectively. As shown in Figure 8.2, this means delighting all our stakeholders: associates, investors, customers, and society.

Our emphasis on and efforts at organization building so far are reflected in our motto, "Our people make the difference." We deeply believe in and practice this. As our customer base increases and our experience is enriched, we find that the best vantage point is to view things from the customer's perspective. Further, we

Figure 8.2   At our core, every Satyamite is a leader

believe that satisfying all our stakeholders is important, while also creating value for our customers. Thus, we strive to achieve:

- associate delight;
- investor delight;
- customer delight; and
- society delight

Associate Delight

Associates have a stake in how enjoyable, convenient, and satisfying the value-creation process is. Staff retention is one of the highest challenges for all companies in our industry, so delighting our associates is core to our continued success.

Investor Delight

Investors fund our ability to create value. At the corporate level, investors are the people who and institutions that invest in Satyam stock. The enterprise invests in integrated groups of businesses. Leaders of integrated businesses invest in value-creating entities. Investor delight comes from healthy, reliable, and continuous return on investment through consistently delivering value.

Customer Delight

Customers are the recipients of the value we create. We have both internal and external customers. Internal customers include associates, relationships, service offerings, processes, and projects. External customers are the people in the companies and organizations that we serve by helping them to plan and implement lasting business solutions. Customer delight in every interaction is core to our existence.

Society Delight

We believe that wealth creation is incomplete unless it contributes to the improvement of society. For that reason, Satyam strives to be a good corporate citizen and regards helping society as our fourth stakeholder.

FULL LIFE-CYCLE LEADERSHIP

Entrepreneurship, innovation, quality, and measured risk are all elements that contribute to rapidly growing enterprises. Satyam has grown from 100 associates in 1992 to almost 40,000 associates today. So, how does an organization sustain growth by embedding into its design the elements of entrepreneurship, innovation, quality, and measured risk that allow for such great success? Fast-growing enterprises need a new paradigm for leadership. At Satyam, we call this new paradigm full life-cycle leadership (see Figure 8.3). Full life-cycle leadership empowers associates to continue to lead sustained growth. The company is divided into logical parts, called full life-cycle businesses (FLCBs). Leaders of the approximately 1,500 FLCBs operate them much like CEOs of independent businesses. Full life-cycle leadership and the FLCB model shifted the organization structure from teams to independent, yet interdependent, businesses. We evolved from an emphasis on growth to an emphasis on balancing assets and outcomes for greater value creation. This value creation allows the organization to continue rapid growth, encourages entrepreneurship, expands innovation, and sustains quality. The interdependence of the FLCBs comes from their having a common brand, a "one firm experience," and consistent measures. Full life-cycle leadership is based on a holistic view. From a corporate perspective, it is balancing strategy, operations, and relationship building with one's ecosystem and, at the same time, emphasizing collaboration.

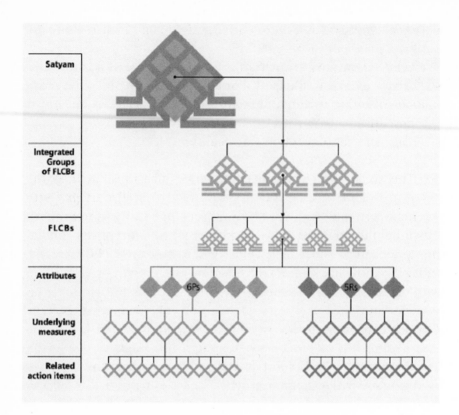

Figure 8.3   Satyam's full life-cycle business structure

"MEASURE AND LEAD"

"Measure and lead" is a paradigm at Satyam. The measurement framework consists of assets and outcomes. A common language of metrics ensures a "one Satyam experience." The most important metric is the "North Star" – the three- to five-year mission. Satyam's North Star is "to be one of the five most valuable global integrated IT services and BPO companies within the next three years." Every FLCB has a North Star that aligns to Satyam's North Star.

The Six P Model

The six P model measures structured assets:

- *People* – the right associates with the right competencies who are proud to be part of Satyam.
- *Process* – demystify knowledge.
- *Product* – put technology to work.
- *Proliferation* – benchmark and apply best practices.
- *Patent* – find a better way.
- *Promotion* – let perception lead reality.

The six P model has many tangible measures, such as the Associate Delight Index (people), the number of intellectual property patents won (patent), or white papers published (promotion), which help to measure progress and create action steps for the full life-cycle leader. The six P model ensures that every FLCB has the right assets in place to reach its business goals.

The Five R Model

The five R model (each ends with an "r") measures the outcome used to assess value creation:

- *Faster* – compress cycle time.
- *Better* – always exceed customer expectations.
- *Cheaper* – use limited resources well.
- *Larger* – maximize scale opportunities.
- *Steadier* – be predictable.

The five R model has many tangible measures, such as the Customer Delight Index (better), greater discounts negotiated due to increasing size (cheaper), or growth in revenue (larger), which measure progress toward the right outcomes. The five R model monitors how well the FLCB's actions align for intended stakeholder impact. Each month, structured asset and outcome measures are tracked in our online, web-enabled system called Startrac. These measures evaluate how effectively full life-cycle leaders are building and maintaining their assets. Having the right assets doesn't guarantee results. Having the right balance of six P assets, combined with the right balance of the five R outcomes, ensures the success of an FLCB. So, depending on how well an internal business of Satyam utilizes its people, creates a rock-solid process, finds a way to automate it (product), finds a way of sharing and contributing its best practices (proliferate), develops its knowledge into an internal intellectual property (patent), and then creates visibility for itself within the organization (promotion), the organization will be able to produce an outcome that is better, faster, cheaper, larger, and steadier.

THE REAL TIME LEADERSHIP CENTER AND SATYAM SCHOOL OF LEADERSHIP

The Real Time Leadership Center (RTLC) and Satyam School of Leadership monitor and develop full life-cycle leaders. The RTLC facilitates timely identification and resolution of issues, and provides full life-cycle leaders with the requisite information to steer their businesses toward achievement of their North Star. The RTLC is the center of excellence founded on the principles of SatyamWay to foster and propel distributed leadership. It is a virtual shared platform that is essential for creating Satyam's next generation of "CEOs" by providing them with access to critical business management and measurement tools and leveraging the "best practice" experiences of colleagues across the organization. It significantly boosts the leader's chances of success and helps to steer Satyam toward meeting its North Star.

For more than a decade, Satyam has focused on addressing both its leadership development needs and the general learning needs of the organization through its dedicated, award-winning Satyam Learning Center. Capable of training thousands of associates a month, Satyam Learning Center is located on 120 acres on the outskirts of Hyderabad, at the Satyam Technology Center. The state-of-the-art learning facilities include classroom buildings, a conference center, and onsite dormitories. In addition, the learning center deploys much of its learning virtually in order to maximize reach to associates located around the globe.

Satyam's primary objective is to grow leaders faster than the competition. Through its proprietary full life-cycle leadership model, Satyam has stepped up efforts toward achieving an integrated focus for leadership development. Launched in 2005, the Satyam

School of Leadership is built on the philosophy of expanding the entrepreneurial energy at Satyam in order to help keep pace with the ever-changing business environment. The full life-cycle leadership framework and Satyam School of Leadership, as well as other leadership initiatives, are a significant step toward Satyam's goal of strengthening leadership practices and extending the leadership pipeline. The strategic intent behind the evolution of the Satyam School of Leadership is to create an establishment that engenders full life-cycle leadership capabilities: leaders are responsive in real time, consistent in decision-making choices/decisions that delight stakeholders, action-oriented, and have the ability to work collaboratively in a networked environment. Leaders must be able to provide integrated and innovative business solutions to their stakeholders and ensure a "one Satyam experience."

The joy in the journey is defined by whom you are traveling with. We are already traveling with our future leaders.

At Satyam we have always known that technology can be learned in a structured manner. We now recognize that leadership can also be learned in a structured manner. At Satyam we develop people who can take control of a situation from end to end while continuing to innovate. Growing our leadership pipeline will help to preserve the culture and DNA of the organization, while helping us to achieve our goal of being one of the top five system integrators in the world. We are proud to be path makers, rather than path takers.

 ## Global Leadership Viewpoints

In this chapter, B. Ramalinga Raju ("Raju"), founder and chairman of Satyam Computer Services, Ltd., outlined Satyam's emergence as a global firm. Along the way, he shared several global leadership viewpoints:

- Think with a global mindset.
- Embed entrepreneurial enthusiasm and the ability to think outside-of-the-box into the organization's DNA.
- Customers can teach you a lot of things, provided you are willing to learn.

- Constantly raise the performance bar and get managers to strive ever harder.
- Hire the right people.
- Organizational design needs to channel entrepreneurial energies effectively.
- Believe passionately in nurturing individual leadership capabilities.
- All companies exist within a societal framework, to which they must contribute.
- Organizational design needs to be adaptive to geographic and market differences.
- Businesses depend on the quality of their people and thus require an investment in capacity building.
- Leaders must be trusted to prioritize and take action.
- Leaders must be viewed through consistent measures.
- The joy in the journey is defined by whom you are traveling with. You are already traveling with your future leaders.
- Be path makers, not path takers.

Endnotes

1 BPO India: www.indobase.com/bpo/global-market-of-bpo.html.
2 www.sei.cmu.edu/cmmi/general/general.html.

Chapter 9

Transitioning to a Global Mindset

V. Shankar

V. Shankar is the global head of corporate finance at Standard Chartered Bank and chairman of the Private Bank at Standard Chartered, based in Singapore. Prior to joining Standard Chartered Bank in September 2001, Shankar spent 19 years with Bank of America where he last held the position of managing director – head of Asia-Pacific investment banking and chief executive officer of BA Asia Limited, based in Hong Kong. He has extensive experience in mergers and acquisitions, and in debt and equity capital markets across Asia and the United States. Shankar completed his MBA at the Indian Institute of Management, Bangalore and has a Bachelor's degree majoring in Physics from Loyola College, Madras.

V. Shankar
Global Head
Corporate Finance
Standard Chartered Bank
www.standardchartered.com

Standard Chartered is an international bank that operates in over 50 countries and employs 44,000 people representing over 89 nationalities. Combining deep local knowledge with international capability, Standard Chartered offers innovative financial products and services in many of the world's fastest-growing markets. It is ranked in the top 25 among FTSE-100 companies by market capitalization.

Although Shankar is based in Singapore, the global nature of Standard Chartered Bank's corporate finance business means that he travels extensively and is often working from "35,000 feet up in the air." He has held leadership positions for more than 20 years. Although Indian in nationality, and fluent in English, Tamil and Hindi, Shankar is a "global citizen." In the past two years he has traveled to over 20 countries in the course of work, and has lived and worked in Hong Kong, Singapore, and the United States during his career.

Global Leadership Insights
- Think "glocal" – global expertise + local insights.
- Create a talent factory – hire people better than yourself.
- Embrace diversity – hire people who are different from you and from the rest of your team.

View diversity as a source of competitive advantage. Actively encourage such differences and give people a voice on issues that face your company, whether it is hiring policy, branding, product launch, or advertising and promotion. This will add richer context and content to your discussions.

WHAT IS A GLOBAL MINDSET?

A global mindset is not an entirely new phenomenon or concept. History is replete with examples of individuals – emperors and explorers, priests and merchants – who considered the world their oyster and displayed a global mindset. Alexander the Great, Vasco da Gama, the traders who plied their wares along the Silk Road, and the apostle St. Thomas who carried Christianity to India are but a few examples of early globalists. These individuals ventured beyond their own shores to expand their empire, sphere of influence, or market share, and, in order to do so successfully, had to recruit, negotiate with, and lead a diverse group of foreigners and counterparties: rival kings, traders, heathens, slaves, or natives.

What is new, however, is the need for large organizations, as opposed to a few individuals, to transition to a global mindset. If organizations are viewed as a collection of individuals united by a common purpose, they have existed in some form or shape through many centuries, with the army and the church possibly representing the oldest-surviving forms of "organizations." However, in historical times such organizations existed primarily to service a local demand. The forces of globalization, technology, and the information explosion have changed the economic landscape. As a result, organizations across the spectrum, both big and small, are having to rethink their strategy and their parochial mindset.

- Who are your clients?
- Who are your competitors?
- Where are the next big opportunities?
- What are the new big threats?

It is no longer sufficient for just a few individuals in your organization to have passports, to speak foreign languages, or to have completed a "study abroad" program. In terms of sheer scale and scope, companies have never had to face as monumental a challenge as they do today in creating and nurturing a global mindset.

In the context of an organization, a global mindset has been defined as one "that combines an openness to and awareness of diversity across cultures and markets with a propensity and ability to synthesize across this diversity."[1] It is the ability to look at businesses, opportunities, risks, and implications through the prism of your home country/culture, and through a multicultural, multinational, and multi-contextual lens. Global mindset is about having a sense of balance between "the way we do things in our company" with "what aspects do we need to fine-tune to make it

Figure 9.1 A global mindset combines global skills with understanding of local culture

work in this country?" (see Figure 9.1). Truly enlightened global companies will be prepared to change or tweak their "horses" to suit the "course conditions" ("horses for courses"), but will not allow "courses" to dictate a change from "horses" to "camels"!

Companies, and individuals, with a global mindset have the ability to consider both "hard" and "soft" business issues. "Hard" business issues to consider may include:

- How do we have a common process and common sets of controls?
- What should be the right minimum hurdle return for a product, irrespective of location?
- How do we optimize advertising spend by having a common theme and branding?

"Soft" business issues may include:

- Does the name sound right in Mandarin Chinese?
- Will the musical score in the advertisement have negative overtones in the Arab world?
- Could a country manager from country A succeed as the country manager in country B?

The quest for such balance often manifests itself in phrases such as "think global, act local," or "be glocal." HSBC positions itself as "the world's local bank." Singapore reflects its quest to become a global destination with the "Our Global City, Our Home" tag line. The challenge, then, is to become neither a "prisoner of diversity"[2] nor a "business case fundamentalist," and to use the holistic insights to deliver faster speed-to-market differentiated offerings that don't compromise overall branding. Ikea, the leading Swedish furniture retailer, provides a cautionary tale of what could go wrong when balance goes awry.[3] When Ikea first entered the United States, the company tried to replicate the formula that helped it succeed in Sweden, including having a Swedish-style cafeteria and selling beds that conformed to Swedish sheet sizes. The sales were disappointing, resulting in the company having to revamp its offering to suit American tastes and sizes.

By contrast, SAB Miller, one of the world's largest brewers, has followed a deliberate strategy of acquiring and promoting local brands. There is never an attempt to eradicate an acquired local brand and substitute it with a Miller or Castle Lager. In China, the company's biggest seller is "Snow." In India, where SAB Miller has achieved the second-largest market share in beer sales, it acquired Shaw Wallace's beer units and left the brands intact. Coca-Cola bought, retained, and promoted a rival brand, Thumbs Up, which continued to out-sell Coke in India for many years after.

DO ALL ORGANIZATIONS NEED A GLOBAL MINDSET?

The need for a global mindset will generally depend on the organization's nature of business and aspirations ("mission" or "strategic intent," in business-speak). Clearly, General Electric, a company with manufacturing and sourcing in many countries and a customer base that spans the globe, has no other option than to have a global mindset (see Figure 9.2). However, a chain of barbershops in Beijing probably wouldn't require a global mindset. Some younger clients who hold a recently minted American degree might demand a "Tom Cruise cut" instead of a "crew cut," but basic skills, good implements, and a few subscriptions to fashion magazines will resolve the issue. On the other hand, if you are a domestic manufacturer whose primary markets are domestic, yet your products are not immune to imported competition, then certain elements of the operation may need to have a global mindset. In the 1980s and 1990s, Reliance Industries catered primarily to the Indian market for polyester fiber and yarn, and had most of its manufacturing facilities in India. But it still had to consider the competition from imports, notwithstanding tariff protection partially afforded by import duties. Reliance's strategic planners had to conceive and implement manufacturing facilities that were world-class in scale, size, and technology, which would match, if not exceed, the cost competitiveness of Taiwan's Formosa Plastics and other competitors. While Reliance's marketing could afford to have a local mindset, its engineers and planners, who envisioned and built the plants, needed to have a global mindset.

Figure 9.2 is a useful way of thinking about the need for a global mindset. The danger inherent in any such simplistic framework, however, is that it provides merely an "as is, where is" freeze frame. It doesn't say anything about the future, or about the external forces that might reshape your industry and, consequently, the competitive positioning of your company within that industry. Consider an apocryphal leading manufacturer of wooden furniture in 1900 we shall call the "Carpenter Company of Charlotte," based in North Carolina. Its key rival is "Furniture Inc.," based a few hundred miles away in Raleigh. Carpenter enjoyed a competitive advantage through access to some valuable timber concessions from the state. The company could make a good living serving its customers in North Carolina without worrying about competitors in California or Canada. Under this scenario, Carpenter could have legitimately plotted itself in the lower left box of the grid shown in the figure. However, fast forward to 2006 and we

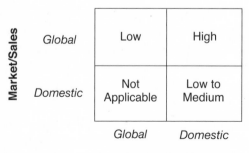

Figure 9.2   The need for a global mindset

see that Carpenter has vanished. Meanwhile, Furniture Inc. is thriving because, sometime in the 1980s, its senior management started researching global production and labor costs and ended up investing in manufacturing facilities in far-away China while simultaneously shutting down its plants in North Carolina. This story is about outsourcing, which is already implemented in many sectors of the economy. Merely replace "wooden furniture" with "garments" or "program development" or "call center," for several contemporary instances.

THE GROWING NEED FOR A GLOBAL MINDSET

Several factors are driving the need for organizations to develop a more global mindset. A fundamental understanding of these factors is essential for any company leader:

- open markets;
- interconnected financial markets;
- "blue-collar" blues;
- "white-collar" woes;
- television and travel; and
- convergence of standards.

Open Markets

Global trade and investments are increasing – exceptions, and failures of certain aspects of free trade agreements, notwithstanding. Some economists predict that by the next decade, trade between countries will exceed total commerce within nations. China's exports to the United States more than doubled between 2000 and 2004, rising from US$52 billion to US$125.1 billion.[4] Markets previously closed to foreign investment now invite it. Foreign financial institutions are now able to open branches – and even to buy up to 20% of the share capital – of Chinese financial institutions. India is the largest growth market for mobile telephony today, and many foreign players, including Singapore Telecommunications, Vodafone, Hutchison, and Maxis, are already participating in that growth. Zambia openly welcomes and benefits from the migration of Zimbabwean farmers displaced by recent events in their country. In most of the Third World, enlightened self-interest and economic pragmatism have replaced the nationalistic sentiments and protectionist tendencies that dominated political thinking during most of the Cold War era.

Interconnected Financial Markets

As demonstrated by the Asian financial crisis of 1997, the financial circuits of most markets are interlinked and connected. What started as a simple devaluation of the Thai baht turned into a full-scale contagion in Korea, Indonesia, Malaysia, and many other countries in the region. Compare the events of 1997 to the events of Black Monday, October 19, 1987, when the US Dow collapsed by 23%, from 2,247 to 1,739, but the Bombay Stock Exchange index barely moved. (It went from 462 to 452.) It would be difficult to imagine that happening today. Most companies outside Europe and the United States, even as recently as two decades ago, secured funding in local markets from local individuals and domestic institutions. Today, the most prevalent traders on most stock markets in Asia are foreign institutions and funds. The world economy is so interconnected that events in New York, London, Tokyo, or Mumbai have an immediate and visible impact on the psyche of overseas investors/financiers. Less than ten years ago, India's leading financial newspaper, *The Economic Times*, had minimal coverage of international financial news. While still dominated by local news, today it devotes several pages to happenings in the global markets. CNBC and Bloomberg television are watched as much by financial pundits in Asia as by their counterparts in the United States.

"Blue-collar" Blues

A shirt purchased at Saks on New York's 5th Avenue epitomizes the new global order. The fine cotton likely came from Egypt, the thread from India, the buttons from Bangladesh, and the fusible interlinings in the cuffs and collar from China. The shirt was designed in Italy, by a person of French ancestry, tailored in Hong Kong, and retails under an American brand name. I once overheard a woman of Chinese origin complaining to the manager of a sporting goods store in Los Angeles, "I'm going to Shanghai tomorrow to meet my relatives and am looking for some sneakers as gifts for my nephews. Every sneaker here has a 'Made in China' stamp. Don't you have any 'Made in USA' stuff? I want to give them an 'American' present." Outsourcing of manufacturing has been made possible by key enablers, including advances in global logistics brought about by more and better ports, and faster ships, planes, and trains; by logistics providers such as DHL and FedEx; and by the emergence of supply chain specialists such as Li & Fung.

"White-collar" Woes

Just as advancements in logistics have enabled the growth of outsourced manufacturing, the emergence of improved information and communications technologies has spawned the phenomenon of services outsourcing. Labor shortages in many developed countries are alleviated by an abundance of well-educated labor pools in emerging countries. This is bringing about a global economic smoothing as many jobs shift from developed countries to emerging countries. The customer hotline operator answering the Pittsburgh caller's installation queries about her recently acquired PC may very well be located in the Philippines. Over time, as the concept has been proved to work, outsourcing has gone beyond the migration of call center activities, to full-scale business processes. The fancy pitch-book the Wall Street investment banker just delivered to the CEO of the Fortune 500 company in Chicago was likely produced overnight by a third party firm in India.

Television and Travel

Growing consumer wealth and the declining cost of travel are resulting in more people traveling more often. From 2002 to 2005, the number of Chinese outbound tourists rose 87%, from 16.6 million people to 31 million.[5] With the advent of low-cost carriers, the cost of a round-trip from Singapore to Bangkok can be less than the hire of a cab to and from Singapore's Changi airport. The number of students who are seeking an overseas education is growing rapidly. The number of Indian students in American universities doubled between 2001 and 2006. Furthermore, the emergence of now ubiquitous television channels such as CNN, Discovery, and National Geographic, and of globally syndicated programs such as *Lifestyles of the Rich and Famous* or *Travel and Living*, are creating consumers with a set of aspirations and desires that transcend national boundaries. Consumers are benchmarking products and services against international standards, not just domestic ones. On the negative side, a molehill in one country can develop into a mountain of a problem globally. News travels faster than ever. The financial impact globally of the negative publicity generated recently by the alleged high levels of pesticides in the Coke and Pepsi that is sold in India is not yet known. However, an earlier episode involving Coke's business practices in India and Colombia generated such outrage among the students of the University of Michigan that they suspended the sale of Coke on their campus.

Convergence of Standards

We are witnessing a convergence of many industries. Who would have thought a few years ago that one of the biggest sellers of cameras would be Nokia through its mobile phones? My 21-year-old son believes watches are redundant, since his mobile phone performs all the functions of a standard watch and more, including an alarm clock function, showing world times, and so on. Similarly, in the financial markets, conventions and rules are converging. The International Financial Reporting Standards and the *Sarbanes-Oxley Act* are two recent examples. Irrespective of where they are regulated, banks with cross-border operations are increasingly subject to international supervision standards. Non-government organizations and environmental groups expect banks to comply with and apply the same set of standards – for example, the Equator Principles – irrespective of whether the new oilfield being financed is located in Abu Dhabi, Angola, or Australia.

SIX KEYS TO CREATING A GLOBAL MINDSET

Embrace Diversity

This is not just a nice-to-have because you want to appear to be an enlightened employer. Diversity is as much a business need as it is the right thing to do. If you want to expand into the Nigerian consumer market, you need local Nigerians who have lived and worked there. If most of your future growth is going to come from India or Mexico, you need to nurture some senior Indians and Mexicans in your ranks. While expatriate managers from the head office can provide the "hard" business skills and discipline, the antenna on "soft" issues comes predominantly from local leaders. The person from headquarters can help bring efficiencies into the buying of corn, the layout of the factory, and the manufacture of cornflakes, for example. However, a local steeped in Indian eating habits can provide you with the added insight into the need to manufacture crispier cornflakes for the Indian market, because most Indian consumers of cornflakes have them with hot milk, which would render the standard American formulation too soft and mushy.

Embracing diversity also involves understanding of and appreciation for cultural nuances. It involves understanding your customers. This won't happen unless you have a diverse and sensitive workforce. The events of 9/11 and their aftermath in the Arab world have shown that culture and religion are more important issues than ever. Negotiation styles vary across Japan, Korea, and India. There is no "Asian style." Gifts may be appropriate in one society, and deemed inappropriate in others. Tapping your colleague on the shoulder may be acceptable in one country and not in another. In Thailand, even accidentally exposing the soles of your shoes to your future business partner may stymie a deal. McDonald's, while establishing a foothold in India, overcame serious religious objections to its staple beef burger by replacing it with a chicken burger, appropriately named the "Maharaja" burger. Its competitor, Burger King, has stores that look and feel the same throughout the world. Yet, Burger King also specializes in introducing local additions to its offerings, such as the "Rendang" burger in Singapore, which caters to South-east Asian tastes. It is important to remember that as demographics change, tastes change, too. In the early 1990s, when an American entrepreneur opened Hong Kong's first chain of coffee parlors, the general wisdom was that they would appeal only to *gweilos* (the local term for "foreigners"), as the local Chinese drank tea, not coffee. Many years later, there were as many Chinese patrons as *gweilos*. Why? There was a new breed of Hong Kongers who had gone to foreign schools, lived abroad, and been introduced to the addictive aroma of Starbucks' coffee. There was no Starbucks in Hong Kong before 2000; Pacific Coffee started a new wave.

Hire Foreign Talent if Necessary

To develop an effective global mindset, senior management must embrace diversity in the composition of its senior ranks. Companies without a diverse top team may need to mandate diversity or target the hiring of foreign talent to address the imbalance. Companies should be open to bringing in outside talent if they don't have the appropriate internal candidate. History tells us that King Ferdinand II and Queen Isabella of Spain hired an Italian explorer who went on to make one of the most significant discoveries of the last millennium. His name was Christopher Columbus.

American corporations have excelled at being race-agnostic in their appointment of CEOs. The recent elevation of Indian-born Ms. Indra Nooyi at PepsiCo follows the appointment of an Australian, Doug Daft, to the top job at Coke several years ago (since resigned). Asian companies have been laggards in this regard, although in recent years the enlightened Singaporean shareholders have appointed foreigners to CEO positions at major financial institutions such as DBS and OCBC, and at companies such as NOL. The Singapore government is now taking this one step further by making the pursuit of foreigners who will make Singapore their home one of its key goals (see Box 9.1). India's leading airline, Jet Airways, bucked the trend by appointing foreigners to its CEO, COO, and other senior positions, although until recently the airline operated only on domestic routes. For Jet's founder, Naresh Goyal, this probably was a quintessential ingredient of his vision to create a world-class airline with top-notch service right on India's doorstep.

BOX 9.1   SINGAPORE INC. – BECOMING A GLOBAL CITY

For the small island country of Singapore, attracting and retaining foreign talent has always been an important driver for greater population and economic growth. As a nation poor in natural resources, Singapore's greatest asset is its people and there is much focus on maximizing its human resource potential in order to boost competitiveness. With declining birth rates and a small local population of only three million (and an additional one million expatriate permanent residents), attracting immigrants has become important for the country and was highlighted as a key initiative by Prime Minister Lee Hsien Loong in his August 2006 National Rally speech, an annual "State of the Union" address.

Embracing Diverse Talent

Prime Minister Lee Hsien Loong stated: "We must look for all kinds of talent. It is not just numbers. You are looking for people with ability, with drive, initiative and ideas, and not just one kind of initiative and ideas. Not just graduates, professionals, bankers or lawyers, but all kinds." As a multicultural society consisting primarily of Chinese, Malays, Indians, and Eurasians, Singapore has always encouraged diversity among its citizens and has maintained a common Singaporean identity. The education system inculcates this from a young age – although English is used as the medium of instruction, all students are required to study a second language to help promote knowledge of their mother tongues. Diversity is also actively celebrated through various holidays/festivals, food, and the sharing of ideas. As a result, Singaporeans "retain what is unique about them and the links which they have back to their own cultures, their own homelands, and their own sense of identity."[6] By embracing and accepting the differences between multiple cultures and religions, Singapore aims to position itself as an attractive environment for immigrants from diverse backgrounds. Singapore will draw strength from this diversity to succeed in its quest to become a truly global city.

Immigration Initiative

A new Citizenship and Population Unit has been set up under the Prime Minister's Office to promote Singapore's immigration program and attract global talent to Singapore. As part of the initiative, the government aims to make the immigration process more transparent and user-friendly and has announced the following measures:

- creating an online self-assessment system for would-be applicants to check their eligibility for citizenship or permanent residency, and the provision of information on how to meet eligibility criteria;
- introducing personalized employment passes linked to the person, rather than to the employer, thereby eliminating the need to reapply for an employment pass in the event of a job switch; and
- extending the validity of social passes for foreigners looking for jobs in Singapore (pending consideration).

Cultivating a Global Mindset

In order for Singapore to become a global society, the government is focusing not only on attracting immigrants and foreign talent in a bid to create a vibrant and cosmopolitan society; it is also working at cultivating a global mindset in its citizens. The examples below highlight how Singaporeans/Singaporean companies are contributing to the country's global ambitions. Given the limitation of a small home market, Singaporean companies are increasingly looking to foreign markets for growth. Singapore Telecommunications, a leading Singapore-based telecommunications provider, now derives over 70% of its revenues from overseas operations. Telecommunications is one of many domestic industries that have responded to the government's call to "internationalize" Singapore's economy by expanding operations overseas and competing at a global level. Another initiative, introduced by the government to promote a global perspective, is the well-instituted scholarship program, at the tertiary level, that sponsors promising young Singaporeans for overseas education at leading institutions around the world. These merit-based scholarships aim at providing Singapore's future leaders with opportunities to immerse themselves in a foreign environment. With the cultivation of a global mindset and the targeted "import" of diverse foreign talent, Singapore will certainly be moving up the ranks as one of the world's most global cities.

Going by the accolades Jet receives from its clients on the quality of its offering, he was right. Howard Stringer's appointment as CEO of Sony Corporation is a rare instance of a large Japanese corporation appointing a foreigner to the top job, although this follows the trail blazed by Carlos Ghosn, with his well-documented and successful turnaround of Nissan.

Expose Your Team to Global Experiences

Building a cadre of experienced international executives is the basic bedrock of creating a global mindset. Different companies have chosen various methods to build that experience level. HSBC and Standard Chartered recruit international trainees and expose them to foreign postings very early in their careers, encouraging them to remain mobile throughout their careers. Many of them live and work in as many as 10 different countries across a number of continents during their careers. Olam International, a leading commodity trader listed in Singapore, adopts a similar approach. Its trainees spend the first few years with the company in remote locations and plantations where the products traded by Olam are grown and harvested.

Numerous companies use expatriate assignments to build global experience. While these assignments are valuable and well intentioned, many high-fliers resist such moves, believing their careers may suffer if they distance themselves from the sources of power (also known as headquarters). Returning employees sometimes find it difficult to obtain good positions, which compounds and reinforces the negative perception. Companies such as Samsung Group use immersion experiences and stints of up to one year to gain insights into a chosen country, not by on-the-job training, but by learning the language, traveling across the country, and spending time with local people in local places. If you really want to learn about South Africa, you are more likely to do it by learning Afrikaans, making some African friends, and visiting museums and pubs, than by working in Samsung's Johannesburg office alongside other Koreans, and hanging out with them eating kimchi and bulgogi in a local Korean eatery.

In the case of Standard Chartered, senior managers attend specific week-long courses devoted to understanding China or India in all its dimensions – history, politics, culture, and business. To get my team excited about business prospects in Africa and the emerging trade corridors between Africa, China, and India, I held a meeting at the Kruger National Park. The sheer serenity of the park and the majesty of its carnivorous and herbivorous denizens convinced them we should have a presence in Africa. Planned knowledge building creates a strong understanding of key markets.

Holding board meetings as well as major company get-togethers at various international locations, a practice common to many international companies, is another useful tool.

Use the World as Your Ideas Factory

The number zero was an Indian invention. By some accounts, chess was first played in Egypt. New products and ideas are no longer the monopoly of any country or race. The popular drink Red Bull, developed in Thailand, required an Austrian entrepreneur to realize its full potential. The first major challenge to Microsoft operating systems came from Linux, an operating system developed in Finland. This is why perceptive companies such as GE and Microsoft are setting up research laboratories in India, Singapore, and Ireland. Companies are also testing, in the United Arab Emirates and Malaysia, their Islamic banking products and services that have global applications and market potential. J.P. Morgan first built its investment banking capabilities in the United Kingdom, a capability that was then transferred to its home country once the restrictions imposed by the *Glass-Steagall Act* – namely, the separation of investment and commercial banking – were rolled back. Innovative developments in the low-cost delivery of ATMs and electronic banking are more likely to emerge in India and South Africa than in the developed world, because a vast majority of the population in those countries cannot afford to pay high fees. Once developed, such a banking model could have ramifications and applications not only in the Third World, but in the developed countries as well.

The challenge for business leaders is three-fold.

1. Ensure that ideas or products are not prematurely abandoned based on inadequate appreciation of current and future business drivers. In the early days of the World Wide Web, one of the most popular search engines was AltaVista (do you remember?), a business that was part of Digital Equipment Corporation (DEC). DEC was taken over by Compaq, which then merged with Hewlett-Packard (HP). Along the way, AltaVista was sold. The new HP-Compaq has a market capitalization of US$112

billion as of December 31, 2006. The search engine of choice for the world today is Google, a company that didn't exist when AltaVista was a force. Comparatively, Google's market cap is US$140 billion, and all they have done is build a great search engine. They don't make computers or printers. What did Sergey Brin and Larry Page see and do that DEC/Compaq/HP missed?

2. Ensure that good ideas emanating from remote outreaches are not disregarded by a "not invented here" syndrome, which is pervasive at most headquarters.

3. Develop an effective process and methodology to cross-pollinate ideas seamlessly across the firm. Bank of America in the 1980s and 1990s had an "Ideas in Action" program. Employees around the world suggested process improvement or cost-cutting ideas, which were evaluated by a global team. Good ideas adopted across the bank resulted in the employee who made the suggestion receiving a special reward equating to a percentage of the savings or additional revenue. The program got attention and worked when some junior employees started receiving checks for amounts up to US$50,000.

Seek Alliances and Organize to be Global

If you don't have the international bench strength and the experienced team to go it alone, seek partners who can plug that gap. This is what Bank of America did when it invested in a 9% stake in China Construction Bank. Chairman Ken Lewis stated in his call with analysts and investors in May 2006, "I don't think we have the talent to go run a bank in China."[7] Bank of America is now using the alliance to launch co-branded credit cards and has sold its retail banking operations in Hong Kong and Macau to its new partner. Bank of America's strategy differs from that of HSBC or Standard Chartered, both of which have long business experience in the country and a cadre of well-trained local staff and foreigners with China experience.

If the performance metrics used by the chief financial officer of your company only look at country-level numbers, it will be a challenge to go global. Conversely, if every function is run globally and the local country becomes an afterthought, you will lose local touch and feel. The challenge is to strike a delicate balance between having global processes, standards, values, and discipline, and still appreciating and leveraging local insights and perspectives. The product/functional lens and the geography lens need to work in tandem to create a winning position with clients. In regulated industries such as banking and insurance, there exists a higher risk of regulatory infractions if there is a lack of local oversight.

Distributing senior leaders across the world is another useful tool for building a global mindset. Standard Chartered subscribes firmly to this view. Two executive board members of Standard Chartered, as well as many global product and support functions, are based in Singapore. Key back offices are located in Chennai and Kuala Lumpur.

Senior management at Standard Chartered also possess significant international experience. Standard Chartered CEO Peter Sands, an Englishman, grew up in Asia and has worked extensively in banking sectors in a wide range of international markets. The non-executive chairman, Mervyn Davies, a Welshman, lived and worked in Asia for almost a decade and, although now based in London, is still a frequent traveler to Asia and the rest of the world.

Think Global from Day One (or Today)

Companies are being born global. India's software icons – Tata Consultancy Services, Infosys, Wipro, Satyam, and others – were born to serve the needs of customers outside India by arbitraging on cost differentials between American and Indian software professionals. The market for their services within India lags well behind the export market. These companies are now setting up operations in Europe, the United States, and China as the next stage of their development. First Quantum Minerals, a Toronto-listed mining company, is fast becoming an important global producer of copper. Started in 1996 by Philip Pascall, a UK resident of Zimbabwean origin, and Martin Rowley, an Australian, First Quantum Minerals first mined copper in Zambia. Its operations have now expanded to include Mauritania and Congo. First Quantum is listed on the Toronto Stock Exchange with a market capitalization of US$3.6 billion as of December 31, 2006.

The Chartered Bank of India, Australia and China, which is now Standard Chartered Bank, was founded in 1853 in the United Kingdom to conduct banking operations in overseas territories (as its original name implies), and not the UK. Its first branch anywhere was in Calcutta (see Box 9.2). Even today, it has no banking branches in the UK or Europe. The corporate finance practice at Standard Chartered, started in 2001, strategically began as a global company from day one.

If you are an existing company with many decades of operations, at first blush this rule may seem irrelevant. I would argue that it still applies. You could apply it to any new product range or offering you are creating. For instance, if you are a commercial bank with a global footprint that is investing into the mergers and acquisitions or the commodity derivatives business, it may merit considering a global, rather than a country-by-country, approach from day one. This is what we did when we started the corporate finance practice at Standard Chartered in 2001. Or, if you are a consumer goods company that is launching a new product line, you may want to consider a global approach to that new line. On another scale, incumbent companies set targets for the percentage of profits they will generate overseas by a stated year. Barclays, at its annual general meeting in 2006, set a target of achieving "an approximately even balance between UK and international profits over the next three years."[8] The acquisition of Absa Bank in South Africa was consistent with that objective. Jeff Immelt, CEO of General Electric, has also publicly disclosed that he hopes to see an eight-fold increase in GE's revenues from India by 2010, and a doubling of revenues from China over the same period.

BOX 9.2   STANDARD CHARTERED BANK: LEADING THE WAY IN CREATING A GLOBAL ORGANIZATION

Diverse Origins

Formed in 1969 through the merger of two banks (the Standard Bank of British South Africa and the Chartered Bank of India, Australia and China), Standard Chartered is one of the world's most international banks, employing over 44,000 people, representing 89 nationalities in over 50 countries. The Standard Bank, founded in Cape Province of South Africa in 1862, had a network of offices across Africa, while the Chartered Bank, founded in 1853, started with an Asia-Pacific presence, which expanded to include the Middle East in the 1950s. The formation of Standard Chartered Bank through the merger created a business with an extensive and diverse network across Asia, Africa, and the Middle East and without a true "home base." As a result, Standard Chartered Bank operated as a global organization right from the beginning.

Creating a Global Organization

Although Standard Chartered London is where the group CEO is based, the bank's business in the United Kingdom is relatively limited (over 90% of the bank's revenues is derived from its footprint across Asia, Africa, and the Middle East), and the London office acts primarily as a governance and regulatory center. Singapore is an important international hub for the bank, where global product heads for both the front-office and operational support units are typically based. Because of this "decentralization," reporting lines within the bank often transcend borders. However, dual country and product reporting lines are in place to ensure that business is run globally while taking into account local considerations. With such a diverse network, how does the bank maintain and cultivate a global mindset throughout the organization? Standard Chartered Bank's emphasis on having an international outlook is reflected and reinforced through its strategic intent to be "the world's best international bank; leading the way in Asia, Africa, and the Middle East." Developing an international mindset is also one of the five core values of the bank, along with being responsive, trustworthy, creative, and courageous. To promote a global mindset among its employees, the bank provides growth opportunities for employees through international and cross-functional development moves, encouraging individuals to gain exposure to different divisions and locations within the bank's network. In 2005, nearly 40% of high-potential employees had a development move and 16% moved internationally. As a result, 60% of senior managers and 10% of junior managers have worked in more than one country within the bank's network.

Leveraging Diversity within a Global Organization

Recognizing the importance of employee diversity in its goal to be a pre-eminent international bank, Standard Chartered actively recruits talent worldwide at all levels of the organization. In 2005 the International Graduate Program, which was set up to recruit and train talented graduates globally, included candidates from 22 nationalities, and saw its intake increase by 47% year-on-year. As part of the two-year program, which includes on-the-job training, in-depth business training, and ongoing performance coaching, the graduates are provided with three international residential workshops to provide them with a global perspective.A Diversity Council, underscoring the importance that the bank places on attracting, training, and developing diverse talents across its network of offices, oversees all matters relating to the issue of employee diversity within the bank. Standard Chartered believes that its diverse employees represent an incomparable advantage in driving its growth and is determined to attract, develop, and retain the best and to leverage the strength their diversity provides. The unique combination of deep local knowledge created by diversity, and an international mindset inculcated throughout the organization, has resulted in Standard Chartered becoming the leading international bank that it is today.

 Global Leadership Viewpoints

In this chapter, V. Shankar, global head of corporate finance at Standard Chartered Bank, provided context and key steps to follow in transitioning to a global mindset. Along the way, he shared several global leadership viewpoints:

- Organizations across the spectrum, both big and small, have to rethink their strategy and mindset in order to respond to the forces of globalization, technology, and information explosion that have changed the economic landscape.
- The need for a global mindset is growing, given the increasingly open and interconnected markets, the growth in outsourcing of manufacturing and services, greater travel opportunities, the growing influence of the media, and the convergence of standards.

- Companies and individuals with a global mindset show an ability to consider both "hard" and "soft" business issues. The challenge is to use holistic insights to deliver faster speed-to-market differentiated offerings that don't compromise overall branding.
- There are six keys to developing a global mindset:
  - Embrace diversity.
  - Hire foreign talent if necessary.
  - Expose your team to global experiences.
  - Use the world as your ideas factory.
  - Seek alliances and organize to be global.
  - Think global from day one (or today).

Endnotes

1   Anil K. Gupta and Vijay Govindarajan, *The Quest for Global Dominance: Transforming Global Presence into Global Competitive Advantage* (San Francisco: Jossey Bass, 2001), p. 111.

2   Ibid., p. 118.

3   Ibid., pp. 113–14.

4   Based on data from WTO.

5   Based on data from United Nations World Tourism Organization.

6   Excerpt from 2006 National Day Rally Speech by Singapore's Prime Minister Lee Hsien Loong.

7   Prudential Equity Group analyst and investor call with Ken Lewis on May 3, 2006.

8   Statement for Barclays' Annual General Meeting on April 27, 2006

Chapter 10

Booz Allen Hamilton's Global People Strategy

Dr. Ralph Shrader

Dr. Ralph Shrader is chairman and chief executive officer of Booz Allen Hamilton, Inc. An active participant in public forums, Dr. Shrader has spoken at major international conferences and graduate business schools in the United States and Europe, including those sponsored by the World Economic Forum and Aspen Institute. His perspective is regularly sought by major news media outlets around the globe.

Dr. Shrader has served in leadership roles in, and been honored with prestigious awards from, a number of professional and charitable organizations, including: the Armed Forces Communications and Electronics Association (AFCEA); The Neediest Kids charity, which helps school-age children; Abilities, Inc., an organization dedicated to improving career opportunities for individuals with disabilities; and ServiceSource, the largest community rehabilitative program in Virginia, in the United States.

Before he joined Booz Allen, Dr. Shrader held senior technical positions with Western Union and RCA. Dr. Shrader received his B.S. degree in Electrical Engineering from the University of Pennsylvania, and his M.S. and Ph.D. degrees in Electrical Engineering, with minors in Mathematics and Nuclear Physics, from the University of Illinois.

Ralph W. Shrader, Ph.D.
Chairman and Chief Executive Officer
Booz Allen Hamilton
www.boozallen.com

Booz Allen Hamilton has been at the forefront of management consulting for businesses and governments for more than 90 years. With more than 18,000 employees on six continents, the firm generates annual sales that exceed US$3.7 billion. Booz Allen has been recognized as a consultant and employer of choice. In 2005 and 2006, Fortune *magazine named Booz Allen one of the "100 Best Companies to Work For," and since 1998,* Working Mother Magazine *has ranked the firm among its "100 Best Companies for Working Mothers."*

Ralph Shrader works in the United States, which is also his country of citizenship. He has held leadership positions for more than 35 years. In the past two years, Ralph has visited more than 15 countries.

Global Leadership Insights
- Lead by listening first, then bringing closure and leading action.
- Have a clear leadership vision and deliver consistent messages.
- Be disciplined – it's a sign of respect for others and yourself.
- Establish your priorities, make them a part of your life, and then live by them.

Personal integrity and authenticity are universal, but leadership style and communication methods should be matched to the culture and situation. In some countries, a more indirect style of communication is appropriate; while in others, a very direct style is appreciated. There is no substitute for travel and personal connection – you need to be able to look into someone's eyes and watch their body language to really understand and reach them. All successful people share these attributes: positive *relationships; responsibility* for their decisions and actions; and *resilience,* the ability to overcome setbacks. Great leaders have these same qualities plus: clarity of vision; ability to lead and serve followers; and strong adherence to core values.

INTRODUCTION

In the foreword to Booz Allen Hamilton's corporate history, which we published to celebrate our 90th anniversary in 2004, I describe the firm's founder, Edwin G. Booz, as an enterprising recent college graduate.[1] Putting his degree in psychology to work with fresh new ideas about management, he started a one-man consulting business in 1914, operating out of two rooms in a rented office in Chicago. Ed Booz believed passionately that to be successful, companies needed an outsider's impartial and expert guidance.

In 1929, Ed Booz joined forces with Jim Allen (who would later coin the term "management consultant"), and with Carl Hamilton in 1935, to grow the organization known today as Booz Allen Hamilton. Although they applied the most sophisticated management theories and tools of the day to provide that perspective to clients, Ed Booz always insisted that "people, not products" are the heart of a management consultant's work.

Leadership scholar Warren Bennis writes in his book, *On Becoming a Leader,* "The release and full use of an individual's potential is the organization's true task."[2] Ed Booz understood this in 1914. And it has endured as a philosophy guiding how we advise all clients (whether they are corporate or government, large or small, European, Asian, African, or Latin American) and how we manage ourselves. Indeed, at the best of times and during difficult junctures in the firm's history, leaders have looked critically at how our culture, our management processes, and our leadership influence the way Booz Allen's people behave and perform.

From our beginnings as a one-man, two-room operation, Booz Allen has become a global strategy and technology consulting firm with 18,000 employees, offices on six continents, and US$3.7 billion in revenues.[3] Based in McLean, Virginia, Booz Allen is a privately held company, owned by its officers, providing expertise to help government and commercial clients solve their toughest problems. The firm's major services span strategy, operations, organizational transformation and change, and information technology.

This unique portfolio of assets includes global reach, prestigious relationships, in-depth knowledge of the public and private sectors, and the best and brightest people in our industry. Yet, maximizing the collective value of these assets has always been challenging for us. While Booz Allen has always had a single identity and structure as a firm, we have historically had two distinct operating units – one serving commercial clients, the other serving government. Each was tailored to serve the specific and unique requirements of our commercial and public sector value propositions, and each had developed its own, quite different, subculture. This changed in 2006, when we implemented our "One Firm" strategy to bring the full range of consulting capabilities to all clients; but the process of bringing the previously separate organizations and cultures together was challenging.

Since the mid-1990s, we have taken on more engagements that bridge the once largely separate commercial and government domains. That has required us to develop a new strategy for a "One Firm Evolution," putting our expertise in organizational change to work on ourselves. As president of the firm's government business from 1994 to 1998, and chairman and chief executive officer of the global firm since 1998, I have worked with dedicated Booz Allen people throughout the world to move our evolution forward. Through re-examinations of our corporate values, changes to our career development strategies, and other means, we have made it our organization's task to cultivate mutually reinforcing value for the firm, for our people, and for the client (see Figure 10.1).

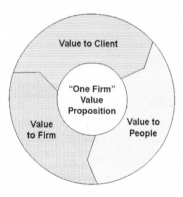

Figure 10.1   Booz Allen's value proposition is a self-reinforcing cycle

This recent period in our history has been especially exciting. Although most of my early career was spent in the government business, I worked on commercial assignments as early as the 1980s; and my belief in the importance of having a unified business spans my entire 32-year career at Booz Allen. Starting in 1974 as an engineer specializing in computer communications and later focusing on global telecommunications, I was involved in projects ranging from the divestiture of AT&T to the development of the US Defense Department's National Communications System. Because I have always worked with government and commercial clients, I have a deep appreciation for the unique power Booz Allen has when we come together – organizationally and geographically.

TWO VISIONS LEADING UP TO 2000

Although Booz Allen is an American firm by origin, it has served international clients and had offices outside of the United States for more than 50 years. We have grown to become the global firm we are today as a direct result of meeting the needs of our clients – the world's largest corporations and government organizations – and changing as they changed.

Sometimes compelling visions for cultural and organizational change emerge when a business's relevance in the marketplace is challenged. In the early 1990s, our commercial business was working to distinguish itself in a market crowded with strategy consulting firms. A few years later, our government business faced its own market challenge as its growth slowed. These challenges were the impetus for a strategy that became known as "Vision 2000," which contributed greatly to improving our institutional capabilities in matching assets as a global firm to market demand.

One dimension of "Vision 2000" began during the recession of 1991, when a group of senior commercial business partners began a review of the state of the business to get at the source of the problem. They discovered that consultants were guarded about their client relationships; teamwork and knowledge sharing had broken down. At the annual officers' meeting held in 1992 in Barcelona, Spain, our then chairman and CEO, Bill Stasior, asked every officer to write a letter to him laying out their vision for the firm. A team of senior officers helped craft a new vision statement from the responses for the commercial business. In October 1993, a new strategy and vision were presented, with these mandates: pursue only clients that want to work with Booz Allen and that want to make a difference in the world; grow global business lines;

create an accessible, centralized repository of intellectual capital; and couple our strategy expertise with Booz Allen's classic strengths in operations and technology. (We called this the "Triple Crown" strategy.)

New people strategies were crucial. The "Triple Crown" strategy was to be executed by forming new multidisciplinary teams. We also renewed our commitment to training and changed our compensation methods and appraisals so that people were more accountable to each other and to the business. We introduced Knowledge On-line, Booz Allen's first intranet, which included a directory of in-house experts and a library containing reports, informal write-ups, project summaries, briefings, case studies, marketing materials, and other information related to client engagements. Much of the Knowledge On-line content was eventually repackaged for training courses.

As our commercial business was undergoing change and showing signs of renewal, the government business was contending with its own issues. Seeing the positive effects of "Vision 2000" on the commercial side, leaders on the government business side decided to launch their own state-of-the-business self-examination, which included interviews with all the officers. The survey showed that the officers were not achieving their aspirations.

As several task forces dug into the diagnosis, problems in the culture and structure became clear. Across the firm, and the government business was no exception, we were too focused on "every one (or practice) for him or herself." At that time, the government business was organized around groups, divisions, and practices. Practices operated almost as independent "business units." This behavior was spurred by the motivational mantra of "How do we get bigger to match our competitors in size?" The government business at the time was around US$500 million in revenues, and our stated goal was to be a billion-dollar business. Some people were building their own revenue bases and competing against each other with sharp elbows to get their share. There was little collegiality. We didn't appreciate our collective capabilities because there was too much fragmentation. Our revenues were flat, while some of our competitors' revenues were growing.

When I was given the responsibility of leading the Worldwide Technology Business (our name for the government business) in

1994, I tried to consider carefully what the officers were saying. At the end of the day, they were unhappy because we were not working as a partnership. Our starting point for change had to come from the leaders: What did we want to be? How did we want to act? What were the things we needed in order to feel fulfilled, rather than just reacting to what the marketplace was telling us?

The survey data was a guiding light for me in terms of what we needed to do to create success in the organization. I felt my first leadership challenge was to get everyone to stop chasing revenue. To do this, we had to stop being 50 officers of 50 different businesses. We had to truly become a team, and we had to communicate better. We had been having very inefficient dialogues inside the leadership.

We created a team of officers with diverse backgrounds to talk about how we would move the organization forward. The process was iterative: we met every two weeks in small groups, asking each other what we had heard in different groups. It was a rich, interactive dialogue, and over three to four months, we started to understand ourselves better and to change our perspective. I heard people say, "We don't want to be a big systems company working large, commodity-type contracts. We want to distinguish ourselves by playing in those places where we can be the best at what we do." That's when it became clear to me that our vision should accentuate what we wanted: to be the *best*, not the *biggest*.

When we launched "Vision 2000," we formally stated our goal: "To be the absolute best management and technology consulting firm, measured by the value we deliver to clients and by our spirit of partnership." In the government business, I also introduced the concept of "Quality Growth." The idea was that we were no longer interested in growth for growth's sake. Like our colleagues in the commercial sector, quality growth would focus on the kinds of clients we wanted, how we wanted to perform, and our desire for unity. We created a new team structure; initially there were eight "client-focused" teams (for ongoing work) and "campaigns" (for new projects). Each of the teams chose its own leader.

We changed from the hierarchical appraisal process we had been using, to 360-degree appraisals by peers, which were followed by group appraisal meetings. By changing the assessment process, we aimed to create a collaborative process in which everyone got to participate. We were interested in the complete picture of what people accomplished, and how they interacted with and related to others.

At this time, I also launched a new "People" strategy to attract and reward the best people at all levels in the organization. All of these aspects of Booz Allen's performance – brand reputation, competitive success, and financial performance – depend on the same thing: *the best people.* We brought in an outside research firm to administer broad internal surveys and focus groups. We probed different groups – minority groups, affinity groups, regions, and all levels – to understand what the staff saw as the barriers to Booz Allen becoming the employer of choice among the best people.

Because we didn't want to be the biggest, we could begin to grow on our own terms. We articulated three interlocking value propositions for our people based on our markets and reflecting the needs of our staff and partners. The unifying principle was: "Here's what the organization will do for you, and here's what the organization expects from you." We also articulated 10 core values, which became the standards we set for ourselves as individuals and as an institution (see Figure 10.2).

As we progressed with "Vision 2000," we took every opportunity we could find to communicate this message to everyone. One of our regular events to connect with employees was "Lunch with Ralph." Since I couldn't meet with thousands of people but wanted to be in closer touch with staff members, we randomly picked groups of 20 people to have lunch with me. We asked them to be prepared to ask questions and to share with their colleagues what they learned – good, bad, or indifferent.

ONE-FIRM EVOLUTION

Over the next couple of years, the impact of our actions to change the culture within the government business was evident. From 1995 to 2000, half of the 50 officers in that sector left Booz Allen, and 25 new ones were promoted from within the firm. Those who didn't want to play by a new set of rules left, and those who stayed were rewarded. In 1997, Booz Allen revenues globally exceeded US$1.3 billion; the government business was a critical engine of

Core Values

Our core values provide a clear view of what we value as an institution. They also provide a model for behavior for leadership and staff. Behavioral definitions for the Core Values are shown in the chart below.

Values and behavioral definitions

Business	**Client service:** Holds client service and the client's interest as a top priority. Considers long-term client needs as well as short-team demands. Makes and delivers on commitments to clients. Takes personal responsibility for improving service to clients.
	Diversity: Respects cultural and individual differences. Furthers the firm's diversity programs and goals. Is inclusive in work activities. Recognizes and utilizes the contribution of different perspectives. Does not discriminate.
	Entrepreneurship: Accepts and rewards risk taking in order to pursue opportunities that will benefit overall team. Encourages creative thought and action. Capitalizes on opportunities created by changes in the market. Inspires with a compelling vision of the future. Demonstrates motivation to take on new responsibilities and skills
	Excellence: Insists on excellence in all things; sets the example. Provides recognition beyond wins and billability. Makes objective, quality service to the client a top priority; sets the example. Continuously strives to improve work processes, products, services. Provides timely effective, accurate, constructive performance feedback to team. Recruits and develops quality staff with potential. Contributes to and stays current with developments in the field.
	Teamwork: Builds strong and positive working relationships. Maintains positive work climate. Involves other in planning activities and decisions. Makes optimum use of inputs of others; uses full resources of firm on client assignments. Helps others. Encourages, recognizes, and celebrates success of team and its members. Supports career mobility. Engenders enthusiasm, excitement for the work and the future. Rewards appropriate team behavior.
Individual	**Professionalism:** Seeks out and listens to honest feedback from others. Gives candid and constructive feedback to others. Identifies and takes opportunities for maintaining/increasing skills. Takes future organizational needs into account in planning own development. Shares own expertise and experience. Actively supports, mentors, and coaches others.
	Fairness: Is consistent in treatment of staff. Distributes information as equally as is appropriate. Uses inclusive work and decision process. Adheres to firm's standards. Does not play favorites. Recognizes the merit of individuals and their performance.
	Integrity: Keeps commitments and promises. Demonstrates courage to present and hear the truth in appropriate manner. Acts best interests of the client, the firm and the team. Displays and reinforces the highest ethical standards. Accurately represents own competencies.
	Respect: Practices patient and active listening. Is sensitive to other people's time. Recognizes and credits the contribution of others. Is empathetic to other's motivations and feelings. Supports work/life balance needs of staff and self. Treats others with dignity. Shows patience, tolerance, and concern for people at all levels and from all backgrounds.
	Trust: Promotes open communications. Builds trusts by being honest, fair, and consistent; sets example for others. Keeps confidences and information at appropriate levels. Accepts and acts on open and honest feedback. Does what is right even if it involves risk or conflict. Takes responsibility for actions and admits mistakes.

People Strategy
at work for you

Booz | Allen | Hamilton

Figure 10.2   Booz Allen Hamilton's core values

that growth. On the commercial side, Booz Allen was experiencing the same fate as other strategy consulting firms that were hit hard by the dot-com bust in early 2000. It was a difficult time for our commercial business, and one of the things that kept us strong during the period was an engagement with the Internal Revenue Service (IRS). It was the biggest job we had ever done in the United States applying commercial consulting skills, and the first time we had taken on a commercial-style strategic transformation with a government client. The IRS engagement was highly successful. But a number of our commercially trained staff felt it wasn't the kind of work they wanted to do. This pointed out some of the key challenges we needed to face in bridging our cultures.

When I took over as the chairman in 1999, I pointed out to my colleagues that the values-based culture we had built in the government business should be exposed to everyone across the firm. The meeting of all the officers in Vancouver, British Columbia, in 2000 was my first chance to address the entire leadership worldwide as the chairman, and my opportunity to promote the potential in blending our commercial and government expertise.

Once again I began by focusing on our people and our culture. We built the meeting around the 10 core values. As a symbol of unity I used a talking stick – a totem-like object used by the leaders of America's First Nations peoples. Ten symbols are carved into that talking stick, which I still keep beside my desk. At the Vancouver meeting, we had our senior officers come to the stage and make a short, informal speech, evoking each of the core values. I know there were skeptics in the room, but after 10 senior vice presidents got up and talked, I felt the entire group, skeptical or not, was impressed.

In the months that followed, the officers kept working on the problem of bringing the two businesses together. As leaders from around the world, we recognized that removing borders would make us a more powerful global firm. Some people seemed to go along because they wanted to be on the same train. But others looked around and realized the positive effects the values and strategy were having in other parts of the organization. Either way, the officers knew these values were my priority. Once again, we asked people who were productive in the business but not aligned with the values to leave.

In 2001, when the commercial business's revenue was down sharply because of the dot-com bust and the aftermath of September 11, we cut costs aggressively. At the same time, I saw this tightening as another opportunity to bring the two businesses together. I asked Dan Lewis, the president of our commercial business, to adopt a streamlined regional structure and to downsize the 28-person commercial partner leadership team into a smaller, more focused group. (We often tell our own clients that they let their top executive teams get too big, and in this case we had violated our own counsel.)

The next step to reinvigorate growth was to get scale, and we knew we couldn't do it by acquiring another firm. But this was Booz Allen's chance to bring the commercial and government businesses together to do things that no one else could do. We asked a senior vice president from the government business and one from the commercial business to lead a major task force, identifying market opportunities for which we could create a joint agenda, and go after specific engagements that would capitalize on Booz Allen's collective strengths.

My plan was to let transactional success with the joint agenda build. I wanted people to see what was working, not tell them what would work. I presumed if they liked what they saw, they would ask for more, and they did. I initiated a meeting in November 2004 where I brought the commercial and government leadership teams together. To my surprise, instead of just acknowledging the success of the joint agenda and moving it along, the group wanted to focus on making it structural. This was the real beginning of what has become known as our "One Firm Evolution." It was a big cultural breakthrough.

No doubt several other unifying initiatives we pursued during the first years of the new millennium bolstered our efforts to foster our global strength. In 2001, we also completed a global rebranding project. This included adopting a new business definition incorporating our government and commercial heritage ("global strategy and technology consulting firm") and a new, unified mission statement ("Booz Allen Hamilton works with clients to deliver results that endure"). We updated our logotype and graphic identity and agreed that this single firm-wide identity – not dozens of "sub-brands" around offices and business units – would be used globally.

Today, virtually all of our large assignments draw on the capabilities and people from more than one business area. Increasingly, Booz Allen is addressing the world's toughest global problems – problems that require bridging public and private concerns in such areas as national and international security, health care, and transportation. In November 2005, I announced that, going forward, we would organize and manage Booz Allen in a unified manner with a single leadership body. With this move, we eliminated regions as part of our organization model, replacing this structure with global market and functional teams.

A NEW PEOPLE MODEL

In January 2005, we began work on a new people model to support this unified business. Over the course of 90-plus years, Booz Allen developed two distinct career development models for our commercial and government businesses. These models have always been based on the market for talent and the prices that different clients (commercial and government) would pay for expert services. Although we had a common people philosophy – for example, the drive to employ top talent and a passion for results – we had differences in day-to-day management practices and approaches, such as leadership styles, compensation systems, career progression models, and a variety of human resources (HR) policies and procedures.

These differences have become more apparent as the firm has pursued engagements and markets requiring staff with different backgrounds and skill sets. We needed more flexibility and adaptability as a firm to apply the right elements of our portfolio to diverse market opportunities. And we needed to have career development models that were independent from our organizational units. We appointed a global task force to lead the development of this people model. In its first year, the task force interviewed more than 100 officers and 150 staff members from around the globe. The task force conducted focus groups and workshops with hundreds of additional employees at all levels. We did this to understand client and talent market requirements, the challenges we have faced to date, the best practices we have created in the trenches, and the options for moving forward. We have also reviewed in detail the people side of every joint engagement to date and benchmarked competitors and other relevant professional services firms. The task force has tried to blend, as much as possible, a strategic view on our future people portfolio, and a pragmatic "don't break what isn't broken" attitude.

The power of one firm is to develop and nurture staff members with distinct skills across a spectrum, but also to be responsive to market differences. So, replacing our two (government and commercial) career models are three new career models (strategy, design, and transformation) designed to help us develop the types of talent and skills needed for many different types of assignments, and to encourage a workforce with diverse motivations and expertise to work together more effectively. Globally, the new career development models apply common human capital management tools and principles, such as competency-based, 360-degree assessments, market-based compensation, world-class global training, and respect for work–life balance. Policies and procedures are adjusted as appropriate by country.

LEADING PEOPLE GLOBALLY

It has taken five years to get people from across the firm working effectively together, and in some places divisive attitudes between our operating units still exist. But we are making real progress. For me, it is now a matter of nurturing our firm and helping it continue to grow. I don't know what my leadership style would be if I were the CEO of a large public corporation. If you have to respond to the market every quarter, you have to have a more command-and-control style because you have less time in which to build consensus. In the end, I have tried to develop a style attuned to our culture and industry environment. That said, from my experience, the following are some principles that have worked for me as I have led people in a global company.

Visualize the Vision

You can't just present a vision; you need to help people visualize what it means for them and how we can get there. I like to get people excited about what they will need to do and how they will be a part of the vision. As we develop our new people model, its success is dictated not by the precision of our blueprint but by how effectively we explain the benefits of the model and what it means for individuals. Staff members look to their leaders for confirmation, guidance, and support, as they try to understand what these changes will mean for them.

Listen and Engage – Without Having to be the "Smartest"

I have always felt it is important to step back so that networks form and debates start. I crystallize my thoughts and ideas through conversation and dialogue, but I don't have the belief that I am the smartest guy in the room. I listen, and from listening I can chart a course. In both the "Vision 2000" and the "One Firm" strategies, the officer dialogues were designed to get everyone who was going to play engaged, and to get the people who weren't going to play out of the mix. I don't think the changes we achieved could have happened any other way. You can't keep too many dissenting voices around the edges without becoming distracted from your mission.

Be With the People

This is my single highest priority. With any organizational change, once the leaders have agreed on a course of action, talking to our people, listening to them, and understanding their needs is key. I prefer face-to-face communications to stay in touch with staff members, help them understand our vision and strategy, and make them feel they are an integral part of our success. For me that has meant working side-by-side with members of forums that represent our diverse employee base, such as the Workforce Diversity Council and the Women's Leadership Initiative.

INSTITUTIONAL VALUES CREATE A HEALTHY GLOBAL CULTURE

Booz Allen is a diverse community on many levels, but our core values unite us. They were written to translate across business and geographic cultures, and to accommodate distinct policies from one country to another. Labor laws may be different, and nationalism is a factor everywhere, but the institution's values endure. Teamwork, for example, has become a binding norm because people know it is the path to success in our firm, and we have a pay system that rewards only team success and not individual success. The same is true for our 300 officers worldwide.

In 2004, the Aspen Institute and Booz Allen jointly surveyed and conducted phone interviews with senior executives from 365 companies in 30 countries to expand on the research about the relationship of values to business performance, and to identify best practices for managing them. In that study we defined corporate values as a corporation's institutional standards of behavior.[4] That research confirmed my belief that the organizations that most effectively garner their institutional strength from the quality of their people – especially when they operate globally – are those that articulate core institutional values and principles that translate across geographies and cultures, and which are made manifest in the behaviors of employees through recruiting, performance appraisals, career development, recognition and reward systems, and compensation.

Booz Allen's 10 Core Values

At Booz Allen, our 10 core values have been essential to the growth, success, and reputation of our global business. We know our people around the world are paying attention to these values, and to the effect that they are having on our work environment, because we use an internal People Survey to ask them. According to the most recent survey, employee satisfaction and pride are at an all-time high. We have also received external recognition. In 2005 and 2006, *Fortune* named us in its prestigious list of "Best Companies to Work For"; and in 2006, *Working Mother Magazine* chose Booz

Allen as one of the "100 Best Companies for Working Mothers" for the eighth consecutive year.[5] We also have the distinction of being named #1 in *Training Magazine*'s top 100 rankings in 2006.

Our promise to our clients is to deliver results that endure, and that is the bar by which we measure ourselves. Every one of our staff undergoes a detailed appraisal process once a year, which begins with an assessment of his or her performance against our 10 values and a set of performance metrics. We commit a great deal of time to these appraisals. Each person is given a 360-degree appraisal by colleagues – from the boss to the executive assistant. In addition, we gather opinions from our clients.

When we talk about our business value of diversity, we mean diversity in every sense – teams that are mixed groups not only in terms of gender but also with regard to religion, nationality, and so forth. Our clients are demanding this, too. When we define excellence as going beyond the current standards, we take this seriously in our recruiting. David Newkirk, a former senior vice president in our London office (now the CEO of executive education at the University of Virginia's Darden School of Business), noted that successful Booz Allen people share two traits – first, of course, is intellect. But the second trait is a lot less obvious, and he looks for it at the bottom of a resume, usually under the heading of sports or other interests. He said, "I look for people who have done something very hard and very well – like compete in a marathon, or climb a mountain, or sing in an opera – something at which they strive to excel for the sheer self-satisfaction of the quest." It's those people who are driven to excel for the feeling, that personal satisfaction of being the best, who really make it at Booz Allen.

Cultivating the Best in People in an Organizational Setting

Inside the entrance to our McLean, Virginia, headquarters, three large panels placed on one side of the entrance trace Booz Allen's history. Life-size photos of and quotes from Ed Booz, Jim Allen, and Carl Hamilton hang on the other side. If you turn left from the atrium, you enter the Allen building; if you turn right, the Hamilton building. Straight ahead is our newest, the Booz building. I don't think that, back in 1914, Ed Booz imagined a huge headquarters campus outside of Washington, DC, with hundreds of other offices around the world. I don't think he imagined that Booz Allen Hamilton would grow to be a US\$3.7 billion professional services firm. Nor do I think he imagined that we would have 18,000 people in offices on six continents.

But, every day, when I walk through the atrium, I see Ed Booz's face on the panel and something meaningful in his eyes. Maybe he *did* envision all of this. For me, that is inspirational. Like our founder, I believe success isn't just the bottom line. The task of management consultants is to learn and to teach the fine art of cultivating the best in people in an organizational setting. Success is about who you are as a person and what you stand for as an institution. We are the strategist ... the realist ... the technologist ... the thinker ... the doer ... the transformer. These are Booz Allen's intrinsic values, its capabilities, and what keeps our global company strong.

 ## Global Leadership Viewpoints

In this chapter, Dr. Ralph Shrader, chairman and CEO of Booz Allen Hamilton, provided insights into the development of Booz Allen's "One Firm" global people strategy. Along the way, he shared several global leadership viewpoints:

- Leaders should look at how the culture, the management processes, and the leadership influence the way the organization's people behave and perform.
- Meet the needs of your clients – change as they change.
- Sometimes compelling visions for cultural and organizational change emerge when a business's relevance in the marketplace is challenged.
- Create a team of leaders with diverse backgrounds to move the organization forward in an iterative way.
- Show interest in the complete picture of what people accomplish, and in how they interact with and relate to others.

- Adopt a global business definition that incorporates the organization's heritage and history, and develop a new, unified mission statement.
- Blend a strategic view on your future people portfolio, and a pragmatic "don't break what isn't broken" attitude.
- Develop a leadership style attuned to your organization's culture and the industry environment.
- Crystallize thoughts and ideas through conversation and dialogue without having the belief that you're the smartest person in the room; listen, and from listening chart a course.
- Organizations that most effectively garner their institutional strength from the quality of their people – especially when they operate globally – are those that articulate core institutional values and principles that translate across geographies and cultures.

Endnotes

1   Art Kleiner, *Booz Allen Hamilton: Helping Clients Envision the Future* (McLean, VA: Greenwich Publishing Group, Inc., 2005), p. 6.
2   Warren Bennis, *On Becoming a Leader* (New York: Addison-Wesley Publishing Company, 1995).
3   Fiscal year ended March 31, 2006, p. 187.
4   The Aspen Institute and Booz Allen Hamilton, *Deriving Value from Corporate Values*, survey and analysis, February 2005, p. 3.
5   *Working Mother Magazine*, October 2006, p. 132.

Chapter 11

Global Risk Strategies

Geoff Taylor

Geoff Taylor is the director of risk management for Nike Europe, Middle East, and Africa and has overall regional responsibility for the Environment, Safety and Health, Security, Business Continuity, Risk Financing, and Incident Management teams based in Hilversum, The Netherlands. Prior to Nike, Geoff's experience includes responsibility for managing risk management strategies at oil and gas and power projects in the Middle East and Europe for Bechtel, Inc. and for Levi Strauss & Co., the US jeans company, throughout Europe, the Middle East, and Africa. Geoff started his career in the UK insurance industry, holding various underwriting positions with the Sun Alliance Insurance Group and the Prudential Assurance Company.

Geoff is a Fellow of the Institute of Risk Management and is currently chairman of AIRMIC (the Association of Risk & Insurance Managers in the United Kingdom). He serves on the steering committee of the Conference Board's European Strategic Risk Council, and is on the British Standards Institution Committee discussing the creation of a UK risk management standard. He is a notable speaker at conferences and has presented many papers covering a broad range of risk management subjects, including on integrating a risk management culture, risk assessment for non-financial risk, business continuity, and corporate governance.

Geoff Taylor
Director of Risk Management
Nike Europe, Middle East, and Africa Region
Nike European Operations Netherlands BV
Nike, Inc.
www.nike.com

Nike, Inc.'s principal business activity is the design, development, and worldwide marketing of high-quality footwear, apparel, equipment, and accessory products. Nike is the largest seller of athletic footwear and athletic apparel in the world. The company sells its products to retail accounts, through Nike-owned retail stores, and through a mix of independent distributors and licensees, in over 160 countries around the world. Virtually all of its products are manufactured by independent contractors. Most footwear and apparel products are produced outside the United States, while equipment products are produced both in the United States and abroad.

Geoff Taylor works in The Netherlands, and his country of citizenship is the United Kingdom. He has held leadership positions for more than 10 years. In the past two years, Geoff has visited 13 countries. During his career, he has lived and worked in Belgium, The Netherlands, and the United Kingdom.

Global Leadership Insights
- Keep an open mind.
- Listen carefully to your team.
- Appreciate and learn from the diversity of your surroundings.

Take the time to value the environment that you are working in. Different cultures approach the same issues in different ways, and this is a learning opportunity. You will be appreciated and respected for your flexibility, willingness to learn, and ability to be part of the team as you lead.

For those who aspire to be global leaders, expose yourself to as many cultures as possible, take the time to explore new businesses and leadership styles, and be confident that being respectful and open will bring dividends over the long term.

INTRODUCTION

Risk management is emerging as a key profession in the 21st century. As a business leader, you are used to executing your business strategy with collaboration from your financial advisors, supply chain experts, and human resource managers. As an emerging field, there is a certain skepticism about what a risk manager can do for you – there is a concern that they might alert you to things you don't want to know about or prevent you from taking a course of action that you know intuitively will bring results. These fears should be dispelled, as a truly professional risk manager will be as focused as you are on bringing about positive outcomes for your enterprise. In this chapter, we will demonstrate how an enterprise risk management strategy led by a risk management professional enhances global leadership decision-making.

As successful global business leaders, we tolerate risk to reap rewards. Risk, in business as in personal life, can be viewed as tolerable or intolerable, depending upon the outcome(s) sought. Many multinational firms do an admirable job of managing risk and avoiding major damage to either their business or their reputation. However, recent catastrophic failures – such as WorldCom and Enron – and reputation disasters – such as Shell Brent Spa and Coke in Belgium – have highlighted the damage that can result from improperly managed risk exposures from both internal and external threats to our enterprises. As a result, the global business community has a new focus on risk awareness and management.

Risk generally falls under the framework of corporate governance. Regulations in almost every country, from the United States to Ukraine, require better standards of corporate governance. Some standards explicitly require a risk management strategy to be explained and confirmed; others merely imply what may be needed.

All stakeholders expect that the enterprises they interact with, whether as shareholders, employees, consumers, or communities, have taken the right approach to managing risks. So, what *is* the right approach to managing risks? Let us explore what we need to know in the modern enterprise, to ensure that we understand and manage risks effectively, by viewing both positive and negative risk and how to prioritize and manage all risk for competitive advantage.

MOVING FROM RISK MANAGEMENT TO RISK STRATEGY

Risk management has evolved since the 1960s, when some clever folks realized that the insurance premiums they paid could be reduced considerably by implementing systems and processes that focused on preventing loss, rather than on simply reacting to it. An effective strategy of prevention includes prediction of potential loss and preparation for it – rather along the lines of the old aphorism, "hope for the best, but prepare for the worst." To begin implementing a new strategy of loss prevention and disaster preparation, the focus was initially on the physical – better building materials and designs, better automatic fire detection and sprinkler systems, and so on. Subsequently, processes focused on safety training and equipment to reduce the risks of workplace injury and accident. Additional benefits of the proactive risk management strategy included reduced downtime and faster recovery, in turn leading to more employee satisfaction, improved productivity, and greater loyalty. Risk management had moved from being somewhat of a necessary evil to providing a significant competitive advantage to those companies smart enough to use it strategically. Nonetheless, risk management was still very much focused on stopping bad things from getting in the way of doing business, and not on giving us an edge with which to beat our competitors. Intense focus on preventing catastrophe in areas such as security, health safety, the environment, property protection, brand protection, product safety, corporate responsibility, and corporate good citizenship resulted in "silos" of risk management for specific areas, rather than holistic management of risk for the organization as a whole.

Although one might assume that by now global leaders have seen the advantages offered by strategic risk management and are acting accordingly, this isn't always the case. What might move us to the next phase of risk management as a tool for competitive advantage?

ENTERPRISE RISK MANAGEMENT

Enterprise risk management (or ERM, as it is widely known) is the next phase of development, when the risk management approaches integrate into all of the operations and business units in a consistent and controlled manner (see Figure 11.1).

Figure 11.1   Integrated risk management

The first step toward an ERM approach requires a shift from managing risks in silos, to a more integrated approach to risk management. Disciplines with a risk aspect within the company centralize with one leadership; this can include security, health safety, the environment, property protection, brand protection, product safety, corporate responsibility, and so on. These functions then feed all the risks into a common approach that gives the senior leaders a risk profile, or a picture of the operational aspects of risk. This stage is important to ensure that management time isn't taken up with receiving too many reports on different aspects of risk, and it allows focus to be directed at the risks that are important to the organization as a whole.

The second stage is bringing this integrated risk approach together with the commercial and financial risk into a seamless enterprise risk management system. From my point of view, the following are the main elements that an ERM approach will deliver:

- a consistent and controlled framework for approaching risks;
- improved decision-making;
- efficient allocation of capital and resources;
- volatility reduction;
- protection and enhancement of assets;
- developing and supporting people;
- competitive advantage; and
- an enterprise-wide, integrated approach to all risks.

Box 11.1 illustrates how two companies chose different approaches to the same issue, and the outcomes for each.

BOX 11.1   CASE STUDY: ENTERPRISE RISK MANAGEMENT

In March 2000, the worldwide demand for mobile phone handsets was peaking, when a thunderstorm over New Mexico became the initial trigger in a chain of events that would eventually lead to one of the dominant forces in the market being displaced. On March 18, a lightning bolt hit a power line that caused a fire in the furnace of a Philips semiconductor plant. The fire was under control in minutes, but eight trays of silicon wafers – enough for thousands of mobile phones – were destroyed. The fire damage was relatively contained, but the smoke and water damage extended over the entire stock of millions of chips.

The plant was closed until March 31, but didn't resume full production until May 15. Nokia and Ericsson, who accounted for 40% of the plant's output, were put at the top of the priority list for supplies. However, each followed up the closure differently, leading to very different outcomes.

Ericsson
- The plant was a sole supplier for Ericsson's Handset division and left it with substantial unfinished handsets.
- Ericsson didn't sustain any property damage, but the six-week halt in production caused it severe difficulties.
- Ericsson didn't inform market analysts of the need to halt production for four months.

The result: Ericsson's stock price dropped approximately 35%, lost sales amounted to US$400 million, and all production was sold to another company.

Nokia
On March 20, Nokia's event management systems indicated that something was amiss.

- Nokia immediately contacted the supplier to discover there had been a fire.

- Without overreacting, they dispatched engineers to the plant.
- Nokia increased its monitoring of incoming supplies.
- When it was apparent that the problem was very serious, contact at the highest levels was made to secure supplies.
- Nokia sent teams to the United States and Japan to secure priority status for alternative supplies. The company set about reconfiguring its handsets for different chips from other suppliers.

The result: Nokia maintained its dominant market position.

What is the Lesson Learned?
From an enterprise risk management approach, both companies would have been very aware early on of the effect of a slowdown in chip production and perhaps would not have been so reliant on a single design. ERM, when fully applied, delivers a solution before an event occurs. The company is then in a resilient position when or if an event occurs, as alternatives have already been explored when designing the risk management processes.

KEY ELEMENTS OF THE ERM FRAMEWORK

A solid ERM framework addresses both upside and downside risks. The process of risk management begins with a clear understanding of an organization's core competencies, strategic goals, and philosophical values. Without this basic understanding, any risk management strategy will fail, as it is only possible to identify and assess the risk by determining what would be most catastrophic to lose. The risk assessment process used by organizations can vary and should be adapted to meet the needs of your own organization. However, in essence, it will include a review of the impact of various risks on the organization and an assessment of the probability that such events may occur. You may also take into account the effect of controls on the risks when making the assessment, although some organizations may be able to differentiate between gross risk (risk impacts and probabilities without controls) and net risk or residual risk (risk impacts and probabilities, taking into account existing controls and their effectiveness). (In my experience, most executives focus on net risk.)

Figure 11.2 depicts a commonly accepted approach to the risk management process.[1]

Figure 11.2   The risk management process

ERM AND GLOBAL LEADERS

To enable the ERM framework to deliver the consistent and controlled approach to risk that is required in a risk-aware organization, the leadership of that organization must take at the very minimum the following steps:

- appoint a risk champion at the board level;
- define the risk appetite of the organization;
- identify probability and risk aversion versus risk predilection;
- drive the risk assessment process through decision-making; and
- engage in reporting risk to stakeholders.

Appointment of a Risk Champion

The risk manager is a trusted advisor who helps drive a consistent approach to risk-taking. The title for this role can vary. We are seeing the appointment of a "chief risk officer" becoming quite prevalent in financial firms, where the risks are more easily quantified, but the term is also being adopted across the corporate world.

Risk management, when done well, includes all the business leaders of the enterprise getting together on a regular basis to discuss the full breadth and depth of risks. The risk leader's role is to facilitate the process and ensure that all of the opportunities that are available are taken. The process prioritizes investments and helps us to allocate resources to those openings that will enhance both revenues and the reputation of our enterprise, as well as reduce the possibility that an unexpected event will take us off course.

Defining the Risk Appetite

We must set our risk appetites; all other activities may otherwise become meaningless or fail. Risk appetite is the amount of risk an enterprise is ready to accept in the course of its operations. Risk appetites can be set in financial terms. This option is popular with financial institutions, where risk is inherent in the products and services they provide. However, it may not work for organizations that are publicly owned or which provide essential services such as medical facilities or energy. While most financial engineers believe that a price can be put on all risks, I don't subscribe to that view, for a number of reasons. First, I believe that it is a truism that all financial models will fail at some point in time. Either there is a change in market behavior, or there is a new variable that hadn't been considered. Whatever the reason, a new and improved model will emerge and be dominant and useful until that, too, falters or goes out of fashion. A good example of this could be the failure of Long Term Capital Management (LTCM), the model for which was developed by Nobel prize-winning minds but nonetheless failed spectacularly through human error. Ultimately, despite the market-rocking debacle of LTCM, hedge funds have prospered, as they can deliver high returns for clients who are prepared to tolerate the concomitant high risk.

Second, I believe that many of the most important risks have too many variables to be accurately modeled or priced. These include social, political, and health risks. Generally, there is a lack of historical data and/or there is no statistical basis for analyzing the historical data to suggest future trends. Even portfolio managers with decades of regression analysis under their belts are fond of pointing out that past performance isn't a guarantee of future results. For instance, an emerging risk might be the alleged health effects of electromagnetic fields – we don't really know what the long-term effects will be, just as miners didn't know what would be the long-term effects of coal dust on their lungs when they first entered the industry. The only way to manage these potential risks is to set a framework for acceptable risk levels. This can include financial measures and must include aspects for human, environmental, reputational, and operational risks.

Risk appetite can be set using financial measures (as it most often is in financially driven organizations); however, it may not be the right approach for all organizations. Consider a construction project involving many workers, where ensuring safety is of paramount importance – would it be acceptable to plan for one work-related death in five years? I would suggest that it is not acceptable, from a human or reputational point of view, to propose such a system. Even in military circles, where casualties may be expected, it doesn't boost morale to tell troops that one in 10 of them will die! Having decided that death isn't an acceptable risk, you are obligated to provide a system of assurance to prevent that event. I have seen zero accidents policies that promote both compliance and a positive environment for safety to exist. This approach applies equally to other areas of risk that cannot easily be modeled or which have a moral or societal dimension. This will form one side of the risk assessment framework – the side associated with the impact of risk. The other side of the framework will concern the probability or likelihood that one of these events could occur.

Identifying Probability and Risk Aversion versus Risk Predilection

In my experience, I have noticed a trend I call the "Kirk vs. Scotty syndrome" – or for those that are too young to remember the original *Star Trek* television series, "the Entrepreneur vs. the Engineer." As you might gather, the entrepreneur in general has a higher tolerance for risk than does the engineer. Entrepreneurs tend to focus on the probability side of risk, as opposed to the impact side. A typical entrepreneur's response to a statement of potential risk is: "That will never happen" or "That is so unlikely that we will ignore it." An engineer, on the other hand, is more likely to respond: "If that happens, it will be the end of us" or "We don't have all the data." Somewhere between these equally valid expressions of risk, predilection, and risk aversion is a truly good risk framework. A risk professional can bring both of these points of view into corporate focus to ensure that a balanced and rational approach to risk-taking is implemented. The framework will encompass both impact and probability, and allow the entire various stakeholder views to be represented equally in the subsequent risk map.

Driving the Risk Assessment Process through Decision-making

In addition to appointing a board-level risk professional, executive management must actively understand and drive the risk assessment process, lead by example, and promote a common understanding of the decision-making process. A leadership that demonstrates a consistent approach to risk will ensure that significant risks aren't taken in one area of the business while restricting risk in other areas. For example, we purchase fire insurance year after year at a premium, but rarely do we have a fire. Why do we do this? We buy insurance first and then think about the risks later. Some of the premiums saved could be easily invested into ensuring we have effective business continuity plans that would seamlessly get our business back on track if an unforeseen event occurs. In addition, because we control the process, we wouldn't need an insurance company to intervene and our coverage wouldn't be restricted to insurable risks. Coverage could cover all events – including reputation, supply chain, people, and any other issues that often arise within an organization.

Proactive, leadership-level risk management can also ensure that business opportunities are not lost due to an abundance of misplaced caution at the managerial level. All too often we hear stories of not enough product being manufactured or of materials not being available to meet demand. If a thorough risk assessment is performed, then not only will we avoid supply-side pitfalls, but we can also bring to light additional benefits.

Engaging in Reporting Risk to Stakeholders

The final, and perhaps the most key, element for leaders to focus on is how and what to report to stakeholders about risk. Risk communication is an area filled with dilemma and is a risk in itself worthy of some risk assessment. Often, we find that senior managers don't want to communicate what they perceive as bad news. This can be a mistake. In addition, perhaps lower and middle managers have not fully communicated their concerns either, compounding the level of misinformation that reaches senior and executive management. Post-hoc reasons often given for failure to report bad news include:

- lack of time or resources;
- not wishing to be the bearer of bad news;
- believing issues are too difficult for the stakeholders to understand;
- believing that we should not communicate if we don't have the answers; and
- believing that stakeholders won't respond to help solve the problem or may create a worse one.

MANAGING EXPECTATIONS

Managing expectations is part of any business function. Waiting three weeks for your new computer to arrive is acceptable if you have agreed beforehand to a wait of three weeks. However, if you expected your computer to arrive overnight, a three-week wait could be intolerable and you may decide to cancel the order. Thus, if we include the stakeholders in the proactive risk discussion, we can defuse any alarm over the risks. In fact, many risks will be explored even more thoroughly when we give people the chance to air their views and share their experiences. The issues may involve technical aspects, and we must not confuse stakeholder dissent with misunderstanding. Take the time to explain the issues and involve stakeholders in the strategy that affects them. Taking the time to listen and learn early will pay dividends, as you won't have your time taken up later by stakeholder activists or interest groups trying to derail your strategy.

Work *with* groups, rather than against them. Remember to be open and honest about the risks, while at the same time ensuring that the technical and scientific data is accurate and backs up your decisions. Also, be aware that different groups will require differing styles of communication. The corporate culture will influence the communication style with stakeholders. For example, a marketing organization needs a story, whereas an engineering organization will prefer to hear about a process. If there is still conflict or dissent, then it may be time to bring in external experts to help facilitate the debate over the key risks. However, avoid appearing to be biased by ensuring that these resources are considered credible by all stakeholders.

Typically, the media are more interested in the politics of decisions than in the risk driving the decisions. Nevertheless, it is a fact that the media won't report on safety procedures and/or risk management until there is a catastrophic failure. If we engage the ERM process, we have what is required to speak with authority, from the heart. While there will always be some who don't agree with us and/or the decisions we have made, they can still respect our decisions.

Finally, I would like to reiterate that if the executives and the board don't communicate their support and sign off on the ERM approach, then the program will eventually be undermined. Key processes for successful ERM include:

- communicating with the stakeholders;
- promoting ownership of ERM processes; and
- ensuring use of a common, company-wide language to describe risk.

When utilizing experts within the organization, demonstrate your recognition of their technical skills (for example, health and safety, environment, treasury, and so on) and only seek outside consultants if the skills don't exist internally. (If you upset a key business area, the whole process of risk management becomes flawed.)

The way forward for global leaders is to engage with and build the ERM approach within your organization, and to be seen as the architect and creator of the risk-based decision-making process at the strategic level. If you move early, ERM competitive advantage will accrue to your organization and stakeholders. Be positive about risk, and the entrepreneur's approach to balancing opportunities with potential pitfalls will deliver optimal results. Moving your leadership on risk to this new level will drive more value through the consistent and efficient risk process and raise the profile of your organization to a global leadership position.

 ## Global Leadership Viewpoints

In this chapter, Geoff Taylor, director of risk management, Nike Europe, Middle East, and Africa Region, Nike European Operations Netherlands BV, provided essential information for global leaders regarding risk and the need for a solid risk strategy. Along the way, he shared several global leadership viewpoints:

- Successful global business leaders must focus on risk awareness and management. A risk strategy results in reduced downtime and faster recovery, which in turn leads to more employee satisfaction, improved productivity, and greater loyalty.
- Enterprise risk management (ERM) integrates all of the operations and business units in a consistent and controlled manner.
- A solid ERM framework addresses both the upside and the downside of risks.
- The chief risk officer is a trusted advisor who helps drive a consistent approach to risk-taking.
- Risk management, when done well, includes all the business leaders of the enterprise getting together on a regular basis to discuss the full breadth and depth of risk.
- Proactive, leadership-level risk management ensures that business opportunities are not lost due to an abundance of misplaced caution at the leadership level.

- The ERM process provides what is required for leaders to speak with authority and from the heart.

Endnote

1   Risk Management Standard, published by AIRMIC, ALARM, IRM 2002 (available for free download at www.airmic.com). Further information on each of the steps is available free of charge for The AIRMIC, ALARM, IRM Standard; or for nominal cost for The Australia and New Zealand Standard; *COSO Guide to Enterprise Risk Management*.

Chapter 12

Vodafone Change Leadership

Antonio Alemán

Antonio Alemán is the business unit managing director and has been Vodafone's director of unity of companies since August 2002. Almost his entire professional career has been developed in the sector of information technologies and communications, assuming various positions of responsibility in companies such as Hewlett-Packard and Siemens. Before joining Vodafone, he was delegate counsellor with Lucent Technologies Spain. He majored in Exact Sciences in the Universidad Complutense de Madrid.

Antonio Alemán
Business Unit Managing Director
Vodafone Spain
Vodafone Group
www.vodafone.com

Vodafone Spain is part of the Vodafone Group, the leading mobile phone company in the world with a presence in 27 countries and with agreements in 33 other countries around the globe. Vodafone provides a complete range of mobile services, including voice and data communication, for its almost 171 million clients.

Vodafone Spain's 13.5 million clients benefit from this leading company's experience and expertise, which help its clients – individuals, companies, and communities – to be better linked to the wireless world. Vodafone is an organization renowned worldwide for its service quality and innovative products.

(Data as of June 30, 2006)

Antonio works in Spain, which is also his country of citizenship. He has held leadership positions for more than 25 years. In the past two years, he has visited 10 countries. Vodafone's official languages are English and Spanish. Antonio speaks fluent English and Spanish.

Global Leadership Insights
• Lead by example.
• Get results through people.

Be close to your employees, invest a lot of time in direct communication, place maximum priority on the development of middle management, and create highly efficient organizations that allow promotion opportunities for internal staff.

Establish fluent communication between global and local management in order to develop mutual professional respect. Create propositions for clients and employees that show the real value of choosing this company.

In this chapter, we will examine the global vision of a multinational company from the perspective of a medium-sized subsidiary. This will demonstrate the need, in a multinational organization, to find a balance between capitalizing on the advantages of globalization while adequately integrating its local subsidiaries. The chapter also reflects on the challenges global leaders face in controlling and directing their local businesses. Failure to do so can produce dissatisfaction among local employees and have a negative effect on the desired outcome.

To illustrate, we will look at how Vodafone Group, a multinational company as well as the world leader in mobile telephony, integrated a medium-sided subsidiary, located in Spain. The integration occurred right after Vodafone's acquisition of the local operator, Airtel.

BACKGROUND

Vodafone Group is the largest mobile community in the world. With a presence in 27 countries (its expansion model is based on the acquisition of existent operators), Vodafone has agreements in 33 countries, on five continents, and its services are provided to more than 171 million customers throughout the world. Vodafone's successful market penetration plan has positioned it as the world leader. Vodafone was formed in 1984, as a subsidiary of Racal Electronics Plc. Then known as Racal Telecom Limited, approximately 20% of the company's capital was offered to the public in October 1988. Vodafone separated from Racal Electronics Plc, becoming an independent company, in September 1991, and changing its name to Vodafone Group Plc. Following its merger with AirTouch Communications, Inc. ("AirTouch"), the company changed its name to Vodafone AirTouch Plc in 1999 and, after approval by the shareholders in a general meeting in 2000, reverted to its former name, Vodafone Group Plc.

The main characteristics of Vodafone Group are:

- global presence and negotiating capacity;
- global brand; and
- specialization in global telephony.

Vodafone works to find new ways of turning these competitive advantages into direct benefits for its customers.

VODAFONE SPAIN

Vodafone Spain, which is part of Vodafone Group, accounts for almost 13.5 million customers who are favored with the experience and capacity of this world-leader company. Previously known as Airtel Movil, S.A., the company was constituted in Spain in 1994. Its second-generation mobile service (2G) was released in October 1995. After taking control of Airtel Movil, S.A. in 2001, the company started operating in Spain, and was one of the first companies in the group to adopt the Vodafone brand.

In February 2002, Vodafone Spain announced Francisco Román as delegate counsellor. Thereafter, a series of new appointments in the directive team resulted in the current leadership team.

In May 2006, Vodafone Spain announced its results for the financial year 2005/06 (from April 1, 2005 to March 31, 2006). Total income reached €5.857 million, a 22.6% increase on the year before. Income from services increased 22% to €5.3 million, of which €4.534 million came from voice services (a 21% increase on the year before) and €766,000 from data services (a 29.3% increase on the year before). Customers numbered 13,521,000 at the end of the financial year. Employees numbered 4,091, of whom 43% are women. Vodafone offers great career development opportunities to its employees – not only in Spain, but also in any of the operators that belong to Vodafone Group.

Spain has 43.1 million mobile users (97% penetration), with three existing mobile operators (TEM, Vodafone, and Amena).[1] Top-line growth in the Spanish mobile market remains one of the strongest in Europe, largely because competition in Spain is based on number portability. Spain is the only country in Europe where number portability is free and able to be implemented in less than a week. In 2005, 3.3 million mobile users took advantage of number portability (+46% year-over-year), representing 8% of total users.

GLOBAL EMERGENCE OF THE VODAFONE GROUP

Vodafone, a United Kingdom-based mobile telephony company, has followed a ground-breaking business model, compared to those followed by other mobile telephony operators. Before Vodafone implemented its current business model, the most common model consisted of former monopolies that were leaders in landline telephony (the business in which they had the most experience) creating a new division for mobile telephony. Existing firms launched mobile divisions in response to the new mobile operators that were beginning to appear in the market. These new divisions were launched as independent operations that shared management and most processes with the already established business.

Vodafone's business model was based on mobile telephony specialization, with global geographical implantation. Vodafone assumed that the mobile technology market would eventually overtake the landline telephony. This model and concentration has turned Vodafone into the world leader in mobile telephony; indeed, the financial numbers of mobile and landline telephony demonstrate a clear evolution toward the transition from landlines to mobile telephones (see Figure 12.1).

Nowadays, companies are merging their landline businesses with their mobile ones. Landline and mobile companies are buying

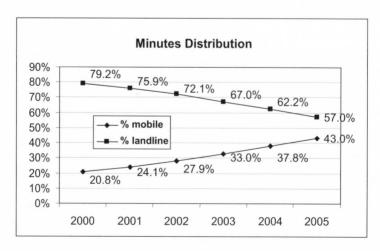

Figure 12.1   Transition from landlines to mobile telephones, 2000–05

each other in order to establish operations that contain both landline and mobile services. At the same time, both are taking advantage of these movements to improve their geographical presence. They are responding to Vodafone's model by attempting to protect the inherent weaknesses of landline telephony by packaging together landline, mobile, and ADSL services.

Vodafone's global growth strategy became the acquisition of local operators. All the local operators acquired had in common that they were independent from landline operators and were responsible for breaking the market monopoly that had existed previously. All these local operators have in common the execution of a successful market strategy and an outstanding share of the available market (sometimes more than 25%) that took less than 10 years to build. In Spain, the selected operator acquired by Vodafone was, as mentioned above, Airtel.

If we take a look at the spectrum of global companies, we will find two different models. First, there are global companies with a global result orientation (one global profit and loss, or P&L, account), serving a global market using local offices located in different countries for distribution and administration. The second type refers to other multinational companies with a multiple result orientation (each country having its own P&L account) accomplished by gathering local results where value and impact is critical. Within this second category, we will find companies such as Hewlett-Packard (HP), which expand by replicating their original models in different countries around the world with homogeneous products and services in all geographical markets. Those companies have a natural tendency to develop, right from the beginning, a consistent company style and a company culture – for example, the "HP Way."

As a subcategory of the second type of company, we find companies such as Vodafone, whose expansion model is based on the acquisition of companies around the world and where there is an attempt to unify products and services even though, at the point of acquisition, the products and services are uniquely local and very different from one market or country to another. Vodafone Group is a successful multinational company with a business model based on extensive acquisition and a focus on integration, which is not easily achieved. Vodafone's success as a global company, in my view, is dependent on the way the leadership works to create the right foundation for the attitude it has to adopt in order for the organization to integrate others in the most effective manner possible.

FROM AIRTEL TO VODAFONE: THE INTEGRATION PROCESS

With so much turbulence in the mobile telephony sector, in order to gain a better understanding of the integration process, let's look at Vodafone in Spain when it was still Airtel. Local employees were uncertain about and defensive toward everything coming from the group. In addition, the local operation's staff were exhausted from having to operate with reduced budgets following cuts in shareholder investments. This exhaustion, though, had caused our main competitor not to consider us as a threat – or, indeed, to pay us much attention. Being aware of this passive attitude, we started the integration process with an opportunity advantage, and therefore we could focus without pressure on fixing the business basics, with outstanding results.

At this stage of the integration process, Spain was a medium-sized country that was normally considered as part of "others" and, consequently, with little or no representation in the governance of multinational companies. Within this context, a new local management team with significant multinational experience assumed the challenge of integrating the local company into the group from the very beginning. The leadership didn't attempt to impose their own ideas and challenges on the group, but instead worked jointly with the global functions.

THE WAY TO INTEGRATION IN A GLOBAL COMPANY

The experience told here is of how local employees in Spain, affected by their loss of power and suffering the loss of their local identity, transformed themselves into a winning team with a global attitude. We became the reference point for successful change within Vodafone Group.

Using this experience, I will highlight the key elements a local subsidiary of a multinational group, based in a medium-sized country, implemented in order to participate actively in easing the transition and their integration into the multinational group of Vodafone. The subsidiary was able to get a head start using the advantages of globalization, without losing its local identity, while at the same time converting its employees into the international environment.

The objectives of the plan of action established were:

1. To re-establish basic business principles with the aim of significantly improving results.
2. To focus deeply on global integration of people, processes, and technologies.

I shall focus now on the second objective, as I consider that the elements of integration are most relevant for global leadership and successful integration. Undoubtedly, all the approaches taken to assist with improving the objectives were fundamental in gaining the time needed for all the required changes to take place in the organization. Most of those changes were behavioral, and arose from the fears and resistance of the local workforce, who didn't know what to expect as a result of the company being acquired and integrated into the global Vodafone Group.

Efficient and effective integration requires a bilateral change. The leadership at headquarters needs to view the workforce in the subsidiary in a positive manner. The workforce in the subsidiary needs to view the leaders from headquarters in a positive manner. Trust from both sides needs to be built through a series of successful communications and small wins. Moreover, for the integration to be successful, consistent, and durable, it is vital for our customers to understand the value to them in becoming part of the larger global business.

Our integration approach had three fundamental focal points:

*   Gain the credibility of the Vodafone Group.
*   Develop and roll out the right value proposition for the workforce in Spain.

- Establish and market the right value proposition for existing and potential customers.

Gaining the Credibility of the Vodafone Group

Global management needs to avoid the tendency to think that because it has the financial capacity to acquire the local operator, it also has the capacity to direct local businesses from headquarters. This behavior results in an almost immediate reduction in trust of the leadership. This leads to the creation of centralized organizational structures that grow very quickly and often have trouble defining a lasting contribution. Well-meaning leaders at the headquarters may overlook this situation, despite the local workforce experiencing some discomfort in the process. There are aspects of an operation, such as finance, and possibly even human resources, where control needs to be centralized. However, in normal business situations, it is a great mistake not to trust the local management to make the right decisions for its market. Even when an operation is centralized, the organization must be flexible and able to adapt to local geopolitical, legal, and cultural circumstances. The local leadership should have the space to move to build a successful team and to meet expected business results.

The key element for credibility is transparency, with all relevant information shared; private agendas are not welcome. In the context of transparency, the corporate headquarters (Vodafone Group) and the subsidiary (in this case, Spain's operations) should play their respective roles in continuously managing relationships and negotiating collaborative outcomes. They should tactically acquire some profits by being smart, but never by endangering their credibility.

Dedication to Vodafone Group by the subsidiary was fundamental. We participated in every forum to which we were invited (even before becoming full members). We had open, free communication and exchange of information about business actions. This was time-consuming, especially when corporate headquarters started asking for information and, at the same time, other subsidiaries wanted to learn more about our early successes. The time was well spent, however, and I highly recommend that local leaders become actively involved. It was a key aspect that assisted us in establishing and retaining our credibility. In four years, we have come from being part of the group of "others" to becoming an integral part of all the governance and leadership of Vodafone Group. The success of the Spain subsidiary's integration into the Vodafone Group is conveyed to everyone as a positive example of how things can work in almost every aspect of the business.

Developing and Rolling out the Right Value Proposition for the Workforce in Spain

The value proposition that the average employee looks for in a company such as Vodafone includes responses to one key question: "What does it mean to me, to be part of a multinational company?" The answer to this question becomes more important as the distance between the employee and the global structure increases. (For example, it will be more important for an employee working in a remote office than for a member of the Spanish executive team.)

Objectively, it is quite easy to build a value proposition. Career opportunities are greater when someone works in a multinational company, and multinational companies invest, on average, more resources in the development of their employees. It is more complicated, however, to transmit adequately the value proposition to employees, and to obtain their positive acknowledgment. This challenge exists because:

- there is reticence about accepting information coming from the new corporate headquarters, especially when people are used to much more independence;
- there is no absolute global vision for local staff to align themselves to; and
- there may be a gap between the profiles of existing staff and the profiles of new employees because of centralized corporate decisions in which local staff may not have had input.

There are three essential steps, which, when applied appropriately, result in a positive outcome from local employees.

1. *Leaders must set the right example* by role modeling the behavior they expect from their teams. Management must represent the whole of the business, Vodafone Group, in a positive way, and act always as an ambassador for the firm.

2. *There must be training programs and suitable budgets aimed at development* to allow local employees to experience their growing potential and become aware of their importance to the enterprise. Companies at both the multinational and national levels are moving in this direction and investing more in training and development programs. Moreover, training and development budgets are applied more efficiently as a result of the larger scale and size of multinational companies. For us, the development program, in its first phase, emphasized the manager's role to ensure that the highest and most influential layers of the organization had the commitment and capacity to assume their roles. The executive local committee was the first assessed and then enrolled in development and formation programs. This set an excellent example for all staff and stimulated interest in the programs throughout the organization.

    Depending on the level of integration, specific training programs were developed. The first and most fundamental level applied to all staff in Spain. It included information aimed at creating a sense of belonging to Vodafone Group as a multinational company. This level included the staff value proposition and demonstration as to how staff would be able to take advantage of development plans. This was fundamental in all employees understanding that they are now part of the multinational company and eased the transition from working for a domestic company to working for a large multinational company. The local leadership's responsibility is to assure that even those employees who don't meet current requirements for the centralized job profiles feel that they can develop their professional careers and that the company will provide support and assistance for them to do so. In regard to those who don't meet the role's criteria and cannot find an alternate role in the company, how the leadership responds, how they support these people, and how they gracefully exit them is viewed very closely by those who remain. The second level was the most critical. Every employee was provided with an opportunity to take an active role in the enterprise (Vodafone Spain). Roles included being a representative of the local company (Spain), contributors to group decisions through the firm's governance, and participation in forums and fluent communication. Each time a local team member contributes their experience, it eases the transition process. The third level is when local employees stop feeling that they belong just to the local organization and feel integrated into the larger enterprise.

It is of great importance in the development program to coordinate with employee evaluation and awards processes. Individual development plans are executed according to the employee's profiles, with practical contributions defined for each employee to meet local and global objectives. With regard to awards, they should not be so generous that the company ends up overspending its capital in the local market.

The development program needs to be accomplished level by level, from high to low, and keeping in mind that there is no total control over one level. Management involvement is a determining factor in the program's success.

3. *There must be continuous, clear communication with employees.* To ensure continuous information flow, periodic meetings are encouraged. First-level managers should meet every three months; all managers should meet every three months; and, finally, all employees should meet every six months. Local communications and meetings are complemented by CEO visits every six months. A high-level to low-level information process is needed and must involve middle managers, who will then be tasked with transmitting the most relevant information directly to all staff. It is also of great importance in the communication program that the executive committee is regularly involved, as their strong dedication, investment of time, and active participation set a positive tone for everyone.

Establishing and Marketing the Right Value Proposition for Existing and Potential Customers

Many of our customers might ask: "What good is it to me that you are world leaders if I live and travel within Spain and you aren't the leaders here?" In our case, in the mobile telephony segment of companies and institutions, our value proposition was built around the functionality of the third generation of mobile technology (UMTS/3G). This proposition would make us unique for our customers. We helped them incorporate the technology in to the core of their businesses, and we enabled them to create new products and services that would help them increase their income and offer better services for their own customers. Vodafone's strength as a multinational company made this innovation possible, because Vodafone now has the largest worldwide investment in information technologies (computer manufacturers, software companies, consultants, and so on).

Vodafone Spain's management team had vast experience in the industry of information technology, and from the first moment it was understood that mobile communications was a complementary technology to information technologies. We knew that mobile functionality would make every computer and mobile device more productive. We knew that usage would improve performance and the results of their employees, and of their business processes in general.

 Global Leadership Viewpoints

In this chapter, Antonio Alemán, business unit managing director, Vodafone Spain, described the integration of a medium-sized subsidiary into a global community. Along the way, he shared several global leadership viewpoints:

- Help people to see that belonging to a multinational company is a professional opportunity.
- Identify and communicate the value proposition for globalization to employees and customers.
- Balance global interests with local requirements.

- Gain the trust of corporate headquarters. Make every effort to use transparency as the basis of the relationship.
- Get local employees to participate in the concept of global, keeping in mind that no employee has decided on their own to be part of the group.
- Personalize the incorporation of each team member, taking into account their development needs and including international opportunities and local business objectives.
- Continuous, clear communication needs to spread across all levels of the organization, with a particular focus on communication to middle management.
- Synchronize development programs with the formal processes of evaluation, awards, and compensation. The development plan and the most tangible elements of the compensation plan must be in synch in order to meet global and local objectives.

At Vodafone Group, "The future is unfolding around us. Over the next decade we will be able to see all sorts of differences that we can barely imagine today."[2]

Endnotes

1   Analistas Grupo Santander.
2   www.vodafone.com, accessed November 15, 2006.

Chapter 13

Managing Your Global Leadership Development

Marjan Bolmeijer and Frank-Jürgen Richter

Marjan Bolmeijer, chief executive officer of Change Leaders, Inc., is a trusted advisor to elite leaders of Fortune 500-size companies worldwide. She is an expert at CEO and board development: turning successful senior executives into even more successful leaders.

Dr. Frank-Jürgen Richter is the president of Horasis: The Global Visions Community. Prior to founding Horasis, Dr. Richter was director of the World Economic Forum, in charge of Asian affairs. Under his leadership, the Forum's summits in Asia and the Asian part of "Davos" have evolved to facilitate the exchange of expertise between leaders in business, government, and civil society. Dr. Richter is also an active scholar and has authored and edited a series of bestselling books on global strategy and Asian business. His most recent books include Global Future, Asia's New Crisis, *and* Recreating Asia.

Dr. Richter has addressed audiences at the World Economic Forum, the Brookings Institute, Harvard University, Beijing University, the Royal Institute of International Affairs, and several high-level corporate events. His writings have appeared in the financial and regional press, such as The International Herald Tribune, The Wall Street Journal, The Far Eastern Economic Review, The Straits Times, *and the* South China Morning Post. *He has been interviewed by several publications and appeared on CNN, BBC, CNBC, CCTV (China Central Television), and the Voice of America. Dr. Richter was educated in Germany (his home country), France, Mexico, and Japan. He is a fluent Mandarin and Japanese speaker.*

Marjan Bolmeijer
Chief Executive Officer
Change Leaders, Inc.
www.Change-Leaders.com

Change Leaders, Inc. specializes in CEO and board development. The company turns successful senior executives into even more successful leaders by leveraging the "soft" factors (e.g. group dynamics, CEO on-boarding, board dynamics) that improve the "hard" business metrics (e.g. growth, value, performance). With 20-plus years' experience and deep insights into the CEO's world, the company is known as an international solution generator.

Marjan Bolmeijer is based in the United States and Europe. She has held leadership positions for more than 20 years. She is fluent in English, Dutch, German, and French.

Global Leadership Insights
- Approach the other, that "different" human being, with curiosity. Be interested. Be inquisitive. Be curious.
- Aspiring global leaders should build on what they already have as skills, experience, or attributes. You probably have and know 75% of what you need. What are the transferable skills and experiences you already have? Which ones need a small improvement?
- Think of a network you assume you can't join. Now, go and do what it takes to get into that network.
- Consider the art of networking as more important to master than finance or sales.

Enlist as sponsors several senior executives who believe that you should become a global leader.

Frank-Jürgen Richter, Ph.D.
President, Horasis
www.horasis.org

Horasis: The Global Visions Community is a strategic advisory on long-term scenarios related to globalization, systemic risk, and Asian business. Horasis is a visions community – together with our clients and partners we explore, define, and implement trajectories of sustainable growth. Horasis provides a range of services to private and public clients who envisage growing into global and sustainable organizations.

Frank-Jürgen Richter works in Switzerland, and his country of citizenship is Germany. He has held leadership positions for more than 15 years. In the past two years, Frank has visited more than 25 countries. During his career, he has lived and worked in China, France, Germany, Japan, Mexico, and Switzerland.

Global Leadership Insights
• Address the key economic, political, and societal issues in a forward-looking, action-oriented way.
• Bring together leaders from different constituencies.

You need the creativity of all kinds of constituents to run the heart of a productive knowledge-based economy.

MANAGING YOUR GLOBAL LEADERSHIP DEVELOPMENT

20th century: "Leaders are born, not made."
21st century: "Leaders are made, and leadership development is a process of self-development."

There is a difference between what you need to "learn" and how you need to "change." Have you ever noticed how the words "team" and "group" and "executive" and "leader" are used interchangeably, although not every group is a team and not every executive is a leader? The same is true for the words "learning" and "change." For our purpose here, we will define these two words as follows:

- **Learning is about a personal ability.** Independent of who you are as a person, you have certain abilities – for instance, the ability to manage a tough meeting or a global advertising campaign, and the ability to feel angry or to calm down.
- **Change is about a personal development.** First, you *learn* intellectually what a "global mindset" is. Then you *experience* "having" a global mindset. Since it is time-consuming to put such a mindset on and off like a coat, you are likely to keep it on and thereby *become* the type of person who consistently has a global mindset as part of their overall persona. This is called a personal development change.

How Do We Learn?

How you master global leadership competencies is influenced by a large number of factors, three of which are:

- *Your personality type.* Extroverts and introverts learn in different ways, as do people who are mostly focused on the past vs. those focused on the future, or people who are more eager to "be right" vs. those who are eager "to win."

- *Type of task.* Leading a global, creative team in cutting-edge product development will develop your chaos management abilities, whereas learning to make complex, global financial statements will develop your intellectual abilities.

- *Type of environment.* Many companies provide their high-potential managers with stretch assignments, during which the manager is put in unfamiliar surroundings (for example, a plant in a foreign country) with seemingly impossible deliverables and deadlines, which forces the manager to operate out of his or her comfort zone.

Although the question "How do we learn?" hasn't been answered fully by the world's leadership development experts, the next question is clearly on the horizon: "How do we change/develop?"

How Do We Change/Develop?

Most people's personal development changes are passive, non-managed, and non-goal-oriented. It is the rare person – someone of the caliber of a global leader – who sits down, thinks about, and plans the type of person they want to become. Here are three tools to assist you to make the personal development changes that will ensure your effectiveness as a global leader.

ACTIVITY 1: GETTING THE RIGHT GLOBAL FEEDBACK

In Hyderabad, India, Ajay is participating in a video-conference with the company's global executive team in Shanghai. It is a long conference and he has almost fallen asleep a few times. But now the company's chief IT officer is speaking and people are paying attention to her every word. Afterwards, Ajay and his colleagues discuss what made her so different from the previous speakers. They decide that it isn't her skills or position of power, or her experience or knowledge; there is just something about the kind of person she is that makes her a leader, someone others are willing to follow.

Leadership is about the person you are and the resulting personal connection others experience with you. Therefore, leadership development is about *personal* development. Yet, knowing *how* to change requires knowing *what* needs to be changed.

To get this information, companies in the West use the 360-degree feedback tool. This is an easy-to-implement, low-cost leadership development tool that can be used at all levels of an organization. It is a simple way to gather ongoing feedback from colleagues spread across the world and provides in-the-moment opportunities for development.

Even if your company hasn't implemented this tool yet, you can implement four of its steps yourself and get great benefits.

The Activity

Step 1: Evaluate Your Global Leadership Strengths and Weaknesses
- Ask yourself: "What are my global leadership strengths and weaknesses? Which specific global leadership skills, experiences, or traits do I still need to acquire?" Be very, very honest with yourself.
- Now, select one aspect of your global leadership behavior that you consider to be weak and which you would like to strengthen. (Just select one aspect; don't try to change everything at once.) An example might be your habit of being late for important meetings.

Step 2: Choose Global Mentors or Coaches
- Select three to five colleagues from different cultural backgrounds who work with you on a regular basis and who you think would genuinely like to see you improve as a global leader.
- Ask these colleagues to be your mentors or coaches, and to give you regular feedback about the one behavior you have selected.
- Discuss and agree to the feedback guidelines (see below) with each mentor.

Feedback Guidelines

- A feedback meeting with a mentor is always one-on-one and confidential.
- Restrict the meeting to no more than five minutes.
- Remain standing during the meeting. This will remind you to keep it short.
- Start each meeting by asking the mentor: "Could you please give me one specific suggestion about how I can become more effective in (this behavior)?"
- The mentor's response should consist of two elements:
  1. One or two feedback sentences, indicating what you are not doing well yet. For example:
     "The feedback is that you are still often late for the monthly sales reviews with the CEO."

2. One or two suggestion sentences on how to improve. For example:

   "The suggestion is that you turn off your phone, PC, and BlackBerry 15 minutes prior to meetings so that there are no last-minute matters to delay you."

- There should be no discussion of non-related business issues.
- Both the feedback and the suggestion should be about one specific behavior. They should *never* be about the person's character, style, or the way he or she thinks or feels.
- Both the feedback and the suggestion should be delivered in an emotionally neutral way.
- The mentor can clarify their feedback/suggestion if it isn't initially clear.
- The session should end with the mentor being told simply, 'Thank you. Goodbye.' Not: 'Thank you. That was very helpful. I will do my best to... This is also useful in situations such as...'

Step 3: Treat Feedback with Respect

People the world over can find it difficult to accept feedback, even if it is given in the form of a gentle suggestion. When that happens, they may reject the feedback and thus lose any benefits it might have provided. Always remember the first and most important rule of feedback: Treat all feedback with respect.

Step 4: Implement. Implement. Implement

Treating feedback with respect means that you follow through on it. Implementation is key.

After completing step 4, repeat the whole process with new mentors/coaches. Taking these basic steps will allow you to be in control and to reap the benefits of the feedback process.

ACTIVITY 2: EXPANDING THE BANDWIDTH OF YOUR CULTURAL SENSITIVITY

"How is the other person experiencing our conversation? I wish I could understand how he thinks, how he perceives things. Then I could understand his point of view."

Do you sometimes wish you could get inside the mind of someone who is so different from you? Well, you can. By fully imagining being that other person – or, as Westerners call it, "walking a mile in someone else's shoes" – you allow yourself to understand the other person better. Go ahead; imagine that you are as tall as that other person. Or that your skin color is like his. Or that you speak his language ... you are that intelligent ... you have that much energy ... you hold those values ....

Developing the ability to strongly imagine being the other person is a sure way to increase your cultural sensitivity and effectiveness in recognizing a broader variety of cultural elements.

The following exercise will help you to expand your insights into how others experience their world and how, as a result, they experience you and their interaction with you.

The Activity

- Select a partner who comes from a different cultural background and environment.
- Each of you starts by choosing one worldview from list 1 on the next page. Make sure to choose an item that *doesn't* represent the way you currently look at the world.
- Spend about an hour acting as if you are someone who completely accepts the worldview you have selected. Act as if you have a 100% belief in this worldview; as if you were born and raised with this view and had never learned anything else. Experience your life with this worldview – physically, emotionally, and mentally.
  Key: *Put your own worldview entirely aside for the hour. This is not an exercise about "defending" your point of view, but about deeply experiencing what it is to hold someone else's point of view.*
- Discuss your experiences and insights with your partner only at the end of the hour. Here are some reflective questions for that discussion:
  - Living with this worldview, what is it like to be you? To do your job? To work at your company? What is different? What is the same? With this worldview, what is it like to negotiate with or be the boss of someone holding one of the other worldviews?

- Since there are no right or wrong worldviews, how would you grow as a person, as a leader, if you were to maintain multiple worldviews simultaneously?
- How would you solve that complicated problem you are dealing with if you were to hold one or more of these additional perspectives?
- When you are done, take an item from list 2 below and repeat the process.

List 1: Worldviews

People across the globe have different perceptions and, consequently, different internal experiences of the world we live in. These worldviews and internal experiences of the world are real and influence our daily actions at the office. Some examples:

1. *The world is a survival game.* Everyone for himself. Be alert to hazards. Trust no one. This is a power-based view of the world.
2. *The world is a combination of a variety of complex systems that need to be understood in order to be a truly free human being.* This is an intellectual-based view of the world.
3. *The world is full of opportunities to improve your situation if you try.* This is a competition-based view of the world.
4. *The world is a place of fundamentally similar people looking for interpersonal connections.* This is a social-based view of the world.
5. *The world is a network of interdependent units forming a global entity whose problems are important.* This is a holistic-based view of the world.
6. *The world is potentially chaotic and needs to be put in order through systems, rules, and loyalty.* This is an order-based view of the world.

List 2: Business Approaches

The following business approaches are real-life examples of how many people approach their day-to-day work:

1. Respect for tradition and sameness/similarities vs. respect for the future and change.

2. Ensuring your own needs will result in servicing our society at large vs. focusing on our society at large will result in ensuring your own needs.

3. Use time pressure and short-term results vs. long-range cooperation and planning.

4. Non-verbal vs. verbal communications.

5. Work the people hard and pay them well vs. work gets done through the people who work here.

6. Emotional and elaborate use of language vs. conservative use of language.

7. Present the problem and seek points of view vs. present facts about the problem and reach an agreement.

8. Straightforward vs. polite, smooth communication.

9. Group orientation vs. being self-reliant.

10. Authoritarian vs. consensus.

ACTIVITY 3: CHARTING YOUR WORLD'S CULTURAL MOSAIC

"When I do business in another language I experience my world as very different. At the outside, my world is still the same, but my internal experience of my external world is very different."

— Executive vice president – international sales,
Fortune 500 firm

Learning languages helps in gaining deeper, intuitive sensitivities to cultural differences. But what if you don't have the time to study languages? In that case, it helps to have a framework for use in deciphering the mosaic of cultural elements you can easily become aware of in your day-to-day environment.

Let's take your company. If it is an international organization, it will have a large number of different cultures all more or less integrated together. First, there are the cultures within the company itself, which differ somewhat between hierarchical levels, divisions, or teams. For instance, in a mid-level sales team the cultural norm is that your status is dictated by your personal accomplishments, whereas the cultural norm for a senior executive is that her status is dictated by her personal connections and standing in the community. Second, there are a variety of ethnic cultures the company's staff bring through the front door. Third, the countries in which the company operates have their own local, regional, and national cultures. For instance, in Japan it is important that you are "esteemed" by others, whereas in the United States it is more important to be "enjoyed" by others. Then there are our global social and cultural elements, such as those we are exposed to through MTV or the internet. Adding it all up, we live in a true mosaic of cultural elements.

As a global leader, you will need to identify differences between cultural elements at a moment's notice on a daily basis.

The following simple, mental framework will be useful in helping you to quickly sort through the different cultural elements you have to deal with.

The Activity

- Read the explanations in the table below.

	Explanation	Example
Micro	The smallest possible unit	You. Or your sales team of 10 people
Meso	The next smallest unit	The entire sales team of 100 people
Macro	A larger unit	The country division you work in, with 1,000 people
Meta	An even larger unit	All the Asian divisions combined, with 15,000 people
Mega	The largest possible unit	The entire global company, with 50,000 people

- Be aware of the four subsections of cultural elements – identities, values/beliefs, abilities, and behaviors – and of how they differ in the examples given for Company A and Company B.
- Select a partner, preferably someone from a very different cultural environment.

- Next, fill in the blank chart for your company: How do you perceive your company?
- Then, fill in the blank chart for your partner's company: How do you perceive your partner's company?
- Ask your partner to complete both sides of the four charts.
- Discuss with your partner these four cultural elements at their micro, macro, and mega levels. In other words, there are four questions to discuss:
  - How do I view myself?
  - How does my partner view him/herself?
  - How do I view my partner?
  - How does my partner view me?

Identities: "I Am"

Human beings develop a variety of personal identities throughout the course of their lives. In English, when referring to personal identities we use the verb "to be." For instance, "I *am* a father," "I *am* a daughter," or in the office, "I *am* a sales guy," "I *am* an entrepreneur."

Teams, divisions, companies, and even countries have their own unique identities as well. For instance, a start-up software company in India can have the identity of "The New Guys on the Block," whereas Nike, Inc. has the identity of "The Competitive Company" and Germany has the national identity of "The Engineers."

	Identities at Company A	Identities at Company B
	Company A wants sales and market share	*Company B wants leading-edge products*
Micro	I am someone who can deliver.	I am someone uniquely different.
Macro	As our company's sales division, we are the company's "Crown Princes."	We, the product development team, are "What's Hot" in our industry.
Mega	We are the market leaders.	We are the product leaders.

	Identities at your company	Identities at your partner's company
Micro		
Macro		
Mega		

Values/Beliefs: "I Believe"

Values, beliefs, rules, or assumptions are those perceptions we think or hope are correct, true, relevant, or important.

	Values at Company A	Values at Company B
Micro	I believe it is important that I deliver what I promised.	I believe it is important that I take risks and act like an entrepreneur.
Macro	The #1 value of the sales division is success.	The #1 value of the product development division is innovation.
Mega	The company values control and stability and we have the reports to prove it.	The company values flexibility and leading-edge innovation.

	Values at your company	Values at your partner's company
Micro		
Macro		
Mega		

Abilities: "I Can"

Abilities are internal or external skills/competencies. For instance, creating daily feelings of fear is an internal skill not every human being can easily copy, whereas reading complex financial reports is an external skill.

	Abilities at Company A	Abilities at Company B
Micro	Our individual contributor knows how to adhere to the company's rules and laws.	Our individual contributor knows how to be creative, to collaborate, and to build consensus.
Macro	Our group knows how to cross-train, keep each other motivated, and drive together for results.	Our group knows how to live in a state of ambiguity and chaos.
Mega	Our company knows how to set measurable market goals and procedures for reaching those goals.	Our company knows how to create flexible procedures that encourage individual initiatives.

	Abilities at your company	Abilities at your partner's company
Micro		
Macro		
Mega		

Behaviors: "I Do"

Behaviors are actions others can see, such as arriving on time at a meeting or closing a sale.

	Behaviors at Company A	Behaviors at Company B
Micro	In a hurry, cuts a conversation short. Talks about the future. Personal goals are located outside the person (sales goals).	Brings his dog to the office. Talks about the present. Personal goals are located inside the person (increased creativity).

	Behaviors at Company A	Behaviors at Company B
Macro	The sales team holds weekly sales review meetings. (Did we meet our goal?)	The group regularly exchanges emails on collaboration tactics for global negotiations. (What else is new/is there to learn?)
Mega	The company gives an annual sales reward trip to the top 10 salespeople and fires the bottom 10 performers.	The company experiments continuously with regular and irregular innovation awards.

	Behaviors at your company	Behaviors at your partner's company
Micro		
Macro		
Mega		

These four cultural elements are somewhat interconnected: the identities we choose tend to influence our values/beliefs/rules, which in turn influence the abilities we develop, which in turn influence our behaviors. But the reverse is also true: perform any behavior (such as talking very loudly) for long enough and it will begin to shift some of your personal values.

CONTINUOUS LEARNING

This book shows that there is a great deal to learn and a lot of personal development required to become a successful global leader. Since globalization has intensified the need for leaders, more executives will experience, more often, more pressure to grow both as people and as leaders. Today's generation of executives will go through more personal development than any prior generation.

The good news is that you have more tools at your disposal than any previous generation, and more companies have the infrastructure to develop global leaders. Plus, there is a lot you can do by yourself. Have fun with these exercises!

Chapter 14

Conclusion

THE NEW GLOBAL FRONTIER

We live in a unique time in history. Individuals and families who had earlier left their countries of origin are now choosing to return for the same reasons they left. They left for social, economic, or political reasons; today, they are returning because of the social, economic, or political changes that are benefiting entire regions of the world. We live in a time when we can travel to all parts of the globe and communicate instantly with people anywhere in the world.

Today's business leaders manage teams and have customers who are from all over the globe. The world is changing rapidly; people are more interconnected than ever, and global leaders have responsibility for continuously moving their organizations forward.

"To be a world-class leader who is successful over many years requires you to renew yourself," says Kent O. Jonasen of A.P. Moller – Maersk A/S in Denmark. "Over time the world and business can change significantly, so you have to be willing and able to change and adapt." Luc J.J. Bollen of Hilton Hefei, China, agrees and adds: "If you are a global leader, you need to understand that you are on a global platform. You must accept that things are not always within your comfort zone. Look for the advantages that differences present, open the door to the global playing field, recognizing your strengths and opportunities. Be willing to evolve as a leader."

In Part 1 of this book, we explored information collected from the Global Leadership Survey. Additional and more detailed insights came from interviews conducted with global leaders around the world. The results can be broken down into five key characteristics leaders need to have in order to be successful on the global frontier: leadership characteristics, global business acumen, worldview, global people leadership, and global business leadership.

Global Leadership Characteristics

Leadership characteristics can be divided into two categories: core values and traits. Leadership traits represent *"who* you are." They develop over time; we don't know exactly how early in life our character develops, but it is safe to say that traits, once formed, don't change quickly. Leadership core values represent *"how* you are" – the guiding principles for how everyone in the organization thinks and acts. We examined both traits and core values from the perspective of world-class leaders who shared their thoughts and successful strategies.

Global Business Acumen

The marketplace is recognizing the need for enhanced global business acumen. The Hay Group has teamed with *Fortune* magazine since 1998 to identify and rank the "World's Most Admired Companies." In 2006, "effectiveness in conducting business globally" was added as a measurement attribute. According to the Hay Group, "It is a timely topic, as operating across geographic boundaries is becoming more and more essential for companies competing in an economy that is increasingly global."[1] The most admired companies in the world are those that understand the importance of developing global business acumen.

We explored, from the perspective of world-class leaders, eight critical global business acumen areas: business terminology, regional and global economics, global finance awareness, strategic marketing, organizational behavior, enterprise knowledge management, operations management, and business innovation.

Worldview

Changing cultures, whether it be through switching companies, traveling, or relocating, challenges leaders to broaden their perspectives. If you are moving into the global leadership sphere, I would advise you first to acknowledge that you probably don't know quite how you are going to make it work, and then to enjoy the adventure!

As a global leader, observe, listen, and learn. World-class leaders use 360-degree views, news, and perspectives to enhance their ability both to expand their global awareness and global understanding, and to engage with all of society.

Global People Leadership

The complexities of global leadership complicate communications and relationships, and this requires interpersonal and intercultural sensitivity. Labor laws are also different from one country to the next. As we continue to integrate teams across the globe, people leadership is at the forefront of our minds. And while many of the people leadership principles you have learned will serve you well, being aware of the complexities and the nuances of leading people from widely differing cultures will aid you on your journey toward global success. Key people leadership areas to master include attracting and retaining world-class talent and helping your organization to be an "employer of choice," demonstrating an interest in others, listening to others and ensuring that everyone is heard, empowering and motivating people, establishing clear goals and roles, and celebrating successes both small and large.

Building a multifaceted workforce allows world-class leaders to be more prepared to take full advantage of opportunities that can result in mega-innovation and limitless creativity. Diverse ecosystems promote enhanced relationships, resulting in continuous organizational benefits. Developing future leaders is a primary responsibility for global leaders. Leaders should look across their entire organization to identify and nurture future leaders.

Global Business Leadership

There are also more complexities when leading business globally. These complexities include the need to have a solid, socialized, and accepted strategy and vision, broader use of technology, alignment across the enterprise, and the ability to network with people from right across the globe. Successful global leaders also recognize that the time it takes to achieve an outcome may differ from one country to the next based on availability of skills, context, and business tools.

Throughout the development of *Leadership Without Borders*, Ibanga Umanah provided assistance as my primary researcher. Since he reviewed all the information collected and assisted in the analysis, I have asked him to share some of his observations (see Box 14.1).

BOX 14.1   INSIGHTS FROM A FUTURE GLOBAL LEADER

Ibanga Umanah

Life is always dynamic and constantly changing; those of us who learn to embrace diversity live rich lives. I was born in 1983 into diversity; my mother was an American veterinary medicine student, my father a political science/economics student from Nigeria. Within three months of my birth, we began to move. I have yet to return to the state of Iowa where I was born. From New York, to Michigan, to District of Columbia, the list goes on, until in 1995 I found myself in Nigeria. It was at that moment, in the middle of the night, as the dense wave of humidity and smell of citrus hit me as I stepped off the airplane, that my global adventure began. By the time I reached university, back in America, "diversity" was part of my nature. I craved it and couldn't understand life without it.

Three majors and one study-abroad program to Denmark later a friend of mine, John Ballantine, asked me: "Would you like to work in India this summer?" The opportunity to move to the other side of the world, to a new culture, to learn about how other people live their lives, sounded too exhilarating to pass up. During my collaboration with Ed Cohen on *Leadership Without Borders*, I have had the opportunity to speak with over 40 world-class leaders from around the world. Their fascinating insights into the world inspired and validated my own views on "what it takes" to lead globally.

"Today, time, and space are collapsing, the availability of information is exploding for anyone, anywhere, with basic electronic communication tools."

— Frederick W. Smith, CEO,
FedEx[2]

Whether produced in the United States, Japan, or South Africa, we live in an age of access to any source of media, about any topic. Innovative content is built by media groups, industry associations, and the local school nurse in her spare time. Gershenfeld argues in his book *FAB: The Coming Revolution on Your Desktop – From Personal Computers to Personal Fabrication*[3] that soon this diffused, innovative capability will move beyond the "digital" toward real goods, as technological changes adjust the means of production.

However, it is not only "who" and "what" that are dramatically different now than at any time in history; it is also "how." In the age of open-source software and wikis,[4] collaboration, creativity, sharing, and the proliferation of ideas are no longer limited to highly literate research or consulting groups. Feats that could be achieved only by mega-organizations in the past can be achieved today, with internet or mobile access, by groups of collaborative individuals based anywhere across the globe.

Tomorrow's organizations will be run by a new generation of professionals, not bound by geographic proximity of ideas, who can communicate and collaborate with individuals and organizations from any location at any time – truly unplugged. As future global leaders, we will face a new set of challenges and will require a new set of competencies in order to be successful.

"Education is the process of learning to see the hidden connections between things."

— Václav Havel,
president, Czech Republic[5]

This "access," as FedEx calls it, allows us to choose from two paths for our learning: (1) we can live inside an information cocoon of confirmation seeking; or (2) we can be exposed to as many points of view and perspectives as we can possibly absorb. For me, one field of study wasn't enough; the world, as Havel noted, is too interconnected – why stop at one lens or point of view, when you can have three? Individuals with extreme curiosity are listening to podcasts, reading broadly, studying a range of subjects, traveling to and experiencing a wide variety of locations, experimenting with the many new tools of this age, and asking questions in search of new ways of thinking, approaching ideas, and reaching markets. These leaders have the greatest global opportunities in front of them. Equally as important for leaders will be the ability to maintain an open, shared approach to idea generation, visioning, and decision-making. Extreme curiosity means you are just as excited about others' ideas, as you are about your own. In Chapter 5, Ed Cohen refers to this as "mega-innovation and limitless creativity."

"If you are sensitive, ambitious, curious, and a learner, it's very hard to shut that off and 'stay home'."

— Elliott Masie, president,
The Masie Center

Balance and success can sometimes seem mutually exclusive, harmony between the two being slightly out of reach. What is clear, however, is that while success as a global leader may require tremendous sacrifices, the best global leaders consider, and deliberately make career choices aligned with, their passions. This holistic type of success comes from a balanced integration of life and work. I learned to teach and relate to people of all ages as a snow skiing instructor. I learned to be creative by inventing recipes as a chef and by writing music with my guitar. My friends live in at least 15 different countries. New leaders need to assimilate many sources of knowledge in their daily lives and use this knowledge to generate positive, mega-creative outcomes. Balance and integration is not a future criterion for success; it is *now*.

SUCCESSFUL STRATEGIES FROM WORLD-CLASS LEADERS

In Part 2 of this book, we had the opportunity to learn from the successful strategies of eight exceptional global leaders.

The Artistry and Science of Global Leadership

"People are able to travel more freely than ever before, resulting in a palpable integration, an irrefutable buzzing and spilling over of borders and boundaries."

— Dr. Mukesh Aghi

According to Mukesh Aghi, the world is no longer an isolationist phenomenon. He goes on to discuss the essence of a leader. The "boundaryless" nature of the world is having the greatest impact on global leadership today, he says. Understanding the needs, beliefs, and cultures of people from all over the world creates a conducive environment in which to conduct business and ensures the healthy and smooth transition to global enterprises. Markets have become global. Companies that are reaching into the global markets need to be able to design global products for narrow, local markets in order to stay competitive. The combination of global communication and global trade has given rise to a business culture that has spread all over the world. Today's global leader is dealing with a global marketplace and a global workforce. True success is about embracing the people and knowledge that are defining the new world of business.

Satyam: The Creation of a Global Company

"The joy in the journey is defined by who you are traveling with. You are already traveling with your future leaders."

— B. Ramalinga Raju

In 1987, B. Ramalinga Raju launched a business that would soon emerge as a global company. While most companies grow primarily on domestic revenues, most of Satyam's revenues came from outside India. A culture of continuous learning quickly became part of Satyam's DNA. Satyam pioneered Rightsourcing™, a global delivery model that offers customers the right mix of global delivery and onsite delivery and development services. Much of Satyam's early success came from keeping its focus on customer needs. Its current business model, full life-cycle leadership, empowers associates to continue to lead sustained growth. The company was divided into logical components called full life-cycle businesses, allowing leaders to operate them much like CEOs of independent businesses. Full life-cycle leadership and the full life-cycle business model shifted the organization structure from teams to independent, yet interdependent businesses. Satyam has grown from 100 associates in 1992 to more than 35,000 associates in 2006. In the process, the company has become a strong competitor in the global technology services market.

Transitioning to a Global Mindset

"The world economy is so interconnected that events in New York, London, Tokyo, or Mumbai have an immediate and visible impact on the psyche of overseas investors/financiers."

— V. Shankar

V. Shankar believes that companies, and individuals, with a global mindset demonstrate an ability to consider both "hard" and "soft" business issues. The need for a global mindset is increasing, with several factors driving that need for organizations, including open markets, interconnected financial markets, "blue-collar" blues, and the convergence of standards. Shankar presented six keys to creating a global mindset: embracing diversity, hiring foreign talent if necessary, exposing your team to global experiences, using the world as your ideas factory, seeking alliances and organizing to be global, and thinking global from day one (or today).

Booz Allen Hamilton's Global People Strategy

"Successful firms adopt a global business definition that incorporates their heritage and a new, unified mission statement."

— Dr. Ralph Shrader

Dr. Ralph Shrader presented the global people leadership strategy that led to the one-firm evolution of Booz Allen, a privately held company, owned by its officers, providing expertise to help government and commercial clients solve their toughest problems.

While Booz Allen had always had a single identity and structure as a firm, it had historically had two distinct operating units – one serving commercial clients, the other serving government. As president of the firm's government business from 1994 to 1998, and chairman and chief executive officer of the global firm since 1998, Dr. Ralph Shrader worked with Booz Allen people throughout the world to evolve toward one firm. This included adopting a new business definition incorporating its government and commercial heritage ("global strategy and technology consulting firm") and a new, unified mission statement ("Booz Allen Hamilton works with clients to deliver results that endure").

Global Risk Strategies

"Successful global business leaders focus on risk awareness and management. A risk awareness strategy results in reduced downtime and faster recovery, which in turn leads to more employee satisfaction, improved productivity, and greater loyalty."

— Geoff Taylor

Geoff Taylor discussed the global business community's new focus on risk awareness and management. Risk appetite is the amount of risk an enterprise is prepared to accept in the course of its operations. The only way to manage these potential risks is to set a framework for acceptable risk levels – this can include financial measures and must include aspects for human, environmental, reputational, and operational risks.

So, what is the right approach to take in managing risks? The first step toward an enterprise risk management approach requires a shift from managing risks in silos, to a more integrated approach to risk management. The second stage is bringing this integrated risk approach together with the commercial and financial risk into a seamless enterprise risk management (ERM) system. A solid ERM framework addresses both the upside and downside risks. Somewhere between these equally valid expressions of risk, predilection, and risk aversion is a truly good risk framework. A risk professional can bring both of these points of view into corporate focus to ensure that a balanced and rational approach to risk-taking is implemented.

Vodafone Change Leadership

"To ensure success, help people to see that belonging to a multinational company is a professional opportunity."

— Antonio Alemán

Antonio Alemán presented the steps taken by both the medium-sized subsidiary, Vodafone Spain, and the Vodafone Group to integrate into one company. He advised helping people to see that belonging to a multinational company is a professional opportunity. He presented the need to identify and communicate the value proposition for globalization to employees and customers. The best change leadership strategy balances global interests with local requirements; it is one where there is transparency as the basis of the relationship between the local and headquarters offices, and that gets local employees to participate in the concept of "global." Continuous clear communication across all levels of the organisation, with a particular focus on communication to middle management, is important for success. Development programs synchronized with the formal processes of evaluation, awards, and compensation are critical.

Managing Your Global Leadership Development

"Globalization has forced more companies to spend more time developing the infrastructure to develop global leaders, the demand for which is already enormous and still growing."

— Marjan Bolmeijer and Frank-Jürgen Richter

Marjan Bolmeijer and Dr. Frank-Jürgen Richter discussed how leading a global, creative team in leading-edge product development will develop your ability to manage chaos; whereas learning to produce complex, global financial statements will develop your intellectual abilities. Most people's personal development changes are passive, non-managed, and non-goal-oriented. Today, derailed careers are unnecessary because personal development tools and experts are widely available to structure personal development opportunities. The authors presented three activities aimed at expanding global leadership awareness. They concluded by explaining that globalization has forced more companies to spend more time developing the infrastructure to develop global leaders, the demand for which is already enormous and still growing.

CONCLUDING INSIGHTS

Our lives, our economies, and our societies are more interconnected than at anytime in the past. Even so, this may well be the most fearful of times in the history of the world. The threat of terrorism hangs over us daily. Traveling on planes and trains, or simply walking down the street, now pose greater risks than ever before. Across the globe, those who have the leadership characteristics, business acumen, worldview, people and business leadership skills to be successful, and who are willing to take these risks, will become more and more marketable. They will find themselves able to choose where they live, who they work for, and the parameters within which they are willing to do so (that is, the work–life balance to which they aspire).

Priscilla and I landed in Luxembourg, on a bright, cold day in November 1989. It was my first international journey outside North America. We stepped off the airplane, walked to the immigration desk, and proudly handed over our shiny new passports. Thirty seconds later, I had my very first international travel stamp! Who could have guessed then, that this would be the start of a lifelong global journey? I have learned so much from so many people during my travels from one part of the globe to another, seeing new places, meeting new people, working, playing, and discovering.

I think of the elderly man whom I spotted sitting at the entrance to the Temple of Confucius in Vietnam and who looked up and smiled nervously while nodding his assent to my request to take his photo. I think also of all the children I have seen during my travels in India who love to have their photograph taken. I recall the global business leaders I have met and learned from in Asia, the Americas, Europe, and Africa. I think about seeing *The Lion King* performed on three continents: on New York's Broadway, in London's West End, and in Tokyo. I recall ringing in the new year in Patzcuaro, Mexico; in Paris, in London, and throughout the United States. And now, living with my family in India, we are experiencing a whole new frontier. Nearly two decades after that first journey out of America, I have had the opportunity to visit and/or work in 32 countries – many of which we continue to return to, and with many more countries yet to be explored.

More than 50 world-class leaders, who have lived in more than 60 different countries, have shared with us their experiences, insights, and successful strategies, allowing us all to discover, learn, and validate how to navigate as leaders in the new global frontier. Success is a journey ... and we wish you awareness, discovery, learning, and understanding on your own global leadership journey.

Endnotes

1   The Hay Group (www.haygroup.com/us/Expertise/index.asp?id=1293), accessed November 27, 2006.
2   "Access: Changing What's Possible," presented by Frederick W. Smith, chairman, president, and CEO of FedEx Corporation, Washington, DC, May 22, 2006.
3   Neil Gershenfeld, *FAB: The Coming Revolution on Your Desktop* (Basic Books, 2005).
4   Wiki is a piece of server software that allows users to freely create and edit web page content using any web browser. Wiki supports hyperlinks and has simple text syntax for creating new pages and cross-links between internal pages on the fly. Wikipedia, the online encyclopedia, is an example of the potential of collaborative creation and coverage of a concept or project from anywhere in the world, free of charge (www.wiki.org), accessed November 27, 2006.
5   *Episode 8*, HBR Idea Cast (Harvard Business School Publishing, August 3, 2006) (www.hbsp.harvard.edu).

Appendix

Research Methodology

The detailed analysis and report from the Global Leadership Survey is available from ASTD at www.astd.org.

GLOBAL LEADERSHIP SURVEY

We developed the Global Leadership Survey in an attempt to gauge the depth and breadth of organizational understanding with regard to global leadership. The participants were asked to provide answers to the following questions:

Demographics
• Organization background, personal background, international experience.

Leadership
• What are the top 5 challenges you face as a leader today?
• Identify the top 5 critical leadership competencies, measured within your organization.
• Identify the top 5 critical leadership competencies, measured within your geographic part of the world.
• In your opinion, what are the top 5 critical leadership competencies needed to be a successful global leader?

We analyzed the information received from the survey participants and then followed up with extended interviews of leaders in order to gather data from across the globe.

LEADERSHIP WITHOUT BORDERS INTERVIEWS

We interviewed more than 50 senior leaders who have lived and worked in more than 60 different countries. The interviewees were asked the following questions:

Demographics
- Organization background, personal background, international experience.

Leadership
- How is leading with global responsibility different than leading domestically?
- In your opinion, what are the top 5 critical leadership competencies needed to be a successful global leader?
- What would you say global leaders should not do?
- How do you manage the people differences (such as culture, language) and their implications?
- How have you used technology to be a successful global leader?
- What are the key challenges you face as a leader today (what keeps you awake at night)?
- What are one or two challenges you expect to face in the future in light of how the world is changing?
- What advice do you have for someone who wants to expand their abilities to become a global leader in the next 5–10 years?

The survey, in combination with interview results, was used to write the practical aspects and advice shared in Part 1 of this book. Experiences and lessons learned from successful senior leaders representing Booz Allen Hamilton, Change Leaders, Horasis: The Global Visions Community, Nike, Satyam Computer Services, Standard Chartered Bank, Universitas 21 Global, and Vodafone are presented in detail in Part 2 of the book.

Index